READERS GUIDES TO ESSENTIAL CRITI

D1145390

CONSULTANT EDITOR: NICOLAS TREDELL

Matt McGuire	Contemporary Scottish Literature
Timothy Milnes	Wordsworth: *The Prelude*
Jago Morrison	The Fiction of Chinua Achebe
Carl Plasa	Tony Morrison: *Beloved*
Carl Plasa	Jean Rhys: *Wide Sargasso Sea*
Nicholas Potter	Shakespeare: *Antony and Cleopatra*
Nicholas Potter	Shakespeare: *Othello*
Nicholas Potter	Shakespeare's Late Plays: *Pericles, Cymbeline, The Winter's Tale, The Tempest*
Steven Price	The Plays, Screenplays and Films of David Mamet
Andrew Radford	Victorian Sensation Fiction
Berthold Schoene–Harwood	Mary Shelley: *Frankenstein*
Nick Selby	T. S. Eliot: *The Waste Land*
Nick Selby	Herman Melville: *Moby Dick*
Nick Selby	The Poetry of Walt Whitman
David Smale	Salman Rushdie: *Midnight's Chidren –The Satanic Verses*
Patsy Stoneman	Emily Brontë: *Wuthering Heights*
Susie Thomas	Hanif Kureishi
Nicolas Tredell	F. Scott Fitzgerald: *The Great Gatsby*
Nicolas Tredell	Joseph Conrad: *Heart of Darkness*
Nicolas Tredell	Charles Dickens: *Great Expectations*
Nicolas Tredell	William Faulkner: *The Sound and the Fury–As I Lay Dying*
Nicolas Tredell	Shakespeare: *A Midsummer Night's Dream*
Nicolas Tredell	Shakespeare: *Macbeth*
Nicolas Tredell	The Fiction of Martin Amis
Matthew Woodcock	Shakespeare: *Henry V*
Angela Wright	Gothic Fiction

Forthcoming

Thomas P. Adler	Tennessee Williams: *A Streetcar Named Desire–Cat on a Hot Tin Roof*
Pascale Aebischer	Jacobean Drama
Brian Baker	Science Fiction
Stephen J. Burn	Postmodern American Fiction
Sarah Haggarty & Jon Mee	Willam Blake: *Songs of Innocence and Experience*
Michael Meyer	John Steinbeck: *Of Mice and Men–The Grapes of Wrath*
Michael Whitworth	Virginia Woolf: *Mrs Dalloway*
Gina Wisker	The Fiction of Margaret Atwood
Gillian Woods	Shakespeare: *Romeo and Juliet*

Readers' Guides to Essential Criticism
Series Standing Order
(outside North America only)

You can receive future titles in this series as they are published by placing a standing order. Please contact your bookseller or, in the case of difficulty, write to us at the address below with your name and address, the title of the series and the ISBN quoted above.

Customer Services Department, Macmillan Distribution Ltd

Shakespeare
A Midsummer Night's Dream

NICOLAS TREDELL

Consultant editor: Nicolas Tredell

First published 2010 by
PALGRAVE MACMILLAN

Palgrave Macmillan in the UK is an imprint of Macmillan Publishers Limited,
registered in England, company number 785998, of Houndmills, Basingstoke,
Hampshire RG21 6XS.

Palgrave Macmillan in the US is a division of St Martin's Press LLC,
175 Fifth Avenue, New York, NY 10010.

Palgrave Macmillan is the global academic imprint of the above companies
and has companies and representatives throughout the world.

Palgrave® and Macmillan® are registered trademarks in the United States,
the United Kingdom, Europe and other countries.

ISBN 978–0–230–23878–7 hardback
ISBN 978–0–230–23879–4 paperback

This book is printed on paper suitable for recycling and made from fully
managed and sustained forest sources. Logging, pulping and manufacturing
processes are expected to conform to the environmental regulations of the
country of origin.

A catalogue record for this book is available from the British Library.

A catalog record for this book is available from the Library of Congress.

10   9   8   7   6   5   4   3   2   1
19   18   17   16   15   14   13   12   11   10

Printed in China

For Angela

CONTENTS

ACKNOWLEDGEMENTS

My deepest thanks are to my beloved wife Angela, with whom I have watched and discussed the *Dream* and other Shakespeare plays for over thirty years.

As always, it was a pleasure to work with Sonya Barker and Felicity Noble at Palgrave Macmillan.

I am most grateful to the anonymous readers of the proposal and the typescript for their comments and suggestions.

NOTES ON THE TEXT

All Act, scene and line references are keyed to the Oxford and Norton Shakespeares and given in Arabic rather than Roman numerals, e.g. 5.1.1–27 rather than V.i.1–27.

In older texts, capitalization, italicization, punctuation and spelling have been silently modified, except where the older usage seems especially significant.

Dates have been supplied for authors, critics and other figures whenever possible, but these were not always available.

Introduction

'Now' is the first word of the *Dream*, plunging us into the present of its fictional time: its last word is 'amends', in which we hear 'end' but which also carries the sense of a plurality of possible conclusions and further aims ('ends') and a suggestion that there are matters which may still need to be put right, amended, in this play of shadows, even though the lovers are now abed (though not, one hopes, asleep) and have the fairies' blessing. Between those two words – those two worlds, perhaps – we have been plunged into a dizzying series of delays, conflicts, flights, dreams, visions, absurdities and awakenings; the proliferating masks of comedy have sometimes slipped to let us glimpse the open mouths and appalled eyes of tragedy; and, at a crucial stage of the play, the human mask has mutated into the beast-head of ancient ritual. At the end, we have witnessed a bravura performance by a magician who is, like Oberon, invisible to mortals, melting into the characters, the situations, the images which his flow of words, his sleights of hand, conjure up. How can we begin to understand this?

That is where criticism starts. The *Dream* is one of the most popular comedies of William Shakespeare (1564–1616). It is a dazzling display which seems brilliantly to render the surfaces and reach into the depths of human existence. In doing so, it also prompts a desire to understand its many meanings and how these are produced; in other words, to interpret the *Dream*. This Guide aims to further such understanding by exploring the key criticism which has, in the past four hundred years, engaged in the process of *Dream* interpretation. This Introduction prepares us for our expedition by considering the date, texts and sources of the play and by mapping the critical journey ahead.

DATE

The *Dream* seems to have been written sometime in the mid-1590s. The clergyman Francis Meres (1565–1647) mentions it in his commonplace book *Palladis Tamia: Wit's Treasury* (1598), so it had already been performed by then, though it would not be published until 1600. It has been suggested that it could not have been written earlier than 1594 because the craftsmen's anxieties about a lion frightening the ladies and the Duchess in the audience (1.2.66–78) relate to a report on the

1

baptismal feast of Prince Henry (1594–1612) on 30 August 1594 at which a chariot was drawn in by a Moor rather than a lion because of a concern that a lion's 'presence might have brought some fear to the nearest' or that the lights and torches might have agitated the lion and made him dangerous.[1] But there is no conclusive evidence for a connection between this incident and the *Dream*. In terms of its stylistic similarity to other Shakespeare plays, the *Dream* has often been placed in the period 1595–6, though the 1988 Oxford *Complete Works* goes for a slightly earlier date, 1594 or 1595.[2] There has been particular interest in whether the *Dream* was written before or after *Romeo and Juliet*, since elements of the *Dream*, especially the 'Pyramus and Thisbe' sequence, parallel aspects of *Romeo and Juliet*; but no secure sequential relationship between the two plays has been established.

Attempts to date the *Dream* more precisely have often become involved with the occasion thesis – the idea that the *Dream* was written and first performed in order to celebrate the occasion of an aristocratic wedding. There is no evidence whatsoever for this, apart from debatable inferences from the text of the play itself. This has not stopped some editors, scholars and critics from assuming it as virtually a fact; for example, John Dover Wilson (1881–1969), in the 1924 Cambridge edition of the *Dream*, states that 'the play must have been written for *some* courtly marriage' (Dover Wilson's italics),[3] though he acknowledges the impossibility of definitely establishing whose marriage it was, and Harold F. Brooks declares in his 1979 Arden edition: 'That [the *Dream*] was designed to grace a wedding is a presumption as strong as it can be in default of the direct evidence that would make it certain.'[4] On the other hand, Stanley Wells in the 1967 New Penguin Shakespeare dismisses the occasion thesis and contends that the *Dream* was 'always intended for the public theatres'.[5] The debate continues: according to the Penguin 2005 edition of the play, David Wiles's *Shakespeare's Almanac: A Midsummer Night's Dream, Marriage, and the Elizabethan Calendar* (1993) offers 'the fullest exposition' of the occasion theory while Gary J. Williams's *Our Moonlight Revels: A Midsummer Night's Dream in the Theatre* (1997) provides 'its fullest refutation'.[6] It seems reasonable to say, however, that the weight of scholarly and critical opinion in the later twentieth and early twenty-first century has swung against the occasion thesis, not only because of the lack of any evidence for it, but also because of changes in the critical interpretations of the play traced in this Guide, especially in the shape of increased scepticism about the attitudes to marriage which it supposedly affirms. As David Marshall remarks, in an essay we shall discuss in Chapter 6, reading the *Dream* in this kind of sceptical perspective 'makes it difficult to imagine that even with its comic scenes the play would have made a very suitable wedding present'.[7]

TEXT

Thomas Fisher published the first Quarto (known as Q1) of the *Dream* in 1600. The play was entered in the Stationers' Register in the standard way, as a means of securing to Fisher the sole right of printing or selling the book. The title page stated that the play had been 'sundry times publicly acted by the Right Honourable, the Lord Chamberlain his Servants' (i.e. the company of actors, the Lord Chamberlain's Men, later called the King's Men, of which Shakespeare was a member). The phrase 'sundry times publicly acted' attests that the *Dream* had now entered the domain of the public theatre, even if the unproven assertion that it had originally been performed at an aristocratic wedding were true. The text of the *Dream* was printed by Richard Bradock and the type appears to have been set from 'foul' papers – that is, from Shakespeare's draft handwritten manuscript, as distinct from the 'fair' copy, the version transcribed after final correction,[8] which the Lord Chamberlain's Men would have retained.

The title page of the second Quarto (known as Q2) bears the date '1600' and gives the printer's name as James Roberts, but was in fact printed for William Jaggard (c. 1568–1623) in 1619. It repeated many of Q1's errors and perpetrated a small number of its own, but restored some mislined passages. The *Dream* next featured in the First Folio collection of Shakespeare's works (known as F1), compiled mainly by John Heminges (died 1630) and Henry Condell (died 1627), who, like Shakespeare, were members of the King's Men (the company formerly called the Lord Chamberlain's Men). Q2 seems to have served as the main copy text for F1, which repeats many of Q2's amendments and errors. But it appears that Q2 was checked sporadically against another source, probably a playhouse prompt book, and that changes were made, mostly with regard to stage directions.

Two of these changes are especially noteworthy: F1 assigns to Egeus all but one of the speeches which Q1 and Q2 give to Philostrate in Act 5; and F1 has Lysander, rather than Philostrate, read out the titles of the proposed evening entertainment, with Theseus providing responses. These alterations have, potentially, considerable interpretative significance. For example, if Egeus is absent from the evening festivities, exiting from the play for ever after Theseus has overborne his will and refused Egeus's plea to apply the law to Lysander (4.1.178), it could emphasize his exclusion from the *Dream*'s reconciliatory settlements or indicate his tacit acceptance of them; if he is present at those festivities as the Master of the Revels, this could emphasize his inclusion or sharpen his humiliation (since, as Peter Holland points out, the Duke overrules Egeus once more when he rejects his strongly urged advice not to watch 'Pyramus and Thisbe'). Lysander's recitation of the titles of the offered entertainments might indicate an usurpation of Egeus's prerogative or a tacit acceptance on Egeus's part of his new son-in-law.[9] *The Oxford Complete Works*, the 1994 Oxford edition of the *Dream* and the 2007 Macmillan RSC Shakespeare all follow F1 in assigning Philostrate's lines to Egeus and the recitations of the titles of the evening entertainments to Lysander and it seems likely that further critical work will emerge in relation to these textual emphases.

SOURCES

The concept of 'sources' is a questionable one in regard to Shakespeare. It suggests that Shakespeare sat down to write his plays with a set of texts in front of him from which he drew plots, incidents, characters and ideas. But as R. A. Foakes points out in his edition of the *Dream*:

■ It is important to ask continually whether Shakespeare needed to go to a source for what was common property, or could have been on tap as flowing from an unconscious or subconscious assimilation of what was, so to speak, in the air, the common materials of the culture and discourse of his age.[10] □

In other words, Shakespeare might never have actually read the texts which scholars propose as sources; he may have picked up the necessary material through conversation, or through an intuition finely attuned to the language, concepts, images and ideas which were circulating in the cultural air of his time. An alternative approach to the concept of sources (though not one which Foakes adopts) is provided by the idea of 'intertextuality': that a text always emerges in, and inevitably relates to, a welter of other texts and discourses, whether or not its writer has read or knows about these. An intertextual reading can point to resemblances between Text A and Text B without positing that the author of Text A actually read Text B. But the more traditional concept of 'sources', provided that its limits are recognized, is likely to remain important to Shakespearean scholarship and criticism.

In contrast to most Shakespeare plays, however, the *Dream* does not have one major source. Moreover, there are significant parts of the play for which no convincing source has been found. For example, the plot of 'Pyramus and Thisbe' comes from Ovid (see below), but the idea of the craftsmen putting on a play seems to be original with Shakespeare. There are, however, a range of texts which have greater or lesser similarities to aspects of the *Dream*, and those most relevant to the criticism explored in this Guide are outlined below.

The Knight's Tale

The Knight's Tale, from *The Canterbury Tales* by the great medieval English poet Geoffrey Chaucer (c. 1343/4–1400), begins by describing a 'Duke' called Theseus (line 2) – a title not given to him in any other known text – who 'conquered all the reigne of Feminy' and 'wedded the queene Ipolita' (lines 8, 10). The tale also describes two young Theban princes, Palamon and Arcite, who fall for the same woman (Emelye, Hippolyta's sister) and finally engage in a combat which Theseus and Hippolyta, out hunting in May, interrupt; Theseus sentences them to death but relents after pleas from Hippolyta and Emelye. Eventually, after Venus and Saturn intervene, Palamon marries Emelye. This story was also employed by Shakespeare and John Fletcher (1579–1625) in *The Two Noble Kinsmen* (first published 1634) (see chapter 8 of this Guide).

North's Plutarch

A second key source is the 1579 English translation by Sir Thomas North (?1535–?1601) of a French translation by Jacques Amyot (1513–93) of the *Lives* of real-life and mythical soldiers and statesmen by the ancient Greek essayist and biographer Plutarch (46–126 AD). Plutarch, and North's translation, highlight differing accounts of Theseus's activities and describe, among other things, the battle of Theseus with the Amazons – he 'slew a great number of them'[11] – and his marriage to Hippolyta (also known as Antiopa). North also contains a range of stories about Theseus's other, often dubious, sexual and marital exploits, for instance with Perigouna, the daughter of Sinnis, who 'lay with him' and whom he afterwards married off to Deioneus;[12] with Ariadne, the daughter of King Minos of Crete, who gave Theseus the ball of thread to find his way back through the labyrinth after killing the Minotaur but whom he abandoned for Aegles, the daughter of Panopaeus; and Phaedra, whom he married after the death of Hippolyta (or Antiopa) and who fell in love with her stepson Hippolytus, the son of Theseus and Hippolyta. There are 'many other reports touching the marriages of Theseus, whose beginnings had no great good honest ground, neither fell out their ends very fortunate'.[13] Some of these exploits are explicitly mentioned in the *Dream* when Oberon refers to Titania's 'love for Theseus' and asks 'Didst not thou lead him through the glimmering night / From Perigouna whom he ravished, / And made him with fair Aegles break his faith, / With Ariadne and Antiopa?' (2.1.76, 77–80). (Here 'Antiopa', an alternative name for Hippolyta in Plutarch, seems to be treated as a separate figure.). It is interesting to ask how far these aspects of the Theseus myth – both those mentioned in the play itself and those in Plutarch and in North's translation – should enter into the interpretation of the *Dream*. Later twentieth- and early twenty-first-century criticism, often, but not necessarily, of a feminist kind, has increasingly felt that Theseus's record as a sexual predator – and the shadow of the tragedy of Phaedra – must be admitted in evidence and that it does affect, to a greater or lesser extent, the significance of the play (see, for example, the discussion of A. D. Nuttall (1937–2007) in Chapter 8 of this Guide).

Huon of Bordeaux

A third significant source is the translation of about 1534, by John Bourchier, second Baron Berners (?1469–1533) of *Huon of Bordeaux*, a thirteenth-century *chanson de geste* (song of deeds). Huon unknowingly kills the son of Charlemagne but is reprieved from death and set a series of seemingly impossible tasks, which he successfully carries out with the aid of a king of the fairies called Oberon, only three feet tall but with the face of an angel, who dwells in a wood. The Oberon of *Huon of Bordeaux* also has strong associations with the Orient, which is significant for the link the *Dream* establishes between Oberon and India and for the postcolonial reading of the *Dream* by Margo Hendricks, considered in Chapter 7 of this Guide.

The Golden Ass

A fourth important source is *The Golden Ass* by Lucius Apuleius (born c. 123 AD), the only surviving complete novel in Latin. It was translated into English in 1598 by William Adlington (active 1556), with a subtitle which ran 'containing the metamorphosis of Lucius Apuleius, interlaced with sundry pleasant and delectable tales, with an excellent narration of the marriage of Cupid and Psyche'.[14] *The Golden Ass* is an extremely entertaining and sometimes bawdy account of the adventures of a man who, in contrast to Bottom in the *Dream*, has his whole body, not just his head, transformed into that of an ass, who encounters many hardships and perils (including the threat of castration), has a sexual encounter with a wealthy and noble matron (toned down in Adlington's translation), and eventually enjoys a vision of the ancient Egyptian goddess Isis. Frank Kermode (born 1919) will relate this passage to Bottom's dream in an essay we shall discuss in Chapter 4 of this Guide, and in Chapter 8 A. D. Nuttall will consider the encounter with the matron in Apuleuis's novel.

Ovid's *Metamorphoses*

The fifth and perhaps most significant source for the *Dream* here is the *Metamorphoses* of the Latin poet Ovid (Publius Ovidius Naso (43 BC–AD 17/18), a rich poetic compendium of more than two hundred ancient legends, often about changes of shape and interchanges between gods, goddesses and mortals. The influential, if sometimes awkward, translation of the *Metamorphoses* into English verse by Arthur Golding (?1536–1605) appeared in 1595–7. The clearest contribution of the *Metamorphoses* to the *Dream* is the story of 'Pyramus and Thisbe', the subject of the craftsmen's play-within-a-play, which appears in Book 4, lines 55–166 of Ovid's *Metamorphoses* and in Book 4, lines 67–201 of Golding's translation. The *Metamorphoses* was also the source of the name 'Titania', which does not appear in Golding's translation but only in the original Latin, where 'Titania' and 'Titanis' are epithets which indicate a female descendant of a Titan and which are applied to Pyrrha (Book 1, line 395), Diana (Book 3, line 173), Latona (Book 6, lines 185, 346) and Circe (Book 12, lines 968; Book 14, lines 14, 376, 382, 438). Golding translates the epithet by the term 'Titan's daughter'. But it can be argued that the relationship between Ovid's *Metamorphoses*, in the original and in Golding's translation, extends well beyond the 'Pyramus and Thisbe' story and the name 'Titania' – that metamorphosis, as topic and poetic technique, is crucial to both Ovid and the *Dream* (Jonathan Bate (born 1958) makes a strong case for the *Dream* as 'a displaced dramatization of Ovid' – see Chapter 7 of this Guide).

Other Sources: Scot, Seneca, St Paul

Other suggested sources for the *Dream* are *The Discovery of Witchcraft* (1584) by Reginald Scot (?1538–99), a sceptical account of superstitions and marvels, which mentions the tales about 'Robin Goodfellow', whose activities include 'sweeping the house at midnight', like Robin Goodfellow/Puck 'sweep[ing] the dust behind the door' after midnight in the *Dream* (5.1.20). Scot also discusses how '[t]o set a horse's or an ass's head on a man's neck and shoulders'. Harold F. Brooks has also proposed links between the *Dream* and passages from the tragedies *Oedipus*, *Medea* and *Hippolytus* by the ancient Roman playwright Lucius Annaeus Seneca (c. 4 BC–AD 65); for example, Brooks compares the account of the plague of Thebes in Seneca's *Oedipus* with Titania's account of the disorder in the elements caused by her quarrel with Oberon. There is also one significant Biblical source for a key passage in the *Dream*: Bottom's account of *his* dream, where the passage 'The eye of man hath not heard, the ear of man hath not seen, man's hand is not able to taste, his tongue to conceive, nor his heart to report what my dream was' (4.1.108–11) echoes, and scrambles, a passage in St Paul's first letter to the Corinthians, chapter 2, verse 9: 'the eye hath not seen, and the ear hath not heard, neither have entered into the heart of man, the things which God hath prepared for them that love him' (this is the translation in the Bishop's Bible of 1568). This echo has aroused considerable scholarly and critical comment – see Frank Kermode in Chapter 4 and Annabel Patterson in Chapter 6 of this Guide.

Any consideration of sources for the *Dream* inevitably involves interpretation, of Shakespeare's text and of the proposed source texts, and of those significant parts of the play which seem to have no source. Such interpretation is likely, if pursued at any depth, to turn into criticism, into explorations of significance and quality. It is those critical explorations of significance and quality which are the main subject of this Guide and it is now time for an overview of the criticism which we shall consider in the chapters to come.

CRITICISM

Chapter 1 of this Guide explores *Dream* criticism between 1662 and 1898. There is a sense in which, as René Girard (born 1923) says, the 'first critical debate' about the *Dream* 'took place during the first performance', in the exchange on the significance and quality of the 'story of the night' between Theseus and Hippolyta at the start of Act 5 (5.1.1–27). But there is no doubt that the diarist Samuel Pepys (1633–1703), among his other claims to fame, has written himself into the history of *Dream* criticism, indeed into its founding moment, with his casual dismissal of the play in a 1662 diary entry. Our first chapter opens with Pepys's remarks and then follows the emergence, from the late seventeenth to the late nineteenth century, of a distinctive repertoire of topics in *Dream* criticism: these include the function and value of its supernatural elements, its representation of women, its portrayal of Theseus, the character and significance of Bottom, the play's treatment of love, its unity and harmony and its genre (is it, for example, a parody, an allegory, or a masque?).

After citing Pepys, Chapter 1 considers observations by the poet and dramatist John Dryden (1631–1700) and Samuel Johnson (1709–84), both of whom try to justify the supernatural aspects of the play. It goes on to discuss Elizabeth Griffith (?1727–93), who both affirms the duty of a child to obey a parent and defends Hermia's defiance of that duty. The chapter then discusses Edmund Malone (1741–1812), who finds that Theseus and Hippolyta fail to live up to their exalted legendary status; and Charles Taylor (1756–1823), who switches the focus to Bottom, whom he sees as a 'coxcomb'.

Chapter 1 goes on to trace the development of Romantic criticism of the *Dream*. In the last decade of the eighteenth century, the German writer Ludwig Tieck (1773–1853) provided a Romantic appreciation of Shakespeare, which was taken up in the early nineteenth century by August Wilhelm von Schlegel (1767–1845), who affirms the unity of the *Dream*. William Hazlitt (1778–1830) elevates the figure of Bottom and lauds Shakespeare's poetic power, while Nathan Drake (1766–1836) stresses the emotional unity of the play and anticipates some feminist themes. Samuel Taylor Coleridge (1772–1834) offers a very brief but intriguing characterization of the mixed genre of the *Dream*.

In the mid-nineteenth century, William Maginn (1793–1842) takes up the topic of Bottom, which is pursued by Charles Knight (1791–1873), who also praises the harmony of the whole play. Joseph Hunter (1783–1861) considers the implications of the idea of the play as a 'dream' and Hermann Ulrici (1806–84) offers a strikingly original account of its unity in terms of interacting parodies. Both Henry Norman Hudson (1814–86) and Georg Gottfried Gervinus (1805–71) are concerned with the unruliness and capriciousness of the *Dream*, and Gervinus goes on to see it as an allegorical comparison of sensuous love and dreaming.

In the later nineteenth century, Sir Daniel Wilson (1816–92) focuses on Bottom and Karl Elze (1821–89) considers the *Dream* as a combination of masque and antimasque. Denton Jacques Snider (1841–1925) offers an interpretation of the play in terms derived from the German philo-sopher George Wilhelm Friedrich Hegel (1770–1831), while John Weiss (1818–79) comes down to earth again with Bottom, whom he sees as an example of a self-made man. Edward Dowden (1843–1913) elevates Theseus to a central role in the *Dream* and Charles Ebenezer Moyse (1852–1924) interprets the play as a symbolic work in which the wood in which the lovers get lost is the world. Julia Wedgwood (1833–1913) considers the relationship between Titania and the mother of the Indian boy, and the significance of the Indian boy himself. E. K. Chambers (1866–1954) regards the *Dream* as a symbolical portrayal of youthful love and Georg Brandes (1842–1927) draws attention to the play's concern with erotic and unconscious elements, bringing Chapter 1 to an end

Chapter 2 considers *Dream* critics from 1900 to 1949. The academic study of English Literature develops in the early twentieth century but initially it devotes much more attention to Shakespearean tragedy than to comedy. The first two critics considered in this chapter, G. K. Chesterton (1874–1936) and J. B. Priestley (1894–1984), write from outside the academy. Chesterton sees the *Dream* as a mystically happy play but registers those darker elements which will be more strongly emphasized in later twentieth-century criticism; Priestley hails

Bottom as a great comic creation. Enid Welsford (1892–1981) takes a more scholarly approach, examining the *Dream* as a creative transformation of the masque. In the 1930s, the focus of critical activity shifts towards the academy. The study of patterns of imagery, which was so crucial to academic literary studies in the mid-twentieth century, is exemplified in relation to the *Dream* by G. Wilson Knight (1897–1985) and Caroline Spurgeon (1886–1942). H. B. Charlton takes a different approach, regarding the play as a comedy exploring the place of love in life, while Donald C. Miller, in 1940, opens up the issue of sexuality in relation to Titania and the Indian boy. But in 1949 Thomas Marc Parrott (1866–1960) reaffirms the benign and innocent view of the *Dream*.

Chapter 3 explores key *Dream* critics of the 1950s, a period of consolidation and expansion in Anglo-American literary criticism. Paul N. Siegel sees the play as an affirmation of a certain set of ideas about marriage. Peter F. Fisher examines the way in which the different worlds of the *Dream* are finally brought into harmonious order. Paul A. Olson further explores the ideas about marriage which he sees the play as presenting. John Russell Brown focuses on the way in which the *Dream* suggests the need to respect both the subjective truth of lovers and the imaginative illusions which drama creates, while C. L. Barber argues that the play both releases fantasies and promotes scepticism about them. By the end of the 1950s, a rich and substantial body of work on the *Dream* had appeared which emphasized order, reason and harmony and which established the play as a highly fruitful object of study.

Chapter 4 considers the *Dream* criticism of the 1960s which developed the interpretations of the 1950s and also began to challenge them. Bertrand Evans is concerned with the way the play exploits the gaps in awareness between the characters in the play and between the characters and the audience. Frank Kermode argues for the visionary quality of the nature of Bottom's dream in relation to *The Golden Ass* and classical and Renaissance dream theory. G. K. Hunter (1920–2008) sees the *Dream* as a dance which highlights the variety and irrationality of love, while R. W. Dent contends that the *Dream* is much more substantial, approximating to Shakespeare's 'Defense of Dramatic Poetry'. All these perspectives emerged within the boundaries of established academic criticism, but Jan Kott (1914–2001) breached those boundaries. His stress on the erotic and threatening aspects of the *Dream* aroused outrage in the corridors of academe and provoked a damage limitation exercise which continues to this day. The later 1960s, however, saw two notable books devoted to the *Dream* emerging from academic contexts. David P. Young's *Something of Great Constancy: The Art of A Midsummer Night's Dream* (1966) stressed the coherence of the play and offered especially interesting accounts of its use of 'picturization' and 'panoramas'; Stephen Fender's *A Midsummer Night's Dream* (1968), in Edward Arnold's Studies in English Literature series, emphasized the play's ambivalence. It is in Fender, more than in Kott, that one can see the beginnings of the kinds of questioning which were to emerge much more strongly in the 1980s.

Chapter 5 examines the significant *Dream* criticism produced during a transitional decade for literary criticism, as established approaches took on a defensive aspect, while alternative approaches struggled to emerge. Alexander Leggatt's analysis of the play in *Shakespeare's Comedy of Love* (1972) is a kind of concealed argument with Kott which contends that the *Dream* exorcises the darker forces which threaten it. In *Dream in Shakespeare: From Metaphor to Metamorphosis* (1974), Marjorie B. Garber boldly reverses the view that the *Dream* ultimately endorses reason, and argues strongly for the play's affirmation of the positive value of dreams, which she links to the power of metaphor and to the act of artistic creation. David Bevington engages in an open debate with Kott, acknowledging his insights but reproving his excesses. In a harbinger of the more politicized readings which would emerge in the 1980s and 1990s, Elliott Krieger's *A Marxist Study of Shakespeare's Comedies* (1979) offers a political reading of the *Dream*, suggesting that the play ultimately endorses a fantasy of aristocratic predominance.

Chapter 6 looks at the key readings of the *Dream* which flourished during the transformation of Anglo-American literary studies in the 1980s. Shirley Nelson Garner analyses the patriarchal, heterosexist ideology of the play and David Marshall raises a host of questions about its representations of women, of marriage, of the craftsmen and of the relationship between plays and audiences. Louis Adrian Montrose, in what is probably the most influential essay on the *Dream* in the last three decades, examines the relationship of the *Dream* to the pervasive cultural presence of a Virgin Queen. James H. Kavanagh interprets the craftsmen's concerns about their projected play as an attempt to produce a performance which is acceptable to their aristocratic audience. Theodore B. Leinwand also addresses this issue in the context of artisan unrest in 1590s England, and in *Shakespeare and the Popular Voice* (1989), Annabel Patterson pursues the matter further by relating it to festive theory. By the end of the 1980s, much has changed in *Dream* criticism, as in Anglo-American literary criticism more generally: issues of sexual politics and class politics, banished beyond the stage door in the 1950s and still largely in the wings in the 1960s and 1970s, have moved centre-stage.

Chapter 7 starts by discussing two books by critics who were drawing together, developing and expanding material on the *Dream* they had published earlier: René Girard's *A Theater of Envy* (1991) applies his concept of 'mimetic rivalry' to the play and James L. Calderwood's

A Midsummer Night's Dream, in Twayne's New Critical Introductions to Shakespeare series, presents the especially intriguing argument that the play should be seen in terms of that form of visual distortion called 'anamorphosis'. The chapter then goes on to consider Terence Hawkes on the significance of the words – and concepts – of 'and' and 'or' in the *Dream*. Patricia Parker, in *Shakespeare from the Margins* (1996) traces images of joining and misjoining across the play, particularly in regard to the craftsmen and the lovers, and Margo Hendricks opens up the question of the *Dream*'s relationship to racial and colonialist discourses. Jonathan Bate, in *Shakespeare and Ovid* (1993), explores the play's intricate links to the work of the Latin poet and Helen Hackett's *A Midsummer Night's Dream* (1997), in the British Council's Writers and their Work series, synthesizes major developments in *Dream* criticism from the 1980s and discusses the play in terms of generic intersections and instabilities.

Chapter 8 focuses on key critical essays of the early twenty-first century. A. D. Nuttall argues that the *Dream* performs an *apotrope*, a turning away, of the malign elements its mythological resonances invoke. Douglas E. Green explores the 'queer' moments and implications of the play produced by reading it 'against the grain', while Alan Sinfield urges the need to distinguish clearly between a 'with the grain' and an 'against the grain' reading of the *Dream* and suggests its limitations as a 'queer' play by comparing it to Shakespeare and Fletcher's *The Two Noble Kinsmen*. Thomas R. Frosch offers a full-blown psychoanalytical interpretation of the *Dream* as one which ultimately affirms marriage and procreation, and Hugh Grady takes it as an example of the 'impure aesthetics' which he advocates as a way of restoring an aesthetic dimension to politicized criticism.

Grady's essay brings us up to 2008, and the final chapter goes back in time to consider the criticism of five key films of the *Dream* which were made in the twentieth century. As this Guide, like the other Guides in the Essential Criticism series, concentrates on critics who are text-centred rather than performance-centred in order to maintain its sharpness of focus, it may seem inconsistent to include a chapter on critical responses to *Dream* films. But there is a crucial difference between a live performance of the *Dream* and a film adaptation. A live performance offers an irreplaceable experience of interaction between the text, the bodies, senses and voices of the actors and the bodies and senses of the audience; but when it has gone, it has gone. It may be partly reconstituted from its traces in memory, in documentation, indeed on film, but the physical and psychological encounter can never be recaptured. We cannot bring the famous 1970 production of the *Dream* by Peter Brook (born 1925) into a seminar room or sitting room but we can bring the 1935 film of the play into any fixed or mobile space which has the appropriate equipment. With today's digital technology, a film, like a text, is, in principle, accessible anywhere and at any time by anybody. This means that films, and the criticism which focuses on them, are more intimately involved with textual criticism than stage productions can be; it is possible to show a film, a primary text, and critical texts, on adjacent screens or on the same screen; and these technological facilities are likely to be enhanced in the future. Thus the chapter on critical responses to film in this Guide is both of intrinsic interest and an acknowledgement of contemporary cultural reality.

'Now'. That word which starts the *Dream* signals the start of our journey through the essential criticism of the play. It is an intellectually exciting and sometimes strange voyage which, like the *Dream* itself, will leave us, at the end, seeing things differently.

CHAPTER ONE

1662–1898: Labyrinth of Enchantment

THE SEVENTEENTH AND EIGHTEENTH CENTURIES

The first and often-quoted critical remark on *A Midsummer Night's Dream* – or on a particular production of the play – comes in an entry for 29 September 1662 in the diary of Samuel Pepys:

■ [T]hen to the King's Theatre, where we saw *Midsummer nights dream*, which I have never seen before, nor shall ever again, for it is the most insipid ridiculous play that ever I saw in my life.[1] □

We do not know whether the production which Pepys saw was adapted; but his response is perhaps indicative of a more widespread uneasiness about the *Dream* in the seventeenth and eighteenth centuries. The supernatural aspects of the play proved a major problem. For example, the poet and dramatist John Dryden, in 'The Author's Apology for Heroic Poetry and Poetic Licence' which prefaced *The State of Innocence: An Opera* (1677), felt obliged to justify Shakespeare's excursions into magic in the *Dream* and *The Tempest* by adducing their foundation in 'popular belief':

■ [P]oets may be allowed the [...] liberty for describing things which really exist not, if they are founded on popular belief: of this nature are Fairies, Pigmies, and the extraordinary effects of Magic; for 'tis still an imitation, though of other men's fancies: and thus are Shakespeare's *Tempest* [and] his *Midsummer Night's Dream*.[2] □

This view would later be partly shared by Samuel Johnson, who accounts for the fairies as a familiar part of 'common tradition' in Shakespeare's time; but Johnson also seeks to legitimate them in high-cultural terms by alluding to their use by the Elizabethan poet Edmund Spenser (?1552–99) in his complex courtly poem *The Faerie Queene* (1590; 1596; 1609):

■ Wild and fantastical as [the *Dream*] is, all the parts in their various modes are well written and give the kind of pleasure which the author designed.

Fairies in his time were much in fashion; common tradition had made them familiar, and Spenser's poem had made them great.[3] □

In his remarks on specific scenes, Johnson's main focus is on the ways in which *Dream* is a play about theatre. He focuses especially on Bottom, whose desire to play a tyrant, 'a part of fury, tumult, and noise' is 'such as every young man pants to perform when he first steps upon the stage'. To Johnson, Bottom 'seems bred in a tiring room' (the Elizabethan term for the place where the actors changed costume and where props were stored). Besides Bottom's desire to play a tyrant, Johnson identifies in him 'another histrionical [acting] passion': he wants to take every part himself and prevent anyone else from aiming at distinction as an actor.[4] With regard to 3.1, where the mechanicals rehearse in the woods and Puck transforms Bottom into an ass, Johnson suggests that this was intended to ridicule incompetent companies of players and thereby to promote the superiority of the theatrical company of which Shakespeare was a part. 'Bottom was perhaps the head of a rival house [company of actors] and is therefore honoured with an ass's head'.[5]

Johnson opens up what would later be called the metatheatrical or metadramatic dimension of *Dream*; Elizabeth Griffith, in *The Morality of Shakespeare's Drama Illustrated* (1775), opens up the question of the representation of women in the play. She praises, in general terms, Theseus's declaration to Hermia that 'your father should be as a god' (1.1.47) and claims that the duty of a child to obey a parent is pious, moral and natural; but she also contends that Hermia's case is exceptional:

■ [T]he particular instance of the daughter's compliance, exacted by the father, in this piece, of resigning an husband of her own choice, *upon equal terms*, and accepting another, chosen arbitrarily for her, *by caprice merely*, was too severe a trial of obedience. [...] When I said that the duty of a child was *natural*, I did not mean to invest the parent with an authority which *was not so*; and I cannot blame Hermia, therefore, upon the severe laws of Athens being declared to her, for the chaste and spirited resolution she frames to herself on that occasion [Griffith's italics; she quotes 1.1.79–82, from 'So will I grow, so live, so die, my lord,' to 'My soul consents not to give sovereignty'].[6] □

Where Griffith had focused on the representation of women in *Dream*, the scholar and Shakespeare editor Edmund Malone focused on the play's representation of its 'higher personages', male and female, and found them disappointing:

■ The manners of Hippolyta, the Amazon, are undistinguished from those of other females. Theseus, the associate of Hercules, is not engaged in any adventure worthy of his rank or reputation, nor is he in reality an agent throughout the play. [...] Through the whole piece, the more exalted characters are subservient to the interests of those beneath them.[7] □

Malone's implication that the less exalted characters in the *Dream* might be more interesting than its higher personages was exemplified by the engraver and writer Charles Taylor, who concentrated on Bottom in a text accompanying an engraving in *The Shakespeare Gallery* (1792). In contrast to Dr Johnson, Taylor sees Bottom not as exhibiting behaviour peculiar to actors but as representative of a type of character to be found 'in all states and ranks of life':[8] the 'coxcomb' (now an archaic term). Taylor defines 'coxcombism' as consisting of 'a frivolous mind, a conceited disposition, a vain estimate of self, and a handsome person'. In Taylor's view, coxcombs often also exhibit 'a supposed merit, or imagined ability, in things not regularly attached to them, nor connected with their direct path of life, and their allotted circumstances of situation'.[9] Taylor sees Bottom as displaying this characteristic in Act I when, though a weaver by trade, he is over-confident in his abilities as an actor, his capacity to play every role. This mobility seems ethically suspect to Taylor, who prefers '[s]teady attention to one thing'.[10]

By the time Taylor's *Shakespeare Gallery* was published, Romanticism was making an impact on the reception of Shakespeare as on many other cultural activities, and the final critic in this subchapter illustrates its impact – the German Romantic poet, novelist and dramatist Johann Ludwig Tieck, who worked with August Wilhelm von Schlegel on his translation of Shakespeare into German. Romanticism was open to the irrational elements of Shakespeare which had proved a problem for the eighteenth century, and the very title of the Tieck essay we shall consider announces this reorientation. It is called 'Shakspeare's Treatment of the Marvellous' ['Shakespeare's Behandlung des Wunderbaren'], written in 1793 and first published as a Preface to Tieck's 1796 translation of *The Tempest*. In the *Dream*, Tieck argues, 'Shakespeare's purpose is indeed to lull his audience into perceiving things as if in a dream' and Tieck knows of 'no other play which in its every aspect answers this purpose so well'. Tieck argues that in this achievement Shakespeare, 'who in his plays so often reveals his familiarity with the faintest stirrings of the human soul', drew on his personal experience: he 'probably observed himself also while dreaming and applied what he discovered here to his poetry'. Samuel Johnson had suggested that Shakespeare, in the *Dream*, drew on his personal experience of the theatre when portraying Bottom and the other mechanicals; but this is, as it were, professional, daylight experience. Tieck changes the emphasis in a Romantic direction when he suggests that Shakespeare drew on his private, night-time experience. Tieck develops this Romantic emphasis further when he suggests the general implications of this private experience by affirming the value to the 'psychologist and the poet' of 'examining the course of dreams'. Such an examination explains 'why certain combinations of ideas have such a powerful effect on the mind'.[11] In dreams 'the poet can most readily observe how a myriad notions are linked together to create a marvellous and unexpected effect'.[12]

In stressing the value of dreams, Tieck helps to provide a new perspective on a play whose title announces that it is a 'dream' and which is, in Samuel Johnson's terms, '[w]ild and fantastical'. For Johnson, the '[w]ild and fantastical' qualities of the *Dream* are not marks of its merit; insofar as the play succeeds, it does so in spite of these qualities. In the perspective suggested by Tieck, however, these qualities are valuable because they provide 'a marvellous and unexpected effect'. It is a crucial change of emphasis as the nineteenth century approaches: from now on, there is less need for critics implicitly to apologize for the *Dream*'s strangeness and singularity, and critical attention can to some extent move elsewhere, as the criticism we shall consider in the next subchapter will show.

THE EARLY NINETEENTH CENTURY

August von Schlegel, the great German critic and translator of Shakespeare, has a high opinion of the *Dream*:

■ [T]here flows a luxuriant vein of the boldest and most fantastical invention [in the play]; the most extraordinary combination of the most dissimilar ingredients seems to have arisen without effort by some ingenious and lucky accident.[13] □

Schlegel emphasizes how these heterogeneous elements form a whole:

■ The different parts of the plot; the wedding of Theseus, the disagreement of Oberon and Titania, the flight of the two pair[s] of lovers, and the theatrical operations of the mechanics, are so lightly and happily interwoven, that they seem necessary to each other for the formation of a whole.[14] □

Part of this interweaving is the way in which the 'extremes of fanciful and vulgar are united when the enchanted Titania awakes and falls in love with a coarse mechanic with an ass's-head, who represents, or rather disfigures, the part of a tragical lover'.[15] Schlegel sees the 'droll wonder of the transmutation of Bottom'[16] as 'merely the translation of a metaphor in its literal sense',[17] but 'his behaviour during the tender homage' of Titania provides 'a most amusing proof how much the consciousness of such a head-dress [presumably on the part of the audience] heightens the effect of his usual folly'.[18]

Like Edmund Malone, Schlegel recognizes the relative inaction of Theseus and Hippolyta, but holds that it serves a quasi-aesthetic function: 'Theseus and Hippolyta are, as it were, a splendid frame for the picture; they take no part in the action, but appear with a stately pomp'.[19] Like seventeenth- and eighteenth-century critics such as Dryden and Johnson, Schlegel sees the supernatural elements of the *Dream* and *The Tempest* – and of *Macbeth* – as based on popular belief in spirits; but he regards these elements not as regrettable superstitions but as ways of coming into closer contact with the sources of nature. He compares Shakespeare's capacity to come close to these sources to that of the medieval Italian poet who wrote the *Divine Comedy*, Dante Alighieri (1265–1321):

■ In general we find, in *The Midsummer Night's Dream*, in *The Tempest*, in the magical part of *Macbeth*, and wherever Shakspeare [sic] avails himself of the popular belief in the invisible presence of spirits, and the possibility of coming in contact with them, a profound view of the inward life of nature and her mysterious springs, which, it is true, ought never to be altogether unknown to the genuine poet, as poetry is altogether incompatible with mechanical physics, but which few have possessed in an equal degree with Dante and [Shakespeare] himself.[20] □

Schlegel implies here a very different way of looking at the supernatural aspects of the *Dream*, and of Shakespeare more generally, from the perspective which was dominant in the eighteenth century. While they are indeed based on popular belief, they can give access to 'the inward life of nature and her mysterious springs' when employed by a poet of the calibre of Shakespeare or Dante.

The English essayist, journalist and critic William Hazlitt, in his *Characters of Shakespeare's Plays* (1817) thought Schlegel's writings on Shakespeare 'very admirable'[21] though he demurred at their 'appearance of mysticism'[22] and their lack of specific quotations from Shakespeare's texts. As the title of his book suggests, Hazlitt's emphasis is on character, and he starts his essay on *Dream* by considering Bottom. Bottom, Hazlitt declares, is 'a character that has not had justice done him'; he is 'the most romantic of mechanics'.[23] Citing Bottom's request to Quince to write him a prologue which will avoid the danger of frightening the ladies by saying that their swords are harmless, that Pyramus is not really killed, and that Pyramus is actually Bottom the Weaver (3.1.16–20), Hazlitt remarks that Bottom appears to understand 'the subject of dramatic illusion at least as well as any modern essayist'. He is equally at home in 'his new character of an ass', instinctively acquiring 'a most learned taste', growing 'fastidious in the choice of dried peas and bottled hay' (4.1.36, 32–3) and becoming familiar with his fairy attendants and assigning them their parts 'with all due gravity'.[24]

Hazlitt challenges the view that Shakespeare is 'a gloomy and heavy writer', contending that his 'subtlety exceeds that of all other dramatic writers' and cites the idea that he is to be regarded 'rather as a metaphysician than a poet'. He affirms that Shakespeare's 'delicacy and sportive gaiety are infinite'[25] and claims that in the *Dream* alone, 'there is more sweetness and beauty of description than in the whole range of French poetry put together'. In accordance with his belief in supporting his points by specific illustrations, Hazlitt provides examples: Helena's 'remonstrance' to Hermia (presumably 3.2.196–220); Titania's 'description of her fairy train' (2.2.5–8); Titania's 'disputes with Oberon about the Indian boy' (2.1.121–37); Puck's 'account of himself and his employments' (2.1.2–31; 42–57); Titania's 'exhortation' to her fairies 'to pay due attendance upon her favourite, Bottom' (3.1.156–66); Hippolyta's description of a hunt in a Cretan wood (4.1.111–17); and Theseus's response (4.1.117–26). Hazlitt finds the last two passages 'as heroical and spirited' as the earlier ones 'are full of luscious tenderness' and offers a general comment on the effect of the play which is, as it were, an anticipatory echo of 'Ode to a Nightingale' (written 1819) by the Romantic poet John Keats (1795–1821).[26] The likeness to Keats, however, indicates how easily certain aspects of the *Dream* could be described in a Romantic critical idiom. As Hazlitt puts it:

■ The reading of [the *Dream*] is like wandering in a grove by moonlight: the descriptions breathe a sweetness like odours thrown from beds of flowers.[27] □

This remark is also significant for Hazlitt's use of the verb 'reading', since he concludes his essay by asserting that, because of its poetic qualities, the *Dream* must be read and cannot work on the stage: 'when acted, [it] is converted from a delightful fiction into a dull pantomime. All that is finest in the play is lost in the representation'.[28]

In the same year that Hazlitt's *Characters of Shakespeare's Plays* was published, the essayist and physician Nathan Drake, in his *Shakespeare and his Times* (1817) called the *Dream* an 'exquisite sally of sportive invention' whose supposed faults are converted into virtues if they are viewed in the perspective which should be applied to Shakespeare's best plays. This perspective is one which makes it possible to discern the *'unity of feeling'* (Drake's italics) which 'most remarkably pervades and regulates their entire structure'. Drake affirms that the *Dream* 'partakes of this bond, or principle of coalescence, in a very peculiar degree'.[29]

Drake sees the title of *A Midsummer Night's Dream* as a declaration of Shakespeare's 'object and aim' – to achieve a dreamlike feeling. In the play, 'the imagery of the most wild and fantastic dream is actually embodied before our eyes'.[30] It is the need to maintain these qualities across the whole play, to achieve unity of feeling, which accounts for the comparative insubstantiality of the human characters of which Edmund Malone had complained. While the *Dream* produces no *'strong character'* (Drake's italics), it does offer 'many pleasing discriminations of passion and feeling'. He focuses on Hermia and Helena, thus pursuing the issue of the representation of women in the *Dream* which, as the previous subchapter showed, Elizabeth Griffith had opened up in the late eighteenth century. He contends that 'the characters of Hermia and Helena are beautifully drawn, and finely contrasted, and in much of the dialogue which occurs between them, the chords both of love and pity are touched with the poet's wonted skill'.[31] Drake also anticipates an aspect of feminist criticism of the *Dream* when he suggests that 'the fairy-practice of purloining children, which, in every previous system of this mythology' was due to 'malignant or self-interested motives, was in Titania the result of humanity and compassion'[32] – he quotes 2.1.121–37, where Titania claims that she wants to bring up and keep the boy because his mother was a votaress of Titania's order who died giving birth to him.

Like Drake, Samuel Taylor Coleridge offers a view of the *Dream* as a unity but for Coleridge this unity comes, not first of all from the feeling which pervades it, but from its combination of two genres – the drama and the poetic lyric. The 'whole of the *Midsummer Night's Dream* is one continued specimen of the dramatized lyrical'. Coleridge draws a distinction between the '[i]nterfusion of the lyrical – that which in its very essence is poetical – [...] with the dramatic' and the interfusion of the lyrical 'in and through the dramatic'. To exemplify the interfusion of the lyrical *with* the dramatic, Coleridge cites the plays of the Italian poet and melodramatist Pietro Metastasio (1698–1782), 'where at the end of the scene comes the *aria* as the exit speech of the character'[33] – an approach in which the distinction between the dramatic (the action in the scene which precedes the aria) and the lyrical (the aria itself) remains quite clearly marked and in which the combination of the two elements occurs in a discrete space, the end of the scene. One of the characteristics of Shakespeare's dramas, however, is that the lyrical is interfused not only *with*, but also *in and through* the dramatic – the linked prepositions 'in and through' suggesting a deeper degree of interfusion than 'with'.

Coleridge's general observations on the *Dream* are tantalizingly brief, and no extended account by him survives. His prestige as a poet and critic meant, however, that his idea of the play as an example of the 'dramatized lyrical' would persist as criticism moved from its Romantic to its early Victorian, mid-nineteenth-century phase.

THE MID-NINETEENTH CENTURY

In the year in which the young Queen Victoria (1819–1901; reigned 1837–1901) ascended the throne, the Irish journalist William Maginn published a paper in the magazine *Bentley's Miscellany* on 'Bottom the Weaver', thus demonstrating Bottom's continued capacity to attract critical interest. Maginn sees Bottom as 'a blockhead'[34] but also as '*the* lucky man [...] on whom Fortune showers her favours beyond measure', contrasting him to Romeo, 'the gentleman', the 'unlucky man of Shakespeare'.[35] During the time he enjoys the favours of Titania, Bottom 'never for a moment thinks there is anything extraordinary in the matter' and 'takes the love of the Queen of the Fairies as a thing of course'. When Titania's enchantment with him is lifted, he is no less 'a favourite of Fortune', no less 'happy and self-complacent'.[36] Afterwards he returns to his ordinary life and although he initially acknowledges that his experience with Titania has been wonderful, he 'soon thinks it is nothing more than a fit subject for a ballad in honour of his own name'. He immediately returns to 'his old habit of dictating, boasting, and swaggering' and does not refer to his experiences in the wood. 'It was no more than an ordinary passage in his daily life. Fortune knew where to bestow her favours'.[37]

Like Maginn, the writer, editor and publisher Charles Knight, in *The Pictorial Edition of the Works of Shakespeare* (1839), is interested both in defining Bottom as a character and in his larger function within the play. Knight shares Maginn's sense that Bottom is a character who remains the same whatever his circumstances, but he sees him, not as a lucky man, but as Everyman:

■ Bottom the weaver is the representative of the whole human race. [...] In every situation, Bottom is the same – the same personification of that self-love which the simple cannot conceal, and the wise can with difficulty suppress.[38] □

Knight's high claims for Bottom are matched by his high claims for the *Dream* as a whole. Like Hazlitt, he sees it as the epitome of English poetic excellence. He also praises it as the most harmonious of Shakespeare's plays:

■ It exhibits all that congruity of parts – that natural progression of scenes – that subordination of character and action to one leading design – that ultimate harmony evolved out of seeming confusion – which constitute the dramatic spirit.[39] □

Striking a note that G. K. Chesterton will later echo in the early twentieth century (see Chapter 2 of this Guide), Knight further maintains that a materialist sensibility will be unable to respond fully to the *Dream*. In the mid-nineteenth century, this idea is approached from a different angle by the antiquarian Joseph Hunter in his *New Illustrations of the Life, Studies, and Writings of Shakespeare* (1845). Hunter suggests that the play escapes from material reality by being presented as a dream. He argues that its title provokes the question: 'Who is the dreamer? The poet, any of the characters of the drama, or the spectators?' His answer is that the characters enchanted by the fairies see their experiences as fit only to be regarded as a dream and that 'it comes before the spectators under the notion of a dream'.[40] So it is not that the spectators are dreaming but that their acceptance of the play as a 'dream' allows them to tolerate incongruities which would otherwise be unacceptable. While the dominant tendency in nineteenth-century criticism was to stress the unity or harmony of the *Dream* rather than its heterogeneity, Hunter's remarks suggest that a strong sense of its incongruities could still remain.

The German philosopher Hermann Ulrici was also strongly conscious of the incongruities of the *Dream* and poses the question which, in his view, the 'rare and heterogeneous elements' of the play immediately provoke:[41] 'whether [the *Dream*] satisfies the first requirement of art that the several parts should round themselves into an organic whole, and if so, what is the centre around which they all adjust themselves?'[42] His answer is ingenious: it is on the 'basis of reciprocal parody that the different and heterogeneous groups first coalesce into unity':[43]

■ Theseus and Hippolyta represent the grand heroic and historically important aspect of human life [but] by seeming to exist for no other purpose than to marry with suitable pomp and splendour, they form with agreeable irony a merry parody on their own heroic importance. [The craftsmen], instead of remaining in their own true station, wherein they at once command respect, worm themselves into the higher domain of tragedy and poetry, and render it as well as themselves ridiculous [The lovers] belong to the middle ranks of life. But instead of behaving agreeably to their station, and regarding life in its plain and sober aspect, they lose themselves in the fantastic humours of a capricious passion, and thereby parody themselves and the class to which they belong. Lastly, the fairy prince, with his interposition in the action, represents that higher power which guides human life with an invisible thread. But even this superintending power is not depicted in its true god-like grandeur and elevation, but [...] either appears as the nimble, frolicsome play of the personified powers of nature, or parodies itself, so far as it is subject to the universal caprice of chance and to its own waywardness; as [...] Titania's passion for the ass-headed Weaver [shows].[44] □

In the mid-nineteenth century, the American Shakespeare scholar Henry Norman Hudson, in his eleven-volume edition of Shakespeare's works (1851–6), partly endorses Ulrici's view but still seems dissatisfied with it, observing that the *Dream* remains a great problem for criticism because it is in a class of its own: 'its very essence is irregularity' and a 'sort of lawlessness is indeed the very law of the piece'.[45] Whereas Ulrici sees the *Dream* as unified by the operation of parody – which we might interpret as a kind of law – Hudson suggests that the play is not wholly governed by this law – or any other that could be codified.

A sense of the unpredictability and capriciousness of the *Dream* is also evident in the account of the German literary historian Georg Gottfried Gervinus, in his *Shakespeare Commentaries* (originally published in German in 1849–50 and first issued in an English translation by F. E. Bunnètt in 1863 and in a new, revised English edition in 1877). Gervinus contends that the 'actions' in the *Dream*, even more than its characters, are treated quite differently than in other Shakespeare plays:

■ The presence of an underlying motive – the great art and true magic wand of the poet – has here been completely disregarded. Instead of reasonable inducements, instead of natural impulses arising from character and circumstance, caprice is master here. [...] these actions without any higher centre of a mental and moral bearing, are compared, as it were, to a dream, which unrolls before us with its fearful complications, from which there is no deliverance but in awaking and in the recovery of consciousness.[46] □

The dreamlike quality of the play, however, is not merely chaotic but carries a moral message:

■ The piece appears designed to be treated as a dream; not merely in outer form and colouring, but also in inner signification. The errors of that blind intoxication of the senses, which form the main point of the piece, appear to us to be an allegorical picture of the errors of a life of dreams. Reason and consciousness are cast aside in that intoxicating passion as in a dream.[47] □

To reinforce his view of the overall purpose of the *Dream*, Gervinus pursues his idea that, in the play, the fairies are the equivalent of

Cupid, the boy-god of classical mythology whose arrows make people fall in love:

■ [T]he actions and occupations of Cupid and of the fairies throughout the piece are interwoven or alternate. And this appears to us to confirm most forcibly the design of the poet to compare allegorically the sensuous life of love with a dream-life; the exchange of functions between Cupid and the fairies is therefore the true poetic embodiment of this comparison.[48] □

Gervinus has thus found a unity in the apparent caprice and chaos of the *Dream*; all its elements contribute to an allegorical comparison of the sensuous love-life and the dream-life, and both of these forms of life are characterized by error, by the sleep of reason and consciousness, by the loss of 'a higher centre of a mental and moral bearing'. Like Ulrici, Gervinus exemplifies the developing critical quest for an overall explanation of the *Dream*. As the next subchapter will show, this quest would be pursued in the later nineteenth century, but there would also be further interest in one particular aspect of the play: the figure of Bottom, whose critical stock rises during the nineteenth century.

THE LATER NINETEENTH CENTURY

In his book *Caliban: The Missing Link* (1873), Sir Daniel Wilson, a man of many parts, focuses on the figure of Bottom. Like Charles Knight, whom we considered in the previous subchapter, Wilson sees Bottom as 'a representative man' who can be found in all eras and social classes:[49]

■ [Bottom is] the very embodiment and idealisation of that self-esteem which is a human virtue by no means to be dispensed with, though it needs some strong counterpoise in the well-balanced mind.[50] □

He is 'a natural genius' who claims the lead because of his 'recognised fitness to fulfil the duties he assumes' and who is never inconvenienced, upset or annoyed).[51] '[U]nabashed by rank, undaunted by difficulties, ready at a moment's notice for all emergencies, thoroughly cool and self-reliant', he is the 'hero' of the *Dream*.[52]

In his *Essays on Shakespeare* (1874), the German scholar and critic Karl Elze brings us back to more general reflections on the *Dream* by focusing, not on Bottom, but on the generic nature of the play. He develops the idea that 'Shakespeare's most charming comedy' is like a masque. Elze argues that masques did not 'aim to solve a dramatic problem', because they were designed as celebrations of key events, such as marriages, among the higher echelons of society. In the masque, action and character, while not excluded, were always secondary. Elze contends that in the *Dream*, 'the two main portions [of the masque], masque and anti-masque are divided' in a manner almost like that of the masques by Shakespeare's fellow playwright, Ben Jonson (1572–1637).[53] Citing Schlegel's claim that Theseus and Hippolyta 'form [...] a splendid frame to the picture', he argues that this frame (which he extends to include 'the Athenian youths') 'corresponds to the actual masque', into which 'the anti-masque is inserted'. For Elze, the anti-masque is 'divided into the semi-choruses of the fairies' and the craftsmen.[54] While masque and anti-masque are often performed together but lack any internal connection with each other, Shakespeare, with great skill, interweaves the two modes in the *Dream*:

■ The anti-masque, in the scenes between Oberon and Titania [2.1.60–145; 4.1.75–101; 5.1.21–30] rises to the full poetic height of the masque, while the [masque itself], in the dispute between Hermia and Helena [3.2.283–345] indeed does not enter the domain of the comic, but still diminishes in dignity, and Theseus in the fifth act actually descends to the jokes of clowns [5.1.106–355].[55] □

Elze thus suggests that not only should the *Dream* be interpreted in terms of the masque and anti-masque but also that it should be seen as improving on the masque and anti-masque by constructing a much more integrated relationship between these two elements than is usually the case. He goes on to contend that, in the *Dream*, Shakespeare also transforms the masque from an elite to a popular mode, thereby making it 'universally attractive' and elevating its artistic status to the highest level.[56]

Elze's claim that the *Dream* was 'universally attractive' was echoed by the American writer and educationalist Denton Jacques Snider in an essay in *The Journal of Speculative Philosophy* (1874): 'There is no work of [Shakespeare] that is so universal, that appeals so strongly to high and low, to old and young, to man and woman'.[57] To support this view, Snider brings an overall philosophical approach – what might today be called a theoretical perspective – to his analysis of the *Dream*. It is an approach derived from the thought of the German philosopher Georg Wilhelm Friedrich Hegel. Like other nineteenth-century critics, Snider stresses the ultimate harmony of the *Dream*; he acknowledges that it can seem like 'a caprice, a dream without necessary connection in thought in its various parts', but affirms that 'a profound harmony' between 'all its essential parts' nonetheless pervades it.[58] Snider outlines

the three 'phases or divisions of the total movement of the play' which
contribute to this harmony:

1. The 'Real World', represented in Act 1, whose 'mediations' and
   'collisions are those of common experience, and are based upon the
   self-conscious Reason of man'.
2. The 'Fairy World, the Ideal Realm', whose 'mediations and collisions
   are brought about through the agency of supernatural beings, the
   creatures of the Imagination'. This comes to an end in Act 4.
3. The 'Representation in Art', which, along with the return from the
   Fairy World to the Real World, occupies the rest of Act 4 and Act 5
   (apart from the final scene). In the Representation in Art, 'the first
   two parts of the play mirror themselves'.[59]

This third phase or division is what later twentieth century criticism
would call the 'metadramatic' element of the *Dream*, the way in which
it highlights and explores itself as a drama and the nature of drama in
general, through the play-within-the play and the discussions which
this provokes.

Snider's interpretation emphasizes abstract ideas and moves at some
distance from the language of the play, rarely supporting its points by
specific quotation – although it would be possible to find quotations
which would support his argument. Moreover, his approach hardly
seems to register the humour of the play or the impact of Bottom's
character – for Snider, the mechanicals are merely stupid.

In *Wit, Humor, and Shakespeare* (1876), the American writer and
Unitarian priest John Weiss provides a useful corrective to Snider in these
respects. We have seen that Bottom has already gone through several
metamorphoses at the hands of critics: for Weiss, Bottom exemplifies the
self-made man who lacks 'a liberal education' and a 'disciplined intel-
ligence'[60] but who is in some ways admirable; for example, he is not
arrogant, has a good temper, and is not sour or cynical. Weiss also registers the humour of the scenes involving the craftsmen and suggests that
this spreads into other parts of the play:

■ [The craftsmen], by passing into the serious portions of the play, infect
it with the element of humor; for the simple earnestness of all their clown-
ishness fraternizes in no offensive way with the more poetical moods of
high society, and we feel the charm that equalizes all mankind.[61] □

Weiss thus endows the humour of the *Dream* with a large function – it
brings together the comic and serious elements of the play and creates
an equalizing charm that dissolves social differences, at least temporarily and on an emotional plane ('we *feel* the charm' [Guide author's

italics]). In a sense, Weiss propounds another version of the familiar nineteenth-century emphasis on the ultimate harmony of the *Dream* despite its apparent incongruities; but his use of the verb 'equalizes' has a different, democratic, perhaps more American emphasis.

In his *Shakspere* [Dowden's preferred spelling]: *A Critical Study of His Mind and Art* (1875), the critic and scholar Edward Dowden was concerned not with the equalizing charm of the *Dream* but with its embodiment of superiority in the figure of Theseus and with the way in which the enthusiastic representation of Theseus demonstrated Shakespeare's impartiality. Dowden's view of Theseus is in sharp contrast to Malone's sense that Theseus in this play is unworthy of his high status and reputation. Moreover, Dowden moves him from the frame of the picture (where Schlegel placed him) to the centre:

■ The central figure of [the *Dream*] is that of Theseus. [He] is to be studied as Shakspere's conception of the heroic man of action in his hour of enjoyment and of leisure. With a splendid capacity for enjoyment, gracious to all, ennobled by the glory, implied rather than explicit, of great foregone achievement, he stands as centre of the poem, giving their true proportions to the fairy tribe upon the one hand, and upon the other to the 'human mortals'.[62] □

Dowden does not see the *Dream* as endorsing Theseus totally, however; Shakespeare takes his distance, Dowden suggests, from this 'grand, ideal figure' when he makes Theseus bracket together the lunatic, the lover and the poet, thus revealing the limitations of Theseus' views on imagination and signalling 'a secret superiority of his [Shakespeare's] own soul'.

Where Dowden places a character, Theseus, at the centre of the *Dream*, the critic, headmaster and university teacher Charles Ebenezer Moyse sees the wood – which represents the world – as 'the centrepiece of the mechanism' of the play. He points out that the metaphor of wood as world is a familiar and enduring one in English and European literature: he cites, for example, the opening lines of Dante's *Inferno* where the poet finds himself in the middle of a dark wood and the opening of Spenser's *The Faerie Queene* where Una and the Red Cross Knight wander in the 'shadie grove' (Canto I, stanza 7, line 2). In the *Dream* itself, the centrality of the wood is shown, Moyse contends, in two ways: 'all the incidents where the tide waves of action run high and fast happen' in the wood and 'every character in the play' is brought into the wood, if we suppose Philostrate to follow in the train of Egeus[63] (or, we might add, if Egeus and Philostrate are one and the same). Moyse concludes that the *Dream* 'is allegorical'; that 'the wood is the world'; that the characters 'are Athenians in fiction, Englishmen in fact'; that 'some members of all groups' in the play, except what Moyse calls 'the earthly imperial' (Theseus and Hippolyta) go astray before harmony is restored; that 'the hero of earthly empire', Theseus, 'performs, as in a Masque, the last, though comparatively unimportant, act which restores harmony', when he overbears the will of Egeus and permits the marriage of Hermia and Lysander (4.1.178–80); that 'the dream is simply the experience of years narrowed to a span by the active mind of the dreamer, and intensified'; and, finally, that 'the tragedy of Pyramus and Thisbe is the diapason', the grand swelling burst of harmony, which 'completes the whole'.[64] Once more, the *Dream* is seen as an ultimately harmonious play.

The writer Julia Wedgwood, in an article on the *Dream* in *The Contemporary Review* (April 1890), changes the focus of earlier critics by concentrating on Titania. Wedgwood sees Titania, 'the central figure' of fairyland, as a large-scale development of the minute Queen Mab of Mercutio's mocking speech in *Romeo and Juliet* (1.4.53–95). For Wedgwood, Titania 'seems as much of a goddess as of a fairy', and her quarrel with Oberon 'might come straight from Homer' – that is, it has an epic, heroic quality befitting the work of the author (or authors) of the ancient Greek epics *The Illiad* and *The Odyssey*. This is a very different view of Titania from that of Edmund Malone, who was disappointed that she did not live up to her exalted station. But in Wedgwood's perspective, Titania is human as well as heroic: she is 'full of human preference, human jealousy; she cherishes [the Indian boy] from the recollection of his mother' and Titania's fidelity to his mother 'puts to scorn the fitful friendship of Helena and Hermia'.[65] Here Wedgwood highlights an issue which some feminist critics will take up in the later twentieth century: the close bonding of Titania and her unnamed votaress.

Wedgwood also homes in on a figure who has no speaking part in the play at all but who has been of considerable interest, as we shall see in Chapters 4, 6 and 7 of this Guide, to later twentieth-century and early twenty-first-century critics: Titania's 'young squire' (2.1.131), the Indian boy whom Oberon wants Titania to hand over to him. Wedgwood finds that this boy 'has a faint affinity' with classical mythology but that 'he is a more of a modern on the whole';[66] she sees him as the origin of a line of children's literature whose most recent avatar is *Alice's Adventures in Wonderland* (originally published as *Alice's Adventures Under Ground* (1865) by Lewis Carroll (pseudonym of Charles Lutwidge Dodgson (1832–98)):

■ With [the Indian boy] the modern fairy tale is born; he survives in that enchanted land where we have all wandered in years gone by; where the happy boy or girl awakens from some mysterious slumber, and finds himself or herself at home amid a quaint bright throng where earth is forgotten. That Indian princeling is the Columbus of fairyland, and all who have trodden its soil since, down to Alice in Wonderland, are followers in his track.[67] □

In calling the princeling 'the Columbus of fairyland', Wedgwood means that he (or Shakespeare through him) is a literary rather than imperialist pioneer; but the image does adumbrate the possibility of considering the Indian boy in a colonial context, as Margo Hendricks does in Chapter 7 of this Guide.

Wedgwood also sees the 'adventures of the night' in the *Dream* as a parable of the confusions of love, and this view is shared to some extent by the Shakespeare scholar and historian of the English stage E. K. Chambers, in his introduction to his 1897 Warwick Shakespeare edition of the play. Chambers calls the *Dream* 'a dramatic fantasy rather than a drama'[68] and places the emphasis on its comic treatment of love:

■ Love, as interpreted by the comic spirit, is a certain fine lunacy in the brain of youth; not an integral part of life, but a disturbing element in it. The lover is a being of strange caprices and strange infidelities, beyond the control of reason and swayed with every gust of passion. He is at odds for the time with all the established order of things, a rebel against the authority of parents, a rebel against friendship, a rebel against his own vows. This is love as it figures in comedy, and in the presentation and analysis of this lies the point of *A Midsummer Night's Dream*.[69] □

Chambers goes on to affirm that Shakespeare treats the theme of love in a symbolic rather than psychological way in the *Dream*. The play's use of the supernatural is part of this symbolic approach; Shakespeare does not really believe in the supernatural but employs it in order to acknowledge a mysterious, inexplicable element in human life which, in the comic perspective of the *Dream*, gives rise to the erratic morals and feelings of lovers.

Like Chambers, the Danish critic Georg Brandes, in the best-selling English translation of his book *William Shakespeare* (1895; 1899), sees the *Dream* as using the supernatural for symbolic purposes, but is more specific than Chambers in identifying what it symbolizes. Whereas Chambers regards the supernatural as symbolizing 'the freakish irresponsible element of human nature', Brandes affirms: 'Oberon's magic is simply a great symbol, typifying the sorcery of the erotic imagination.'[70] This explicit statement of an erotic element in the *Dream* points to an aspect of the play that had been little discussed in the nineteenth century, but was to receive far more attention in the twentieth: its treatment of sexuality. Brandes also sounds a modern note when he speaks of the 'unconscious':

■ [The *Dream*] is a lightly-flowing, sportive, lyrical fantasy, dealing with love as a dream, a fever, an illusion, an infatuation, and making merry, in especial, with the irrational nature of the instinct. [Shakespeare] early felt and divined how much wider is the domain of the unconscious than of the conscious life, and saw that our moods and passions have their root in the unconscious. The germs of a whole philosophy of life are latent in the wayward love-scenes of [the *Dream*].[71] □

Brandes's emphasis on the 'unconscious' is not a Freudian one – Sigmund Freud (1856–1939) was a relatively little-known figure at this time, whose first major independent work, *The Interpretation of Dreams*, would not be published until the end of 1899. But the idea of the power of the unconscious does resonate with what would become one of the key concerns of psychoanalysis.

By the end of the nineteenth century, a critical tradition had grown around the *Dream* and key approaches and topics had emerged. Does the play form a unity or harmony, and if so, how? How might the play be understood in terms of genre? What is the role of the supernatural element? What is the function of the play-within-a-play? How does the play represent women? How does it portray craftsmen? How might the character of Bottom best be defined? How significant is Theseus, and what does he stand for? How useful is it to think of the *Dream* in terms of sexuality and the unconscious? As the next chapter of this Guide will show, these issues, and their possible answers, would be pursued further, and in a variety of ways, in the twentieth century.

CHAPTER TWO

1900–49: Quest for Constancy

In the early twentieth century, the study of English Literature began to emerge as an academic discipline in the UK and critical power started to move away from the man or woman of letters towards the critic employed in and speaking from a university. As a field of study seeking to establish its academic respectability, English Literature would certainly be likely to focus on its major asset, William Shakespeare, but it might not concentrate first on Shakespearean comedy, especially not on the *Dream*, whose fairies might make it look as though it had more in common with the whimsical play *Peter Pan* (1904) by the Scottish dramatist and novelist J. M. Barrie (1860–1937) than with serious and enduring literature. Not until the 1930s would a theory of Shakespearean comedy start to emerge. In the early part of the twentieth century, criticism of Shakespearean comedy – and of the *Dream* – was still the province of the man of letters more than the university teacher. Two key examples of *Dream* criticism which emerged in the 1900–25 period were from outside the academy. In 1904, the poet, novelist, journalist and essayist G. K. Chesterton made high claims for the *Dream*, and in 1925, the novelist, playwright and broadcaster J. B. Priestley – yet to emerge as the best-selling author of the novel *The Good Companions* (1929) – took up a topic which, as we saw in the last chapter, already had a good pedigree: the figure of Bottom. After this, however, the critical initiative does pass to academic scholars and critics, with the work of Enid Welsford, G. Wilson Knight, Caroline Spurgeon and H. B. Charlton.

G. K.CHESTERTON

G. K. Chesterton loved paradox and, in an essay published in the journal *Good Words* in 1904 and collected in *The Common Man* (1950), he affirms, surprisingly, that the *Dream* is not only Shakespeare's greatest comedy but also, from a certain viewpoint, his greatest play. Moreover, he asserts that it is 'perhaps a greater triumph of psychology than

Hamlet'. This may seem even more surprising, given the weight of opinion which had already accumulated in the nineteenth century to the effect that the characters in the *Dream* lacked psychological depth and differentiation. But Chesterton makes it clear that the psychological triumph of the *Dream* does not lie in its study of the psychology of individual characters. It occurs, rather, in its rendering of 'a social and spiritual atmosphere' and Chesterton wonders whether 'any other literary work in the world' does this so vividly. The *Dream* is 'a psychological study, not of a solitary man, but of a spirit that unites mankind':[1]

■ The sentiment of such a play, so far as it can be summed up at all, can be summed up in one sentence. It is the mysticism of happiness. That is to say, it is the conception that as man lives upon a borderland he may find himself in the spiritual or supernatural atmosphere, not only through being profoundly sad or meditative, but by being extravagantly happy. The soul might be rapt out of the body in an agony of sorrow, or a trance of ecstacy [sic]; but it might also be rapt out of the body in a paroxysm of laughter. Sorrow we know can go beyond itself; so, according to Shakespeare, can pleasure go beyond itself and become something dangerous and unknown. [We] cannot have *A Midsummer Night's Dream* if our one object in life is to keep ourselves awake with the black coffee of criticism. The whole question which is balanced, and balanced nobly and fairly, in the *Midsummer Night's Dream*, is whether the life of waking, or the life of vision, is the real life, the *sine qua non* [the 'without which nothing', the absolutely essential thing] of man.[2] □

The exploration of this question is enacted in the design of the *Dream*. Chesterton finds that 'the supreme literary merit' of the play lies in its design, which possesses an 'amazing symmetry' and an 'artistic and moral beauty'. The *Dream* opens 'in the sane and common world', enters 'the tangled wood of young troubles and stolen happiness', penetrates into 'the heart of fairyland', emerges into 'the clean and bracing morning' and almost ends in a triumphant evening party of human laughter and human certainty, before the final scene in which the fairies reappear and suggest that they may be the realities and mortals the shadows after all.[3]

Chesterton finds a further point of 'artistic perfection' in the play: 'the extraordinarily human and accurate manner in which [it] catches the atmosphere of a dream'. 'The chase and tangle and frustration of the incidents and personalities are well-known to every one who has dreamt of perpetually falling over precipices or perpetually missing trains'.[4] Chesterton offers a definition of a dream as a kind of jumbled, arbitrary narrative which is nonetheless unified by the persistence of one emotion throughout. A dream possesses 'an utter discordance of incident combined with a curious unity of mood: everything changes

but the dreamer'. It can start or finish with any event but if the dreamer
is sad or happy at the beginning, the same mood will persist through
to the end. For Chesterton, the *Dream* 'has in a most singular degree
effected this difficult, this almost desperate subtlety.[5]

> ■ The events in the wandering wood are in themselves, and regarded
> as in broad daylight, not merely melancholy but bitterly cruel and igno-
> minious. But yet by the spreading of an atmosphere as magic as the fog
> of Puck, Shakespeare contrives to make the whole matter mysteriously
> hilarious while it is palpably tragic; and mysteriously charitable, while it
> is in itself cynical. He contrives somehow to rob tragedy and treachery of
> their full sharpness, just as a toothache or a deadly danger from a tiger, is
> robbed of its sharpness in a pleasant dream. The creation of a brooding
> sentiment like this, a sentiment not merely independent of but actually
> opposed to the events, is a much greater triumph of art than the creation
> of the character of Othello.[6] □

Chesterton has suggested earlier in his discussion of the *Dream* that
pleasure can 'go beyond itself and become something dangerous and
unknown',[7] a remark which hints at a potentially threatening aspect
of the play. The remarks in the passage which has just been quoted
add a range of other negative aspects and make them more emphatic:
'melancholy', 'bitterly cruel', 'ignominious', 'palpably tragic', 'cynical'.
The *Dream* starts to seem a dark play, redeemed only by the unity of
atmosphere which Chesterton sees as pervading it.

Turning to Bottom, Chesterton produces the most exalted account
of him so far; Samuel Johnson's youthful actor, Charles Taylor's coxcomb, William Hazlitt's most romantic of mechanics, William Maginn's
lucky man, Charles Knight's Everyman, and Daniel Wilson's 'natural
genius' now becomes, for Chesterton, 'greater and more mysterious
than Hamlet' because he has 'a rich sub-consciousness', where Hamlet
has merely 'a rich consciousness'.[8] 'Sub-consciousness' is being used
here, not in any psychoanalytical sense, but to indicate that Bottom
does not have Hamlet's reflective, introspective intellect. This lack of
intellect does not diminish Bottom's greatness. For Chesterton, greatness does not consist in cleverness but is 'a certain indescribable but
perfectly familiar and palpable quality of size in the personality, of
steadfastness, of strong flavour, of easy and natural self-expression'.[9]
Bottom, Chesterton implies, has all these qualities. He also has 'the
supreme mark of this real greatness in that like the true saint or the
true hero he only differs from humanity in being as it were more human
than humanity'. Moreover, his 'sensibility to literature is perfectly fiery
and genuine, a great deal more genuine than that of a great many
cultivated critics of literature'.[10] The exaltation of Bottom would be taken
up and developed, with different emphases, by J. B. Priestley.

J. B. PRIESTLEY

In 'Bully Bottom', the opening chapter in J. B. Priestley's book *The English Comic Characters* (1925), Priestley describes Bottom as 'a gigantic individual creation, the first of [Shakespeare's] really great comic figures'.[11] Priestley cites and endorses Hazlitt's observations, which we considered in the previous chapter of this Guide, that Bottom is a character that has not had justice done to him and is the most romantic of mechanics. Priestley acknowledges Bottom's earthiness in the context of the *Dream*. 'He is a trades-unionist among butterflies, a ratepayer in Elfland'.[12] But he is also 'the enthusiast, the romantic, the artist'.[13] Priestley takes issue with Puck's description of Bottom as 'The shallowest thickskin of that barren sort' (3.2.13):

■ Bottom, though he may be the biggest fool (and a big fool is no common person), is really the least shallow and thickskinned of his group, in which he shows up as the romantic, the poetical, the imaginative man, who naturally takes command. We admit that he is conceited, but he is, in some measure, an artist, and artists are notoriously conceited.[14] □

Priestley pursues the idea that Bottom is to some extent an artist by affirming that, among the craftsmen, 'he is the only one who shows any passion for the drama itself, the art of acting, the enthralling business of moving and thrilling an audience'.[15] His desire to play all the parts in 'Pyramus and Thisbe' 'shows the eagerness and the soaring imagination of the artist'[16] and if it also shows 'a confidence so gigantic that it becomes ridiculous', we must remember that 'vanity and a soaring imagination are generally inseparable'.[17] Bottom is also a kind of humorist who, behind his pose, laughs at his audience as they laugh at him. 'Is he entirely our butt or is he for at least part of the time solemnly taking us in and secretly laughing at us?'[18]

Priestley's focus on character would, however, be repudiated by the emerging academic criticism of the *Dream*, which would examine the play in terms of its relationships to genre, as with Enid Welsford and H. B. Charlton, and to imagery, as with G. Wilson Knight and Caroline F. E. Spurgeon. It is to Welsford's analysis which we turn first.

ENID WELSFORD

In *The Court Masque* (1928), her magisterial history of the origins and development of the masque as a cultural form, Enid Welsford extends the idea that the *Dream* and *The Tempest* resemble masques. The idea that the *Dream* was like a masque was familiar – we saw in the previous chapter that Karl Elze explored it in the nineteenth century – but Welsford is concerned to stress that resemblance is not identity, that the *Dream* and *The Tempest* should *not* be regarded as masques. Rather, they are 'masque-like', 'particularly happy examples of the transformation of the masque by the creative imagination of the poet'. Shakespeare, Welsford affirms, 'perceived, or at any rate acted upon, the principle that the masque must die to live'.[19]

For Welsford, a key element of the *Dream* as a creatively transformed masque is its design, which absorbs 'the scenic splendour of the masque' in 'description and picturesque language' and also in 'a blending of tones, a harmony of colours' achieved 'by a most delicate and subtle handling of the laws of resemblance and contrast'. It opens in the daylight world with 'the two sets of characters who most emphatically belong to that world': 'the genial cultivated rulers, the simple-minded artisans'. The craftsmen serve as 'a foil', the rulers as a 'framework' to the 'poetry and moonshine of the dream'. Welsford's image of the 'framework' is like that of the 'frame' which, as the previous chapter of this Guide showed, Schlegel used in the early nineteenth century. But Welsford pursues the idea further, arguing that Shakespeare's excellent workmanship is demonstrated in the organic connection between the 'framework' and the 'picture' which is evinced by the presence of Philostrate, the Master of the Revels, alongside Theseus and Hippolyta. As Welsford puts it: 'We are in the world of men, but men are in holiday mood'.[20] She traces how daylight gives way to moonlight and suggests that '[m]oonshine is almost as real a personage in Shakespeare's as in Bottom's play'.[21] Welsford then follows the transition from moonlight to dawn, then to evening and finally into the post-midnight zone when 'the colouring changes' and the fairies return – a moment, for Welsford as for Chesterton, when the distinction between the real and unreal becomes unstable: 'dreamland has invaded reality, and who shall say which is which'.[22]

Welsford contends that the whole of the *Dream* is 'musically written'. She contrasts the fairy songs in the *Dream* and *The Tempest* to the 'Sabrina' lyric (lines 858–900) in *Comus: A Masque presented at Ludlow Castle* (1634) by John Milton (1608–74). According to Welsford, 'each word [in 'Sabrina'] is exquisitely right, each word is an entity with its own peculiar value'. By contrast, the words in Shakespeare's songs 'melt into one another, and sometimes meaning is almost lost in melody and emotion'. The 'flowing blank verse' of the *Dream* has 'the same musical quality' and is 'lyrical rather than dramatic; liquid clear, never checked in its course by some sudden, sharp, projecting thought'.[23]

For Welsford, however, 'the rhythmic movement of living bodies' is the 'real soul of the masque'. This element of movement is an integral part of the *Dream* whereas in *Comus* it is incidental. The dances could be left out of *Comus* without much effect on the play but most (though not all) of the dances in the *Dream* 'are vitally connected with the plot'[24] (for example, the dances announced in 4.1.84–91, lines which mark the reconciliation of Oberon and Titania). In the *Dream*, the lines which anticipate or accompany the dance sequences are 'alive with movement, and suggest the repeat and turn and rhythmic beat of dancing'. Welsford sums up the difference in this way: 'in *Comus* we have thought turned to poetry, while in [the *Dream*] we have sound and movement turned to poetry'.[25]

Welsford does not locate the dance-like quality of the *Dream* only in its set-piece songs and dances however, but also, and primarily, in the whole structure of the play. She makes a further comparison with *Comus*: Milton's play 'is a criticism of life' which 'springs from an abstract idea'; the *Dream* is 'a dance, a movement of bodies'. Its plot is 'a pattern, a figure, rather than a series of events occasioned by human character and passion, and this pattern, especially in the moonlight parts of the play, is the pattern of a dance'.[26] It is this dance-like pattern which entails that 'the lovers should be almost as devoid of character as masquers or masque presenters'. A credible display of passion would mar the 'harmony and grace of the action'. Only Bottom, Theseus and possibly Hippolyta rank as characters.[27]

We saw in Chapter 1 of this Guide that Karl Elze, in the nineteenth century, saw the *Dream* as consisting of masque and antimasque. Welsford also locates an important antimasque element in the *Dream*, but whereas Elze argued that this element was divided between the semi-choruses of the fairies and the mechanicals, Welsford finds that it is the mechanicals who perform the same function as the antimasque. She acknowledges that the *Dream* appeared before Ben Jonson had developed and formulated the antimasque, but proposes that 'grotesque dances' were well-liked from the beginning of the masque as a form and that 'the principle of contrast was always latent' in it.[28] But she finds a large contrast between Shakespeare and Jonson's deployment of the antimasque. Whereas in Jonson's kind of antimasque 'the transition is sudden and the contrast complete', Shakespeare aimed to attain beauty by setting up a masque/antimasque contrast through an 'obvious and striking' difference which arose 'out of a deep though unobtrusive resemblance'.[29] This is most evident in the embraces of Titania and ass-headed Bottom.

The transmuted elements of masque and antimasque in the *Dream* contribute to the dance which constitutes a play whose 'underlying motif is harmony'. However sharp the disparities of the *Dream*, its unity is more profound. The presiding deity of the play, Welsford suggests, is Hymen, the ancient Greek god of weddings. In the *Dream*, the fairies are emanations of Hymen and perform his functions. Taking advantage of the deep-rooted link in folklore between fairies and fertility, Shakespeare, in the *Dream*, substitutes fairies for Ceres, Diana and Juno, the ancient Greek fertility goddesses who appeared in pageants, and turns them into 'an expression of the harmony and concord which was the keynote of most Elizabethan revels'.[30]

Welsford's final stress in her discussion of the *Dream* is on harmony. A similar emphasis appears five years later in G. Wilson Knight's interpretation of the play in *The Shakespearean Tempest*, but Knight aims to locate this unity within the greater unity of Shakespeare's drama as a whole and to explore the *Dream*'s resonances with darker Shakespearean strands.

G. WILSON KNIGHT

G. Wilson Knight approaches the *Dream*, not only as a unity in itself, but also, and above all, as a part of the overall unity of Shakespeare's works. This 'true Shakespearean unity' is 'the opposition, throughout the plays, of "tempests" and "music"'.[31] He denounces the approach to Shakespeare's plays which views them 'primarily as studies in characters, abstracting the literary person from the close mesh of that poetic fabric into which he is woven'.[32] Instead he insists that criticism should focus on 'poetic colour and suggestion, thinking primarily in terms of symbolism, not "characters"'. In this perspective, 'each play in turn' will 'appear more and more amazing in the delicacy of its texture', and then, and not before, 'the whole of Shakespeare's work begin[s] to reveal its richer significance, its harmony, its unity'.[33]

The turn from a concern with character to a perspective which focused on poetic symbolism through a close examination of vocabulary and imagery was a crucial shift in Shakespeare criticism in the 1930s, and Knight was one of its pioneers. Among Shakespeare's plays, the *Dream* had attracted less character study than some others because, as we have seen, some of its leading figures, especially the lovers, are not strongly individualized and cannot easily be seen in terms of psychological complexity. Bottom is the character who stands out most, as the weight of critical commentary on him testifies, but, as G. K. Chesterton pointed out, Bottom is no Hamlet. Thus the *Dream* had already aroused critical responses which aimed to analyse it in terms of overall patterns, such as Ulrici's reading of it as composed of interacting parodies, or Welsford's view of it as an ultimately harmonious dance. Knight, however, wants to find a pattern which is not only specific to the *Dream* but also congruent with the 'tempest-music' opposition which, in his view, pervades all Shakespeare's work.

Knight finds that the *Dream* weaves 'all the best of Shakespeare's earlier poetry [...] into so comprehensive and exquisite a design that it is hard not to feel that this play alone is worth all the other romances' (by 'romances' here, Knight means Shakespeare's romantic comedies (*Love's Labours Lost, As You Like It, Much Ado about Nothing, The Two Gentlemen of Verona, All's Well that Ends Well*), rather than the later plays (*The Winter's Tale, Cymbeline, Pericles, The Tempest*) which are sometimes called 'romances'). These comedies, whatever their ostensible setting, are located in 'a land of purely fanciful delight, a fairyland of success-ful, tempest-vanquishing romance'.[34] In Knight's perspective, this 'fairyland' evoked by the imagery of all these comedies must be linked to 'those other images where, in the Histories and Early Tragedies, amid more realistic and tragic stress, the poet makes fleeting sugges-tion of the soul's desire set beyond rough seas of disaster and disorder, fairy riches on far-off Indian strands of the soul'.[35] The *Dream* brings together the 'fairyland' dimension of the other comedies and the 'Indian' dimension hinted at in the Histories and Early Tragedies and combines them with the human dimension:

■ In [the *Dream*] fairyland interpenetrates the world of human action. And that world is varied, ranging from the rough simplicity of the clowns, through the solid common sense and kind worldly wisdom of Theseus, to the frenzied fantasies of the lovers: which in their turn shade into fairyland itself. The play thus encloses remarkably a whole scale of intuitions.[36] □

As well as bringing together the fairyland, Indian and human dimen-sions and enclosing 'a whole scale of intuitions', the 'interplay of imagery' in the *Dream* is the most 'exquisitely varied' of all the romantic comedies, encompassing the beautiful and the alarming.[37]

Pursuing his idea of a 'tempest-music' opposition which runs through all Shakespeare's plays, Knight finds the 'tempest' in the *Dream* in the quarrel between Oberon and Titania, which arises from 'these spirits' desire for human love'[38] and what he later specifies as their 'rivalry for the Indian boy' and their respective jealousy of Theseus and Hippolyta.[39] Knight quotes Titania's account of the impact of their dispute on the weather and on rural life (2.1.81–117) and observes:

■ Unruly floods, disorder in the seasons, storm and mud and all natural confusion result from this dissension in fairyland. And this tempest is at the heart of the play, sending ripples outward through the plot, vitalizing the whole middle action.[40] □

In contrast to this 'tempest' element, music interthreads the pattern of the *Dream*. For example, Lysander has 'sung' verses to Hermia (1.1.30);

Theseus evokes a nun 'chanting faint hymns' (1.1.73); Titania recalls Oberon 'playing on pipes of corn and versing love to amorous Phillida' (2.1.67–8); Titania, wakened by Bottom's singing, finds her 'ear much enamoured of thy note' (3.2.131); her fairies will 'sing' to him (3.2.151); she later asks Bottom if he will hear 'some music' (3.2.27) and Bottom claims to have 'a reasonable good ear in music' and calls for 'the tongs and the bones' (3.2.28–9); Theseus asks Philostrate (or Egeus) 'What masque, what music?' he has to make the evening pass more quickly (5.1.40); picking out the contradictory terms in the mechanicals' summary of their play, Theseus asks: 'How shall we find the concord of this discord?'; responding to Quince's delivery of his prologue, Hippolyta remarks that 'he hath played on his prologue like a child on a recorder' (5.1.122–3).

Knight also examines vocabulary and imagery in the *Dream* which relates to moonlight, 'tempest beasts' (especially the bear), bushes, birds, flowers and jewels. In focusing on the darker aspects of the *Dream*, he reiterates their likeness to *Macbeth*: he finds that the nocturnal world the *Dream* evokes has 'a gnomish, fearsome, Macbeth [*sic*]-like quality [...], just touching nightmare';[41] that the play has 'many sombre *Macbeth* effects';[42] that it 'continually suggests *Macbeth*', with 'elves and gnomes' replacing 'witches and ghosts';[43] that it links 'the *Macbeth* nightmare frenzy' with 'the super-consciousness of love, and poetry';[44] that 'the *Macbeth* dark' pervades it.[45]

Knight backs up these general statements with more specific examples. For instance, when Hermia finds Lysander sleeping, she at first thinks he may have been murdered and says to Demetrius: 'If thou has slain Lysander in his sleep / Being overshoes in blood, plunge in the deep / And kill me too' (3.2.47–9). The imagery is akin to Macbeth's lines: 'I am in blood / Stepped in so far that, should I wade no more, / Returning were as tedious as go o'er' (3.5.135–7). Later, Oberon instructs Puck to make the night dark and confuse Lysander and Demetrius 'till o'er their brows death-counterfeiting sleep / With leaden legs and batty wings doth creep'; Knight links this with the lines in which Macduff, having discovered the dead Duncan, urges Macbeth and Lennox to '[s]hake off this downy sleep, death's counterfeit, / And look on death itself' (2.3.75–6). Towards the end of the play, Puck's penultimate speech evokes the night in which 'the wolf behowls the moon' (5.1.379); his beast-reference can recall Macbeth's speech as he nerves himself up to slaughter Duncan and speaks of 'the wolf / Whose howl's his watch' (2.1.53–4).

Like G. K. Chesterton, Knight does not see the dark elements of the *Dream* as ultimately dominant: the 'atmosphere of gloom and dread' in the *Dream* is 'the playground for the purest comedy', '[r]omance and fun interthread' the shades of tragedy[46] and at the harmonious end of the play 'the two worlds, fact and fairyland, which have been divided in tempest, now embrace to music.'[47] But Knight's interpretation clearly opens the way for darker readings of the *Dream*. A much more benign reading of Shakespeare's imagery in the *Dream* would be offered by Caroline Spurgeon.

CAROLINE SPURGEON

Like G. Wilson Knight, Caroline Spurgeon's focus, in *Shakespeare's Imagery and What It Tells Us*, is on what she calls 'iterative' or 'recurrent imagery' – 'the repetition of an idea or picture in the images used in any one play' and the part these repeated images play 'in raising and sustaining emotion, in providing atmosphere or in emphasising a theme'.[48] She suggests that in the comedies 'this imagery contributes chiefly atmosphere and background, as well as sometimes emphasising or re-echoing certain qualities in the plays'.[49] In the *Dream* 'what we feel overpoweringly is the woodland beauty of the dreaming summer night, and it is only when we look closer that we realise in some measure how this sensation is brought about'.[50]

A crucial contribution to this sensation is the pervasive 'influence and presence of the moon'.[51] Spurgeon locates twenty-eight occurrences of the word 'moon', three-and-a-half times more than in any other Shakespeare play. The term 'Moonlight' also features with unusual frequency: there are only eight references to 'moonlight' in the whole of Shakespeare's dramas, and six occur in the *Dream*. The *Dream* also contains his only reference to 'moonbeams'. The moon is invoked at the start of the play, in the opening exchange between Theseus and Hippolyta, and near the end, in Puck's phrase 'the wolf behowls the moon' (in contrast to Knight, Spurgeon does not mention any sinister, *Macbeth*-like implications in this line). The moon measures time and movement: the lovers arrange to meet the next day 'when Phoebe doth behold / Her silver visage in the watery glass [i.e. when the moon is reflected in water]' (1.1.209–10). Oberon tells Titania: 'We the globe can compass soon, / Swifter than the wand'ring moon' (4.1.96–7). The moon is 'the governess of floods' (2.1.103) and her 'chaste beams' quench 'young Cupid's fiery shaft' (2.1.162, 161). She 'symbolises the barren air of the cloister' where the nuns chant 'faint hymns to the cold fruitless moon' (1.1.73). Hermia would as soon believe that Lysander has stolen away from her while she was sleeping as she would believe that the 'whole earth may be bored, and that the moon / May through the centre creep, and so displease / Her brother's noontide with th'Antipodes' (3.2.53–5).

The moon imagery 'partly supplies the dreaming and enchanted quality in the play' and the effect of 'woodland beauty' reinforces this. This effect is achieved by 'the high proportion of poetical images [...] and the very large number of nature images, including animals and birds'. There are also images which Spurgeon classifies under other headings but which relate to nature. For example, Spurgeon feels that 'the green corn / Hath rotted ere his youth attained a beard' (2.1.94–5) should be classified as a personification but that it primarily evokes, for her, the appearance of the fields at the end of many wet English summers. The account of how 'the spring, the summer, / The childing autumn, angry winter, change / Their wonted liveries' (2.1.112–13) should be filed under 'clothes' but 'really presents us with a pageant of the seasons in their many-coloured garb'.[52] Spurgeon implies here that the lines evoke the familiar 'pageant of the seasons' but the key point is that the seasons are departing from their usual manifestations, their accustomed appearance ('wonted liveries').

Spurgeon also discusses the bird imagery which in the *Dream*, as elsewhere in Shakespeare, serves to indicate a range of movements, sound and colour. For delicate but definite movement, there is Oberon's command to the elves and fairy sprites: 'Hop as light as bird from brier' (5.2.24). For hectic movement, there is Puck's comparison between the mechanicals when they fly away after seeing Bottom transfigured to an ass, and the 'wild geese' or 'russet-pated choughs' that, '[r]ising and cawing at the gun's report / Sever themselves and madly sweep the sky' (3.2.20–3). Bird imagery is used to suggest sound when Helena tells Hermia her voice is '[m]ore tuneable than lark to shepherd's ear' (1.1.184). A sharp colour contrast is conveyed when Demetrius, his vision transfigured by the love-juice, says of Helena: 'high Taurus' snow, / Fanned with the eastern wind – turns to a crow / When thou hold'st up thy hand' (3.2.142–4).

The image-based approaches of Knight and Spurgeon to the *Dream*, and to Shakespeare criticism more generally, would be highly influential in the 1930s, but they were not the only fruitful ones. A productive alternative approach, exemplified by H. B. Charlton, was to see the *Dream* in the context of a broader view of Shakespearean comedy and of comedy in general.

H. B. CHARLTON

In his *Shakespearean Comedy* H. B. Charlton contends that in the *Dream* Shakespeare, for the first time, 'reveals his promise as the world's comic dramatist'[53] and demonstrates 'his power to use comedy for its proper function, to show real man encountering the real problem of the world in which he was really living' – and this problem was, according to Charlton, 'the power felt then to be the primary factor of his existence, his response to the quality and the might of love'.[54] In aiming to define the masterly achievement of the *Dream*, Charlton acknowledges its skilful fusion of three disparate aspects:

■ [The] anachronistic court of a pre-Homeric Athens, the realistic population of a contemporary English countryside, and the realm of a fairy land [In the *Dream*] ancient, mediaeval, and modern have broken through the limits of time to exist together in one and the same timeless moment'.[55] □

But this unity is only the outward and visible sign of 'the real harmony' which 'has been shaped by imaginative insight'.[56] The 'three separate worlds are moulded into one by a controlling point of view, by an idea'. The *Dream* is 'Shakespeare's first masterpiece' not because of its technical superiority to his previous comedies but because 'in it he has seized more securely on the vital temper of his generation and embodied with it more of the essential spirit of his time'. The 'most distinctive mark' of this security is that Shakespeare's 'matter has now acquired a more searching significance for life, and a closer bearing on the facts of existence'. In the *Dream*, Shakespeare attains 'a comic idea', not 'through his work-a-day reason', but 'as an artist, through his imaginative apprehension'.

Charlton suggests that '"What is love?" or rather, "What is the place of love in life?" is the question underlying' the *Dream*.[57] In exploring Shakespeare's dramatization of this question, he offers an intriguing description of Hermia and Helena which covers both of them. 'They are Shakespeare's first real flappers, straight from a lady's seminary'. Here Charlton compares the two young women both to the figure of modern feminine freedom (including sexual freedom) associated above all, in modern literature, with the American novelist and short-story writer F. Scott Fitzgerald (1896–1940), and to the coyly innocent 'three little maids from school' of the comic operetta *The Mikado* (1885) by the librettist W. S. Gilbert (1836–1911) and the composer Arthur Sullivan (1842–1900). Focusing then on Helena, he sees her as having once resembled 'the prim young maiden of the Pre-Raphaelites', working at her sampler – this perhaps alludes especially to the painting *The Girlhood of Mary Virgin* (1848) by the poet and painter Dante Gabriel Rossetti (1828–92). Charlton points out that Helena 'is pale and tall, the traditional emblem of forlorn maiden love', but she is more than an emblem; in the course of the play, she learns from experience and moves from being a 'spaniel' to an assertive young woman who resists Lysander's entreaties and demands guarantees; she is finding 'phrases, modes and ideals more applicable to the needs and situations of the moment'.[58] Charlton finds Hermia 'even more alive'; 'the sprightly sketch of the girlish moods and the feline attitudes of Hermia's jealousy' greatly enhances the 'customary comic play of misapprehension and unexpected confusions in the scene where the four lovers are at odds [3.2.138–345]'.[59]

To an extent, then, Charlton sees Helena and Hermia as modern young women, in terms of the 1920s and 1930s, as his comparison of them to 'flappers' indicates. But only to an extent; they will play out 'the fond pageant of youth', but the 'power' of 'their human nature' must bring them in the end to monogamous, heterosexual, domestic marriage.[60] For Charlton, the alternative to this kind of marriage is represented by Titania and Oberon, who, though married, are clearly not monogamous and not necessarily wholly heterosexual (though Charlton, it should be stressed, does not explicitly raise the question of their sexual orientation). Their mobility, their capacity to speed across the globe in a flash, frees them from the ties of domesticity and lets their mood, whim and fancy run wild, creating a 'state of sentimental anarchy' which 'is never ordered by obligation to the world'. By showing them as unfitted 'for the responsibilities of the settled human institution of marriage', the *Dream* fulfils the 'natural function' of comedy, 'glorifying those settled institutions of man's social existence which owe their persistence to mankind's experience that such as these make for his welfare in the substantial problem of living life in the world as the world is. Marriage is to the comic dramatist the beneficent arrangement through which mankind achieves a maximum of human joy and a minimum of social disability'.[61]

Whereas Charlton is critical of both Oberon and Titania, Donald C. Miller, in 1940, directs his fire upon the fairy queen, and particularly on her relationship with the Indian boy. In doing so, he engages much more explicitly than Charlton – or any other previous critic – with the issue of sexuality in the *Dream*.

DONALD C. MILLER

Donald C. Miller's 'Titania and the Changeling', a short article tucked away in the 'Notes and news' section of the journal *English Studies*, received little attention at the time – in 1940, much of the world had other things to worry about – but, as Dorothea Kehler points out, it 'anticipates sexualized readings' of the *Dream*.[62] Miller is aware that he is challenging the 'idyllic quality' of the *Dream*'s fairies when he poses three questions:

■ Why was Titania so stubborn in refusing to give Oberon the changeling?
   Why was Oberon so determined to have him?
   Why did he employ love-juice to get him?
   To each question there is the same answer: Because Titania had made the boy her lover.[63] □

Miller sees only one objection to this answer: the idea that Titania is equivalent to the goddess of chastity. But he contends that the fact that Ovid uses 'Titania' to mean 'Diana' in the *Metamorphoses* does not entail that Shakespeare does the same. Moreover, the Titania/ Diana of ancient myth was a goddess of virginity, whereas the *Dream*'s Titania is married. And the claim that Elizabethans thought of fairies as beings who refused to tolerate unchastity does not, again, mean that the *Dream*'s fairies – and certainly not their Queen – are similarly strict; Miller suggests that Shakespeare might simply have inverted a popular belief. Miller argues that, in fact, Titania is sexually licentious – that when Oberon, in their first encounter in the *Dream*, calls her a 'wanton' (with its possible connotations of sexual promiscuity), he is near the truth. Miller's interpretation depends on three further words used by Oberon and Titania in their first encounter: Oberon calls Titania 'proud', Titania calls Oberon 'jealous', and Oberon calls Titania 'rash' (2.1.61, 64, 62). Miller sees 'proud' as having not only its most usual meaning but also a connotation of being sexually eager for a male. 'Jealous', Miller contends, refers specifically to Oberon's suspicion that Titania has bestowed her sexual favours on others, especially the Indian boy. He quotes what is still given as obsolete meaning 2 in the online Oxford dictionary: 'Ardently amorous; covetous of the love of another; fond, lustful'. With regard to 'rash', Miller acknowledges that this might have no more than its most usual meaning but could also be associated with sexuality. He cites lines from Shakespeare's *The Rape of Lucrece* in which, he suggests, 'rash' has this kind of connotation: 'Who o'er the white sheet peers her whiter chin / The reason of this *rash* alarm [sudden attack] to know' (lines 472–3); 'O *rash* false heat, wrapp'd in repentant cold' (48); 'Not to seducing lust, thy *rash* relier' (639) (Miller's italics); 'While lust is in his pride no exclamation / Can curb his heat or rein his *rash* desire' (705–6). He also cites lines from *Othello*: Iago says of Cassio 'Sir, he is very *rash* and very sudden in choler' (2.1.280); Lodovico of Othello: 'Where is this *rash* and inconsiderate man?' (5.2.283); Emilia, responding to Othello's accusation that Desdemona was 'false as water', responds: 'Thou art *rash* as fire, to say / That she was false' (5.2.134). Miller also cites the term 'rash-embraced' in *The Merchant of Venice* (3.1.109) and the figure of 'Master Rash' alluded to in *Measure for Measure*.

Miller finally returns to the term 'wanton'. He takes this to mean what the current online Oxford Dictionary calls 'a lascivious or lewd person' and he feels that Titania's behaviour fully justifies such a description. He also implies that the term is equally applicable to the mother of the changeling. Like an aggressive prosecuting counsel in a trial, Miller states flatly that Titania's statement that she will not part with the boy for the sake of his dead mother is 'a lie'. The truth is that 'Titania was in love with the changeling'. He draws attention to the similarity between her treatment of the boy and of Bottom: Puck tells the fairy that Titania 'crowns [the boy] with flowers' (2.1.27) and Oberon later tells Puck how Titania had 'rounded' Bottom's 'hairy temples' with 'coronet of fresh and fragrant flowers' (4.1.50, 51). In order to get Titania back, Oberon, by magic, makes her fall in love with Bottom and while she is enamoured of an ass he asks her for the changeling boy, whom she yields up without question. Oberon then lifts the spell and Titania's love returns to him. He concludes the matter 'with kingly grace' when he says to Titania: 'Now thou and I are new in amity' (4.1.86).

Miller's case is not wholly convincing. It relies to a significant extent on dogmatic assertion – for example that Titania is lying when she says she will not part with the boy for the sake of his late mother – and on questionable interpretations of the meaning, in the context of the *Dream*, of the words 'proud', 'rash', 'jealous' and 'wanton'. It condemns Titania on inadequate evidence while ignoring her charges that Oberon himself has been a wanton with Phillida and indeed Hippolyta. Moreover, Miller does not consider that one possible answer to the question of why Oberon is so determined to have the changeling boy is that he wishes to make the boy *his* lover and that one reason for his jealousy of Titania is that she appears to have done what he would like to do. His victory over Titania in the custody battle for the boy may not be, as Miller implies, a restoration of the conjugal order in which a husband 'is once more master of his wife's affections' but the triumph of a predatory paedophile. Nonetheless Miller does open up the issue of sexuality – and particularly of deviant or perverse sexuality – in the *Dream* in a way it had not been opened up before. But it would be some time before critics would pursue that issue. The Second World War produced, understandably, something of a hiatus in Shakespeare criticism, and it was still possible in 1949 for Thomas Marc Parrott to reaffirm a wholly benign view of the *Dream* in his book *Shakespearean Comedy*:

■ The shadow of death or danger that hangs over [Shakespeare's] earlier comedies, and was to reappear in darker shades hereafter, has vanished in the enchanted moonlight that floods the wood near Athens. Nowhere in all Shakespeare's work do we hear him singing in so carefree a strain as in [the *Dream*].[64] □

This benign view of the *Dream* would continue into the 1950s, but, as we shall see in the next chapter, Parrott's lyrical expression of it would be displaced by more analytical accounts of the play's significance, especially in regard to marriage and to the imagination.

CHAPTER THREE

The 1950s: Concord from Discord

In the 1950s, literary criticism became an established academic discipline and also, at least in the minds of some of its practitioners, something rather more – a means of preserving a sense of value, stability and order in a fast-changing and deeply uncertain modern world, marked, at least in the UK, Western Europe and the US, by a paradoxical combination of the pleasures of increasing affluence and a dark apprehension of a cataclysm through nuclear war. There was a strong emphasis on those qualities in literary texts which marked them off from popular cultural forms and which seemed to conduce to a harmonious balance of opposing forces within an organic whole. This was often linked to a rejection of key aspects of contemporary society and a nostalgia, more or less explicit, for an idealized world of the past (prior to the scientific revolution of the seventeenth century and the industrial revolution of the nineteenth century) in which, it was believed, the dissociated sensibility which characterized modern experience had not existed and the lower orders were happily integrated into a social whole and posed no threat to the cultural practices of more elevated groups. In this context, there was an emphasis, in *Dream* interpretation, on those elements of the play which seemed to produce concord from discord, to create and support a hierarchical civilized order with which literary critics could identify themselves. This is evident in the first key reading of the *Dream* in the 1950s by Paul N. Seigel.

PAUL N. SIEGEL

In '*A Midsummer Night's Dream* and the Wedding Guests' (1953), Siegel starts from the idea that the play was originally written for an aristocratic wedding. He is not concerned to identify whose wedding it was or to offer any specific detail about, or documentary evidence of, what an Elizabethan aristocratic wedding might have involved. Siegel does, however, invite the reader to take up the role of a guest at such a wedding in reading the *Dream*: '[B]y becoming the wedding guests in our imagination, we can recapture something of the total aesthetic experience of its first-performance audience, an experience which adds to the experience of the audiences of all ages a teasing piquancy of its own.'[1]

Considering the opening scene with Theseus and Hippolyta, Siegel contends that the 'wedding guests could not miss the flattering similarity between the Elizabethan bridal couple and the gracious, exalted pair of legendary antiquity'.[2] The young lovers, however, 'are like puppets in the hands of a puppet-master, now jerked this way, now that, now chasing after, now running away from, in an amusing exhibition of the vagaries of love and the absurdities to which it impels its victims'. Love is presented as, in Siegel's term, a 'pixilation' – a term which can mean bewildered, confused and drunk and is a variant of 'pixie-led', literally 'led astray by pixies'. It 'seizes young folk' but they eventually awake from it, 'as from a dream, to find themselves happy in their approaching marriage'. This aspect of the *Dream*, Siegel suggests, reflects the situation of the young aristocrats among the wedding guests in the audience. In contrast to the 'sportive' presentation of the young lovers, 'the love of Theseus and Hippolyta, and by implication that of the august bridegroom and bride whose wedding is being celebrated, is decorously presented on a different level'. On the verge of marriage, Theseus's 'passion is controlled, his love dignified and elevated'. 'From his serene height', he 'looks down with humorous condescension and benevolent tolerance upon the lovers and their moon-struck madness'.[3]

Theseus has his limits, however, and these emerge, for Siegel's imagined audience, in his dismissal of the lovers' tale of their nocturnal adventures. After all, the audience has seen those adventures and knows – within the terms of the dramatic illusion which the play produces – that he is wrong to discount them. But on another level, the audience does know that those adventures are part of a dramatic illusion, and as Theseus continues to discourse on the poet's imagination, he alerts the audience to the operation of that illusion, the way in which the poet 'gives to airy nothing / A local habitation and a name' (5.1.16–17). This is how the fairy creatures of the world have been created but it is also how Theseus himself, a character who only previously existed in 'antique fables' (5.1.3) has been created in the play. In dismissing the poet's creation as fantasy Theseus is also, in a sense, negating himself. Siegel suggests that '[s]ome perception of this paradox must have made the keener members of Shakespeare's courtly audience sense an irony in the large assurance' of Theseus's discourse on the lovers' tale and on the poet. Hippolyta could be right to suggest that there might be something in the lovers' tale. 'Perhaps – on a different level – it is true that the imaginative intuition of the poet can actually apprehend more essential truth than "cool reason" [5.1.6]'.[4]

The entry of the lovers immediately after Hippolyta's remarks in Act 5, however, returns the wedding guests 'to the solid world of human society, of which marriage is the base'. It seems likely to Siegel that the first performance of the *Dream* took place on the evening of the wedding ceremony, between supper and bedtime. In this case, he suggests, the last part of the *Dream*, speeding towards the consummation of the fictional marriages, could have been increasingly synchronous with the progress towards the consummation of the real-life marriage which the play was written to celebrate. '[A]t the conclusion of the play-within-the-play the play itself would end, and both stage-marriage and actual marriage would be consummated.'[5]

Siegel sees the play-within-the-play as 'not merely a burlesque of the performances put on by such groups during Elizabeth's progresses' but as 'a kind of comment on the *Dream* itself'. It could be called 'a presentation in little' of the *Dream* 'seen through a distorting medium'.[6] Citing Hippolyta's remark that 'This is the silliest stuff that ever I heard' (5.1.209), Siegel observes that the 'same might have been said' of the *Dream* 'by a hardheaded businesslike man of affairs who would have no truck with fairies and such'[7] and goes on to suggest that it was in effect said by Samuel Pepys when, as we saw in Chapter 1 of this Guide, he dismissed a 1662 production as 'the most insipid ridiculous play that ever I saw in my life'.[8] According to Siegel, 'Shakespeare was subtly asking his aristocratic audience to regard his play with imaginative understanding and sympathy'. But he goes on to say that no amount of imaginative understanding and sympathy can amend the faults of the performance of Pyramus and Thisbe, with its 'crude literalism' and 'inept explanatory comments'.[9]

Siegel's essay is, on one level, itself a fantasy, offering its contemporary audience (consisting mainly of mid-twentieth-century literary critics) the gratification of an imaginary identification with aristocratic wedding guests who turn out, in their attitudes, to be remarkably like mid-twentieth century literary critics (most of whom would not have been likely to be guests at an aristocratic wedding in their own era but who, through Siegel's essay, can be guests by proxy). He provides no specific detail – or documentary evidence – of what the attitudes of Elizabethan aristocratic wedding guests might actually have been and he tends to assume those attitudes must have been homogeneous, even if some of the guests had 'keener' perceptions than others. Filtering his interpretation of the play through the imagined responses of an Elizabethan aristocratic audience, he tends to edit out the ambiguous or negative aspects of the play. For example, he does not ask whether the representation of Theseus is wholly flattering, even though there are elements in the text which suggest he is forgetful and self-absorbed and arbitrary in his application of the laws of Athens. He does not consider the view of both Edmund Malone, in 1790, and Hermann Ulrici, in 1846, that Theseus and Hippolyta lacked the distinction of their legendary forebears, although Malone judged this simply a failing while Ulrici interpreted it as a contribution to the parodic structure of the play. Instead, he follows in the line of Edward Dowden who, as we saw in Chapter 1 of this Guide, felt that Theseus (if not Hippolyta) was endowed with greatness.

Siegel's sense that the play worked to produce a harmonious whole would be pursued, in different ways, by other critics of the *Dream* in the 1950s, particularly Peter F Fisher and Paul Olsen.

PETER F. FISHER

Peter F. Fisher's 'The Argument of *A Midsummer Night's Dream*' (1957) aims to tackle what it regards as a neglected topic – the argument of the play, 'the meaning of the action, as expressed in the form of its presentation'.[10] Fisher identifies a comic 'problem' – 'the conflict between natural desire and social custom'[11] – and contends that the 'form of the plot' of the *Dream* 'revolves around' this problem and that 'the struggle to resolve [it] is the expression of the argument'. He identifies 'four worlds' in the play: the lovers, who 'represent the irrational force of sublunary passion' (a passion which belongs to this world); the 'rationally ordered world of the Athenian court in the heroic age of Theseus'; 'the earthy and grotesquely matter-of-fact world of Bottom'; and 'the ecstatic and fantastic world of Oberon'. These four worlds 'meet in the wood and emerge in proper perspective'. What Fisher sees as 'the sharp clarity of the formal presentation' in the *Dream* is also evident in the way these four worlds are characterized by the different kind of dialogue which predominates in each of them. The lovers use rhymed verse, Theseus and his court employ blank verse, Bottom and his fellows talk in prose and Oberon's court engages in song. A fifth kind of dialogue -- the 'farcical, short, rhymed line' – characterizes the play-within-the-play.[12]

Fisher also draws attention to the larger context of the play provided by the connotation of 'Midsummer Night' in its title – a connotation which exists whether or not the action of the play is actually supposed to unfold on Midsummer Night. Drawing on *The Golden Bough* (abridged edn, 1922), by the historian of religion Sir James Frazer (1854–1941), he suggests that the Midsummer festival was primarily one of lovers and fire and links it with the May Day spring festival, citing Lysander's reference, in his exchange with Hermia, to the wood to which he proposes they flee as the one 'Where I did meet thee once with Helena / To do observance to a morn of May' (1.1.166–7). Both festivals were linked with a more ancient practice of fire-worship, and Hermia links fire with passion when she invokes Dido, the Queen of Carthage, who burnt herself to death when her lover Aeneas, from the ruined city of Troy which had itself been consumed by fire, deserted her: 'By that fire which burned the Carthage queen / When the false Trojan under sail was seen' (1.1.172–3). These references to ancient ceremony and legend provide a context in which the 'depths of natural impulses are given rein, and an invasion of the elemental world of passion is undertaken'.[13]

Fisher identifies three 'spheres of influence which confront the lovers'. One is the 'classical heritage of reason and social necessity'; the second, with which the first sphere comes into conflict, is the 'elemental power of nature'; and the third, which provides 'both basis and ballast', is 'the workaday world of common sense found in Bottom and his crew'. Fisher is one of those critics who elevate rather than disdain Bottom, although he is less concerned with him as a free-standing 'character' and more interested in his contribution to the whole 'argument' of the *Dream*. For Fisher, Bottom is, in a way, 'the real foundation upon which the whole is based'; Fisher draws his metaphor from Bottom's craft of weaver to call him 'the warp and woof of contact between the three spheres'. Bottom is 'at home everywhere and turns every situation to his advantage. The worlds of nature, of the imagination, and of society and social institutions meet in him. [...] His confidence is that of the man who follows his instincts rather than his passion or his reason'.[14]

The 'blunt nadir' of Bottom and Peter Quince is balanced by the 'polar zenith of fantasy' which Puck provides. Puck's activity 'represents both a unifying and transforming power which changes the wood into the depths of a Midsummer-night's dream'. Through his machinations and the deployment of the love-juice, the misleadings and mistakes of the lovers, in their 'first movement into the wood', 'rise to an ecstatic height of apparent discord, confusion, and inconstancy'. The second movement, however, is 'out towards the revelation of underlying harmony and constancy'. After spreading confusion and thus revealing 'the cult of strife inherent in elemental nature', Puck 'evoke[s] out of his dialectic of deceit and discord a new realization and harmony'. The 'movement towards constancy and order' begins in Oberon's world, when he starts to pity Titania's enthrallment to Bottom, and continues as the dreams of night disperse. 'The complete, awakening orientation runs the gamut' through the four dimensions of 'fantasy, reason, passion, and instinct'.[15] For Fisher, as for Siegel, however, reason, as represented in Theseus's famous speech at the start of 5.1, is limited; after all, the comic problem caused by the conflict between natural desire and social instinct has been resolved, not by reason, but in the world of fantasy, of moonlight and dream; and Hippolyta's response to Theseus's speech 'points to a more profound experience than that of mere fantasy'.

Whatever the nature of that experience, the 'transfiguration' of the four lovers in the wood and the night, it has, Fisher contends, 'ostensibly wrought a final alignment with the approved order of things':[16]

■ The last act [of the *Dream*] presents the various worlds of the play in their conventional relationship. The world of reason and accepted order is seated with Theseus and Hippolyta in the place of honour and power; that of passion and desire is once more firmly within the orbit of rational influence and control; and the world of common life and activity disports itself for their amusement and approval. The world of imagination and fantasy remains as an undercurrent which ends the play.[17] □

For Fisher, as for Siegel, there is a final emphasis on order. In contrast to Siegel, Fisher does not suggest that the significance of the *Dream* which he outlines is one which its supposed original aristocratic audience, or at least its more discerning members, would have particularly appreciated; he implies that it is one which any audience would experience, though it might require a critic such as Fisher to draw out the explicit argument of the play. His aim is to put in abstract terms what the experience of the play provides. A more extended argument for the *Dream*'s endorsement of harmony would be provided three years later by Paul A. Olson.

PAUL A. OLSON

In 'A Midsummer Night's Dream and the Meaning of Court Marriage' (1957), Paul A. Olson, like Siegel, contends that the significance of the play becomes clear if we consider the occasion of its initial performance, as the celebration of an aristocratic marriage. For Olson, as for Siegel, the specific bride and groom are unimportant; it is the fact that it was first presented on the occasion of what Olson calls a 'court marriage' that counts and that, '[c]ommensurate with its occasion', the *Dream* 'speaks throughout for a sophisticated Renaissance philosophy of the nature of love in both its rational and irrational forms'.[18]

Olson proposes two interlinked aims in his essay: to provide a compressed survey of Renaissance thought about 'the function of festival drama and the significance of wedlock' and to outline 'the methods by which symbol and masque pattern, structure and theme, work together to make luminous a traditional understanding of marriage'.[19] The initial audience or audiences of the *Dream*, Olson proposes, would have included those familiar with 'art which builds its meaning from the materials of traditional emblems and allegories'.[20] This art was represented, in drama, by the court comedies of John Lyly (?1554–1606) and the masques of Ben Jonson (1572–1637) and, in poems and prose, by Spenser's *The Faerie Queene, The Countesse of Pembroke's Yuy-Church* (1592) and *Arcadia* (published posthumously as *New Arcadia* (1590) and *The Countess of Pembroke's Arcadia* (1593)) by Sir Philip Sidney (1554–86). The *Dream* can be seen as a skilful combination of references to iconic forms which represent abstract ideas. 'Thus, while the aesthetic of the [play] implies a surrender to modes of looking at the world which do not derive their sustenance from phenomenal fact, it also demands a return to this kind of fact for their expression.'[21]

The abstract ideas about marriage which the *Dream* represents through its imagery and structure descend from the medieval era and also circulate in the sixteenth century in 'sermons, scriptural commentaries, marriage manuals [and] encyclopedias of general knowledge'.[22] Marriage in which the man governed the women helped to maintain social and cosmic harmony and hierarchy and also carried symbolic religious significance, representing the union of the soul with God and of Christ and the Church. Contemporary marriage manuals advised parents not to force their children into marriages without their children's consent but forbade children to marry without their parents' blessing. Olson affirms that modern critics must be aware of these ideas about marriage throughout the *Dream* because, in his view, they 'control the pattern of its action and modify the meanings of individual words and actions'.[23]

The *Dream*, if viewed in the perspective of such ideas, reveals a three-movement pattern like that which Nevill Coghill (1899–1980) discerns in the medieval basis of Shakespearean comedy.[24] The first movement, in Act I, is 'towards an orderly subordination of the female and her passions to the more reasonable male' and is epitomized by the relationship of Theseus and Hippolyta. The second movement, in Acts 2–3, 'passes through the cycle of a Fall which brings the domination of unbridled passion'. The third movement, in Acts 4–5, 'returns to a realization of the charity and cohesive community morality in which [the play] began'.[25]

Like other readings which stress the harmony of the *Dream*, Olson's interpretation involves some editing out of possible ambiguities. For example, he makes no mention of the element of violence in Theseus's wooing of Hippolyta or of Theseus's past reputation as a philanderer (or, put more strongly, a serial rapist). He cites Donald C. Miller's view of Titania, which we discussed in the previous chapter of this Guide, and seems to concur with Miller's judgement that Titania is sexually attached to the changeling boy; indeed, Olson asserts that Titania's 'erotic games with Bottom and the changeling fit the symbolic frame which Shakespeare has placed about her, since she is princess of sensual passion'.[26] Like Miller, Olson does not raise the question of a possible predatory and sexual element in Oberon's wish to possess the boy and interprets that wish allegorically. Oberon represents celestial love and wants the boy in order to establish his dominance over earthly love:

■ [C]elestial love[,] in the form of Oberon[,] attempts to capture the young man [the Indian boy] into his train and bring earthly love under his control in order that the rational and the animal in man may form a proper marriage. [...] Oberon uses love-in-idleness to force Titania to release her hold upon the changeling and to seek only the carnal or physical man, Bottom.[27] □

Olson's aversion to ambiguity highlights a wider question about his adopted approach, which involves matching the *Dream* to a set of pre-existing ideas that, supposedly, it emblematically illustrates, vivifies and widens. This makes the play ideologically coherent but it does not fully address those elements which make the *Dream* different from those texts – the court comedies of Jonson, the masques of Lyly, Spenser's *Faerie Queene*, Sidney's *Arcadia* – with which it may indeed share some ideas and techniques, but from which it also appears to diverge in its texture, resonance, tolerance of ambiguity and inferred audiences. The question of audience is important: by confining himself, like Siegel, to the supposed interpretative framework which an imaginary aristocratic court audience – or at least its more learned and insightful members – would apply, Olson neglects the question of how other audiences who might have seen the play in Shakespeare's time – let alone subsequently – might have interpreted it. There are indeed aspects of the *Dream* which lend themselves to symbolic and allegorical interpretation; but are they the only or most important aspects?

Despite these questions, and perhaps partly because it provokes them, Olson's essay is a rich and significant contribution to *Dream* criticism, giving a deeply informed sense of the broader context of ideas and dramatic, poetic and rhetorical techniques out of which the play emerged and highlighting the more general issue of how far such contexts might relate to and determine it. It was also possible, however, to consider the play without reference to those contexts but within a general perspective on Shakespearean comedy. John Russell Brown takes this approach in *Shakespeare and his Comedies* (1957).

JOHN RUSSELL BROWN

At the start of *Shakespeare and His Comedies*, John Russell Brown briefly surveys the state of Shakespeare criticism and contends that the early comedies are still comparatively neglected by criticism. A considerable critical discourse has grown around the history plays, late romances, tragedies and late comedies (*All's Well that Ends Well, Measure for Measure, Troilus and Cressida*), but the early comedies (including the *Dream*) have received relatively little attention. But a more penetrating discussion of these should, Brown suggests, be possible. On one level, it can be said that they are 'life-enhancing' in their 'delight in human character', their eschewal of satire and moral condemnation, their willingness, at times, to sacrifice characterization in the interests of 'surprising and piquant situations' and, 'above all, the richness and variety of incident, character, diction, and verse'.[28] But to say this is not enough; criticism should go further by inferring the implicit judgement on life which 'must necessarily inform every detail of selection and presentation'.[29]

Brown contends that there are 'three main kinds of clues' to this implicit judgement. Firstly, 'the manner in which Shakespeare ordered his plots, the structure, proportion and shape of his plays', which 'must include his creation of characters' and their 'interplay'.[30] Secondly, Shakespeare's 'choice of situations, actions, and words', which 'must include the colour, tone, and texture of the words, and the metre, rhythm and syntax of the dialogue'. Thirdly, 'the judgement explicit in [Shakespeare's] other plays and poems, especially those written about the same time in his career'. Following these clues entails 'minute analysis and the relation of each detail to the rest of the play in which it occurs and to Shakespeare's work as a whole'.[31] This approach is evidently different from that of Paul A. Olson: both approaches involve careful analysis and the relating of details to larger wholes; but Olson goes outside the play, and beyond Shakespeare, to a broader literary and cultural context, whereas Brown stays within Shakespeare's work.

Brown takes the benign view of the *Dream*. In the wood, 'lasting hardship', 'frustration' and 'suffering' are mitigated, minimized, by moonshine and laughter. But the play nonetheless makes an implicit judgement on life, and this is a judgement about 'the absurdity, privacy, and "truth" of human imagination'.[32] The *Dream* allows the audience to regard the lovers and Titania with a certain detachment; each of these characters is utterly convinced by the 'truth' of what they see and feel when they look at their loved ones, even when that loving perception and emotion is, as in the case of Titania and Lysander, a temporary aberration produced by the love-juice. At the start of Act 5, however, the audience's sense of superiority is, in a way, challenged when Theseus suggests that the poet (or poetic dramatist) also produces illusions which the audience take on some level for truth.

Brown summarizes the judgement which, in his view, informs the *Dream* in this way:

■ [T]he play suggests that lovers, like lunatics, poets and actors, have their own 'truth' which is established as they see the beauty of their beloved, and that they are confident in this truth for, although it seems the 'silliest stuff' [5.1.209] to an outsider, to them it is quite reasonable; it also suggests that lovers, like actors, need, and sometimes ask for, our belief, and that this belief can only be given if we have the generosity and imagination to think 'no worse of them than they of themselves'. ⌐

[5.1.214–15][33]

Brown locates the 'greatest triumph' of the *Dream* in its use of 'our wavering acceptance of the illusion of drama' as 'a kind of flesh-and-blood image of the acceptance which is appropriate to the strange and private "truth" of those who enact the play of love'.[34] It is a 'flesh-and-blood image' because the audience actually have to perform, in relation to the *Dream* itself, the act of acceptance advocated (but not performed) by Theseus in relation to 'Pyramus and Thisbe': 'The best in this kind [i.e. actors] are but shadows, and the worst are no worse if imagination amend them' (5.1.210–11). For Shakespeare, 'the ways in which actors and audience accept the "truth" of dramatic illusion' provide 'an image of man's recognition of imagined truths'.[35]

This aspect of Brown's argument focuses, like the interpretations of Siegel and Olson, on the responses of a hypothetical audience. But whereas the hypothetical audiences of Siegel and Olson are Elizabethan audiences, and Olson's is adept at arcane interpretation, Brown posits a kind of universal audience, unlocated in any specific time or place except that created by a performance of the play, whose members respond to the *Dream*'s portrayal of love and, above all, to its engagement with the theory and practice of dramatic illusion (what some later critics would call the *Dream*'s metadramatic element). In Brown's perspective, the most significant knowledge extraneous to the play itself and which would enrich one's experience of it is a knowledge of Shakespeare's other plays, especially of the play-within-a-play or of less prominent references to dramatic illusion elsewhere in his drama (for example, in *The Taming of the Shrew*, where, after the Induction (introduction or prologue), the play-within-a-play takes over, effectively becoming the main play; *Much Ado*; *The Merry Wives of Windsor*; *Hamlet*; and *Henry IV* Part I (2.5.436–86), where Prince Hal plays King Henry IV and Falstaff plays Hal). Brown's approach seems to get closer to key aspects of the *Dream* (its intertwined concern with the illusions of love and dramatic illusion) than an approach such as Olson's which moves away from it to other texts and cultural practices in order to return to it in ways which can be richly illuminating but which also, arguably, subdue the particularity of the play's actions and words to an interpretation which appears, in its abstraction and remoteness, to miss the point – or rather, the multiple points of energy which the play generates. Of course, Brown's focus on the love/dramatic illusions aspects could also be seen as selective and subduing and to miss some of these points – it might be said there is much more than this going on in the *Dream*, but it does demonstrate the value of an approach which largely excludes explicit consideration of extraneous material. The final interpretation we shall consider in this chapter, however, C. L. Barber's deeply influential *Shakespeare's Festive Comedy* (1959), does go outside the text of the *Dream* to anthropology and cultural history and brings the insights and perspectives thereby gained to bear deeply on the play.

C. L. BARBER

Whereas Siegel and Olson focus on erudite elite culture in their interpretation of the *Dream*, C. L. Barber focuses on popular culture, 'the popular theatre and the popular holidays'.[36] Barber is aware of the sophisticated elite culture which, for Olson, provides the essential context for interpreting the *Dream*, but he sees this as part of a 'highly developed' repertoire of 'theatrical and literary resources' which included 'folk themes and conventions' as well as 'classically trained innovators like Lyly, Kyd and Marlowe'. In the *Dream*, 'his first comic masterpiece', Shakespeare 'expressed with full imaginative resonance the experience of the traditional summer holidays', and in doing so 'found his way back to a native festival tradition' closely resembling that which lay behind the ancient Greek playwright Aristophanes (c. 450–c. 385 BC). But Shakespeare, 'in expressing the native holiday', was 'also in a position to use all the resources of a sophisticated dramatic art'.[37]

Barber identifies the 'general subject' of the *Dream* as 'the folly of fantasy':

■ The whole night's action is presented as a release of shaping fantasy which brings clarification about the tricks of strong imagination. We watch a dream; but we are awake, thanks to pervasive humour about the tendency to take fantasy literally, whether in love, in superstition, or in Bottom's mechanical dramatics.[38] □

The shaping fantasy is especially active in the wood, a zone of 'teeming metamorphoses'[39] where, under the moon and stars, 'things can change, merge and melt into each other',[40] 'where the perceived structure of the outer world breaks down, where the body and its environment interpenetrate in unaccustomed ways, so that the seeming separateness and stability of identity is lost'.[41] Barber's language here might seem to anticipate that of later post-structuralist or queer readings of the *Dream* which emphasize and value the destabilizing of identity; but in his overall perspective, this metamorphic zone is not an unfettered utopian playground but a temporary stage through which the characters pass on the way to greater stability.

In suggesting how the *Dream* distances us from the metamorphic zone, Barber stresses the play's sceptical dimension. This dimension relates to both popular and elite culture: 'in holiday shows, it was customary to make game with the difference between art and life by witty transitions back and forth between them' and there was a 'general Renaissance tendency frankly to accept and relish the artificiality of art, and the vogue of formal rhetoric and "conceited" love poetry [i.e. poetry which used elaborate and surprising similes or metaphors], also made for sophistication about the artistic process'.[42] Scepticism is 'in solution' through the *Dream* and becomes explicit in Theseus's speech (5.1.2–220) which acknowledges the power of the imagination to create out of nothing but also recognizes that such creation may finally be based on nothing. 'A sense of the plausible life and energy of fancy goes with the knowledge that often its productions are more strange than true.'[43] Scepticism is then carried through into the performance of 'Pyramus and Thisbe', in which Shakespeare 'captures the naïveté of folk dramatics and makes it serve his controlling purpose as a final variant of imaginative aberration'.[44] Like John Russell Brown, Barber cites Theseus's lines 'The best in this kind [i.e. actors] are but shadows, and the worst are no worse if imagination amend them' (5.1.210–11), but he sees this as expressing 'part of our response' at this stage of the play – 'a growing detachment towards imagination, moving towards the distance from the dream expressed in Puck's epilogue'.[45] Barber does not share Brown's sense of the metadramatic dimension of the *Dream* and of how Theseus's lines could be seen to ask the audience member or reader to use, rather than increasingly to detach themselves from, their imagination; that the apprehension of the experience of the *Dream* demands identification with, as well as self-distancing from, 'imaginative aberration'.

Barber suggests that in Shakespeare's later work, especially in *The Tempest*, a more developed idea of imagination becomes a much more positive value which transcends the *Dream*'s neat contrasts between appearance and reality. But those neat contrasts are responsible for the *Dream*'s particular kind of festive comedy:

■ The confident assumption dominant in [the *Dream*], that substance and shadow can be kept separate, determines the peculiarly unshadowed gaiety of the fun it makes with fancy. Its organization by polarities – everyday-holiday, town-grove, day-night, waking-dreaming – provides a remarkable resource for mastering passionate experience.[46] □

G. Wilson Knight had already, back in 1932, questioned the idea of the *Dream's* unshadowed gaiety, Jan Kott would do so much more graphically in 1965, and later critics would, in different ways, take this further. But Barber affirms its festive, benign quality.

Barber goes on to identify a 'curious paradox' in the *Dream* whereby its 'full dramatization of holiday affirmations' allows Theseus to cordon off that area of irrational imaginative experience exemplified in those affirmations. If we align ourselves with Theseus, the play becomes 'an agency for distinguishing what is merely "apprehended" [with the imagination] from what is "comprehended" [with the reason]'. Barber compares this to the 'distinction between mind and body' made by the French philosopher and mathematician René Descartes (1596–1650) and suggests that, while we might not want to adopt Theseus's or Descartes' rationalist stance today, it 'remains a great achievement' to have reached that milestone on our road to the present.[47] But Barber is also aware that Theseus in the *Dream* does not quite have the last word; that Hippolyta's point that 'the story of the night [...] / More witnesseth than fancy's images / And grows to something of great constancy' (5.1.23, 25–6) casts doubt upon his rational stance; that imagination gives access to 'a creative tendency and process' that is enacted in the play and in marriage and can be named only by the 'many words [...] in motion' of the *Dream* itself.[48]

By the end of the 1950s, there had been considerable, and impressive, developments in *Dream* studies. Some of the possible original meanings of the play which later criticism and production might have obscured were suggested by the informed imaginative reconstruction of the responses of its hypothetical original audience by Paul Siegel and Paul A. Olson, and by Peter F. Fisher's formulation of its argument; John Russell Brown had explored the relationship between the *Dream's* concern with the illusions of love and with dramatic illusion by looking at the play both in itself and in the context of Shakespeare's dramas as a whole; and C. L. Barber had examined how the *Dream* could be seen to employ the conventions of popular as well as elite culture in order to demarcate the territories of reason and imagination. By the start of the 1960s, there was a well-established body of critical discourse on the *Dream* which critics could develop and challenge. And as the 1960s gathered pace, challenge was in the air.

CHAPTER FOUR

The 1960s: Order and Outrage

As we saw in the last chapter, a substantial body of criticism and scholarship had accumulated around the *Dream* by the end of the 1950s and this was extended in the early 1960s by the influential interpretations by Bertrand Evans, Frank Kermode, G. K. Hunter and R. W. Dent, which we shall consider first in this chapter. But the sense of a smoothly developing discourse, in which discords were resolved in ultimate concord, was shattered by the appearance, in 1964, of the translation of Jan Kott's *Shakespeare our Contemporary*, a very sixties event in its capacity to disrupt, challenge, offend and provoke attempts to control and contain its disruptive force. The critical discourse around the *Dream*, however, continued to grow, even though it was now more conflicted and fragmented. The clearest sign of this increasing critical activity was the appearance, in the later 1960s, of two major books devoted to the play, by David Young and Stephen Fender. We shall consider these later in this chapter. We start our exploration of the exciting developments in *Dream* criticism in this decade with Bertrand Evans's book which, following in the line of H. B. Charlton and John Russell Brown, considers the *Dream* within the broader context of Shakespearean comedy.

BERTRAND EVANS

Bertrand Evans approaches Shakespeare's comedies through what he sees as one of their most striking features – Shakespeare's manipulation and exploitation of 'discrepant awareness' between his audience and the characters – or, to use his own preferred terms, 'participants' or 'persons' – in the plays. Evans identifies three possible ways in which a dramatist can handle 'the relative awareness of audience and participants': 'he can keep the audience less informed than the participants, equally aware, or more aware than they'.[1] Shakespeare adopts the third way, giving the audience 'an advantage in awareness' over the participants and thus opening 'exploitable gaps between audience and participant, and between participant and participant'.[2] The 'ultimate creator of the main discrepancy' in the *Dream*³ is the magic herb which, in touching the eyelids of two mortals – Lysander and Demetrius – and one fairy – Titania – creates discrepancies among all the principal persons, making the awareness of each of them, at some time in the action, less aware than the audience and giving the audience an advantage over one or more persons in seven of the nine scenes. But there are further discrepancies between the awareness of audience and play-persons which are not directly produced by the love-juice – for example, when Puck mistakes Lysander for Demetrius: the audience knows Puck is making an error of which Puck himself, at this stage, is unaware.

The *Dream* is the first example of Shakespeare's use of an 'outside force' – in the shape of Oberon – which intervenes in and directs the other persons in the play.⁴ Evans points out that Oberon gets involved in the problems of the four lovers by chance – he first intended the love-juice for Titania's eyes only. It is while he is waiting for Puck to fetch the flower that Demetrius and Helena enter and Oberon, invisible to them but seen by the audience, eavesdrops. Demetrius and Helena do not know that Oberon is listening to them, but the audience does: this is the first discrepancy in the play between the vision of the participants and of the audience. It inaugurates a cognitive gap that, uniquely in Shakespeare's comedies, stays open at the end of the play: the awareness of the mortal participants is never raised to the same level as that of the audience. The mortals never know of Oberon's existence or interventions.

The audience knows more than the mortal participants in the *Dream*, but it also knows more than Oberon from the point when the Fairy King sends Puck off to put the love-juice on a young man whom he identifies only as wearing 'Athenian garments' (2.1.264). The identifying detail is inadequate because, as the audience is aware, there is more than one Athenian male in the forest – and Puck finds the wrong one, misled by the sleeping Lysander's '[w]eeds of Athens' (2.2.77) and the young man's physical distance from Hermia. Puck interprets this distance as a rejection of Hermia (2.2.78–84) rather than what the audience knows it to be: the result of Lysander's compliance with her desire to retain her virtue (2.2.45–70).

Evans suggests, however, that, in the action which runs from Puck's application of the love-juice to Lysander's eyes to the discovery and correction of this mistake, the primary discrepancy is not between the audience's knowledge and the knowledge of Oberon and Puck but between the audience's knowledge and that of the lovers. As in *The Comedy of Errors*, 'the effects of error are a chain reaction of surprise, misunderstanding, mystification and near frenzy'.⁵ The lines which run from 3.3.122 to the end of Act 3 Scene 3 are, for Evans, 'Shakespeare's finest achievement' so far 'in representing the comic effects of error'.⁶

Crucial to these effects is the presence of Oberon throughout the escalating quarrel of the lovers: the audience's awareness of Oberon gives it 'a vantage-point from which to view the action not merely as a quarrel, but *as a quarrel of mortals overwatched by benevolent omnipotence*' (Evans's italics). The audience can rest assured that, 'however large danger may loom in the view of the participants who lack [the audience's] perspective, no lasting harm will be done and all will at last be well'.[7]

For Evans, the polar opposite of the audience's superior awareness is incarnated in Bottom. Evans sees the weaver as immune to aware-ness, an insulated mind that lacks perspective. The audience always has the advantage over him. 'He steers an undeviating course through the ordinary and the marvellous alike.'[8] His 'unruffled oblivion is the exploitable substance of the first fifty lines'[9] of Act 4, a 'brief scene which complements and completes that of the mortal lovers' quarrel and frantic chase through the forest'. The two scenes 'stand [...] together at the summit of the play'.[10] Evans sums up the effect of the multiple discrepancies he has located in this way:

■ From the perfect vantage-point on which Shakespeare seats us throughout [the *Dream*], we perceive more [...] than the activities of any single group of participants. We are set where our sweep of vision takes in all actions at once – high enough to see that the worlds of fairies, lovers and artisans, quite separate and alone so far as the participants know, are all one world.[11] □

For Frank Kermode, however, the *Dream* does not so much offer a position of superior knowledge as bring its audience up against the limits of knowledge. And, as we shall see in the next subchapter, the figure that marks the limits of knowledge is the very one over whom, according to Evans, the audience always has the advantage: Bottom.

FRANK KERMODE

In 'The Mature Comedies' (1961), Frank Kermode compares the Titania–Bottom relationship to two episodes in *The Golden Ass*: the Cupid and Psyche episode, where Venus uses Cupid to avenge herself on Psyche, as Oberon uses Puck and the love-juice to avenge himself on Titania; and the vision of Isis, and subsequent initiation into her mysteries, which Apuleius has after Isis has freed him from his ass's form. The rich allegori-cal interpretations of both these episodes generated in the Renaissance are, Kermode suggests, part of the living texture of the *Dream*.

Kermode pursues the allusion to Apuleius in order to challenge what he sees as a simplified idea of the moral of the *Dream* – that the lovers pass through a period of irrationality which is especially heightened in the wood and that they eventually waken from their dreams and return to reason and sanity. It is the 'final awakening' – that of Bottom – which complicates this simple moral, this 'neat "love-is-a-kind-of-madness" pattern'.[12] Kermode cites Bottom's commentary on his dream:

> ■ I have had a most rare vision. I have had a dream, past the wit of man to say what dream it was: man is but an ass if he go about to expound this dream. ... The eye of man hath not heard, the ear of man hath not seen, man's hand is not able to taste, his tongue to conceive, nor his heart to report, what my dream was. □
> [5.1.102–4, 108–11; Kermode's ellipsis][13]

Kermode affirms that this is 'a parody' of Chapter 2, verse 9 of the First Epistle of Paul to the Corinthians in the New Testament (Kermode also adds an extract from verse 13 of the same chapter):

> ■ Eye hath not seen, nor ear heard, neither have entered into the heart of man, the things which God hath prepared for them that love him ...
>   Which things also we speak, not in the words which man's wisdom teacheth, but which the Holy Ghost teacheth ... □
> [Kermode's ellipses; he quotes from the 1611 Authorized Version of the Bible here, rather than the version in the Bishop's Bible quoted in the Introduction to this Guide][14]

Just as St Paul sees the difficulty of speaking of 'the things which God hath prepared for them that love him', so Apuleius could not speak of his initiation into the mysteries but received a vision of the goddess Isis. The common elements in the experiences of St Paul and Apuleius are 'transformation, and an experience of divine love'. Bottom's experience is not dissimilar: as Kermode puts it, he 'has known the love of the triple goddess in a vision'. His vision, or dream, is of a different kind from that of the other dreamers in the play.

Kermode draws here on the distinction between two different kinds of dream made by the ancient Roman grammarian and NeoPlatonist philosopher Ambrosius Theodosius Macrobius (c. 400 BC) in his *In somnium Scipionis commentarii* (*Commentary on the Dream of Scipio*); *Somnium Scipionis* (*The Dream of Scipio*) itself is the most substantial, known fragment of *De Republica* by the ancient Roman orator and writer Marcus Tullius Cicero (106–43 BC) and it owes its survival to its incorporation in Macrobius's *Commentary*. *The Dream of Scipio* gives an account, put into the mouth of the real-life Roman general Publius Cornelius Scipio Aemilianus Africanus Numantinus (184–29 BC), of a visionary dream about the nature of the universe and makes a distinction between 'phantasma' – a term which Brutus, in Shakespeare's *Julius Caesar*, uses when he speaks of 'a phantasma or a hideous dream' (2.1.65) – and 'oneiros' or 'somnium' – the kind of dream that Bottom has which is, in Kermode's words, 'ambiguous, enigmatic, of high import'. This kind of dream provides a vision which cannot adequately be grasped by the senses. Such a vision poses a challenge to the idea that blind love is necessarily an aberration.

The view that the blindness of love could provide a kind of mystical vision was held by the Italian thinkers Giovanni Pico della Mirandola (1463–94) and Giordiano Bruno (1548–1600) and the German occultist Cornelius Agrippa (1486–1535), and Kermode suggests that, for these thinkers, 'this exaltation of the blindness of love was both Christian and Orphic'[15] (that is, related to the ancient Greek and Roman mystery religion which took the legendary ancient Greek poet Orpheus as its founder and which lasted from about the sixth or seventh century BC to the fourth century AD and had some influence on Renaissance thought). Drawing on *Pagan Mysteries in the Renaissance* (1958; revised edn 1968) by the German-born and English-based art historian Edgar Wind (1900–71), Kermode observes:

■ Orpheus said that love was eyeless; St Paul and David that God dwelt in darkness and beyond knowledge. Bottom is there to tell us that the blindness of love, the dominance of the mind over the eye, can be interpreted as a means to grace as well as to irrational animalism; that the two aspects are, perhaps, inseparable.[16] □

Kermode is not concerned with Bottom as a character, but his remarks do offer a different sense of Bottom's status – as the figure whose words, in his account of his dream, summon up Biblical, Orphic and Neoplatonic precedents and realign and complicate the meanings of the play.

Kermode's essay is a subtle, erudite exploration of what he calls 'the *skopos* [purpose, target]' of the *Dream* – 'the thematic preoccupation, the characteristic bursting through into action of what seems a verbal trick only (the talk of eyes)'.[17] In Kermode's reading, the imagery of eyes in the *Dream* develops into a central concern with the intricate relations of seeing, blindness and vision (of a spiritual as well as an earthly kind). A more straightforward reading of the *Dream* is provided by the next critic we shall consider, G. K. Hunter.

G. K. HUNTER

In *Shakespeare: The Later Comedies*, G. K. Hunter echoes Enid Welsford's idea of the *Dream* as a dance, although he does not relate the play to a history of the masque as Welsford does. According to Hunter, the *Dream*, 'is best seen [...] as a lyric divertissement [a minor entertainment or diversion, or, in ballet, a short, self-contained dance meant to display a dancer's technical skill], or a suite of dances – gay, sober, stately, absurd'. The *Dream* focuses on love, but 'it moves by exposing the varieties of love, rather than by working them against one another in a process of argument'.[18] Its characters are not 'self-aware' and 'self-correcting' but stay largely 'fixed in their attitudes'; those who do change – Lysander, Titania – do so without inner conflict, as the result of the application of the love-juice or its antidote.[19] The characters lack 'the psychological dimension of inner debate'.[20] The *Dream* is concerned with 'pattern' not psychology:

■ The pattern of the dance is what matters, and the pattern is one which works through an alternation of errors, trying out all possible combinations of persons: Helena in love with Demetrius, Demetrius in love with Hermia, Hermia in love with Lysander, and then (change partners) Hermia in love with Lysander, Lysander in love with Helena, Helena in love with Demetrius, Demetrius in love with Hermia – but this is worse, so change again: Hermia in love with Lysander, Lysander in love with Helena, Helena in love with Demetrius, but completely at a loss when Demetrius seems to be pretending to return her love; finally we settle on the only stable arrangement, where no-one is left out.[21] □

The irrationality of the lovers is stressed, Hunter suggests, when contrasted with 'the rational love of Theseus and Hippolyta, the mature and royal lovers who frame and explain the occasion of the play'.[22] (The idea that Theseus and Hippolyta 'frame' the *Dream* goes back to Schlegel, as we saw in Chapter 1 of this Guide.) Hunter acknowledges that, as he puts it, 'Theseus has also lived in the moonlit wood' but affirms that he and Hippolyta have now attained 'a settled and rational state of loving that has lived through the violent half-knowledge of passion'.[23] Theseus stands for an 'idea of achieved self-possession'.[24]

The lovers' own speech also brings out their irrationality. As one example, Hunter cites Helena's line from 1.1 starting at line 232, 'Things base and vile, holding no quantity' and ending at line 141, 'So the boy Love is perjur'd everywhere' and sees these as fallacious arguments which Helena uses 'to justify her betrayal of friendship and abandonment of reason'.[25] But the lovers' irrationality emerges most clearly, however, in the comparison with 'the parallel situation of Titania and Bottom'. 'Like all the other lovers, [Titania's] first concern is to justify the *wisdom* of her choice'.[26]As Bottom is the only human to see the fairies, so he is the only one in the nocturnal wood to see the rational truth about love: as he says to Titania, 'reason and love keep little company nowadays' (3.2.136–7).[27] But Hunter finds that Bottom's knowledge of the fairies and of the divergence between reason and love is of no use to him – a point Hunter justifies by quoting out of context from Bottom's speech on his dream, 'man is but an ass, if he go about to expound this' (4.1.105; Hunter omits 'dream' after 'this'). There is no sense, as there is in Kermode, that Bottom's belief in the inexpressibility of certain kinds of experience may ally him with distinguished figures such as St Paul and that the idea of 'blind love' can be linked, not only with irrationality and folly, but also with a vision which exceeds the rationality represented by Theseus.

Hunter does not, however, wholly disdain Bottom or his companions:

■ There is an absurd truth in Bottom's dignity [...] which touches an awareness of the genuine limitations on *anyone's* understanding, and catches our involvement even if it does not control our sympathy. Here among the muddled roots of humanity it is dangerous to laugh too loud, for Shakespeare makes it clear that it is *ourselves* we are laughing at.[28] □

Hunter also suggests an uncertainty which remains at the end of the *Dream*: '[w]as the adventure of the lovers true or false, real or imaginary? The play would seem to answer, "both true and false"'.[29]

Hunter offers a simpler view of the *Dream* than Kermode or, in the previous decade, Paul A. Olson. In contrast to those critics, he does not bring any other non-Shakespearean texts specifically to bear on the play. In the next analysis we shall consider, R. W. Dent does probe more widely and deeply into the contemporary cultural context of the *Dream*, by focusing on the idea of imagination.

R. W. DENT

In 'Imagination in *A Midsummer Night's Dream*', R. W. Dent points to the widespread critical praise of the *Dream* for the unity or harmony which it weaves from its apparently incommensurate aspects, but finds this praise lacking in one key respect: it fails to analyse the fifth act, except for suggesting, rather vaguely, that the play-within-a-play roughly parallels the difficulties of the lovers. Despite the praise of the *Dream* as a unified or harmonious whole, critics have rarely considered the whole of the play. Dent proposes 'to reexamine the degree and kind of unity achieved' by the *Dream*. He suggests that 'its most pervasive unifying element, is the partially contrasting role of imagination in love and art'.[30]

Dent considers the critical view that the *Dream* is about love and that it contrasts the irrational love of Hermia, Helena, Demetrius and Lysander with the rational love of Theseus and Hippolyta. In this perspective, imagination in love must ultimately be renounced as unreasonable, disturbing and potentially destructive, 'in simple contrast to the disciplined use of imagination essential to Shakespeare's art'. But Dent finds this contrast too 'mechanical'[31] and suggests that the *Dream* does not show love eventually falling into harmony with reason. Throughout the play, love-choices cannot be explained in rational terms; love may co-exist with reason but it is not rational. It may be, as Helena says, that '[l]ove looks not with the eyes but with the mind' (1.1.234), but the 'mind' here indicates the imagination rather than any reasoning faculty. As Dent puts it: 'the eyes "see" what the lover's imagination dictates'.[32] Although the term 'imagination' – and related words such as 'image, 'imagine', 'imagining' – are not used in the *Dream* until Theseus's speech in Act 5, much of the play prior to that Act 'has concerned the role of imagination in love'. A 'subordinate part' (the scenes with Bottom and his companions) has likewise considered the role of imagination in drama – a role which, Dent suggests, informs the whole of the *Dream*.[33]

Focusing on the rehearsal scene of Bottom and his companions, Dent suggests that

■ the whole rehearsal is concerned with how the mechanicals abuse their own imaginations by a failure to understand those of the audience. On the one hand they fear their audience will imagine what it sees is real, mistaking 'shadows' for reality; on the other, they think the audience unable to imagine what it cannot see.[34] □

The *Dream* itself asks its audience to perform those imaginative acts which the craftsmen fear their prospective audience is incapable of performing. Indeed, the play requires that its audience stretch its imagination further to believe in fairies and 'to accept them as the ultimate source of harmony and disharmony, while at the same time not asking us to "believe" in them at all'.[35]

Dent suggests that their performance of 'Pyramus and Thisbe' in Act 5 exemplifies 'not the follies of love but the follies of abused imagination in the theatre'. For Dent, 'the primary thematic dialogue' of the *Dream* occurs after the exit of Wall:

■ *Hippolyta*: This is the silliest stuff that ever I heard.
Theseus: The best in this kind are but shadows; and the worst are no worse, if imagination amend them.
Hippolyta: It must be your imagination, then, and not theirs. □

(5.1.209–13)[36]

A 'successful production', Dent contends, 'depends on the imaginative cooperation of playwright, producers and audience', but the play of the craftsmen requires its audience to do all the imaginative work – a task which its onstage audience refuses because they can enjoy the play as farce rather than tragedy and because the imaginative effort necessary to amend it 'would take an imagination transcending Shakespeare's own'.[37]

Theseus's view that 'the best in this kind are but shadows' is correct in one sense – Shakespeare's plays themselves often draw attention to the illusory nature of theatre – but the whole of the *Dream* challenges his 'consistently deprecating' attitude to drama. This attitude, however, is no idiosyncrasy but expresses Elizabethan psychology's dominant view of the imagination, which Dent finds helpfully summarized by William Rossky in 'Imagination in the English Renaissance: Psychology and Poetic' (1958):

■ Although instrumental to the healthy operation of the soul, imagination [...] is a faculty for the most part uncontrolled and immoral – a faculty forever distorting and lying, irrational, unstable, flitting and insubstantial, haphazardly making and marring, dangerously tied to emotions, feigning idly and purposelessly.[38] □

In the Elizabethan era, the attempt to produce a more positive idea of imagination involved the use of contemporary cultural materials (often including those from the psychology which distrusted imagination) to create a concept of 'poetic feigning', which Rossky describes as follows:

■ [P]oetic feigning is a glorious compounding of images beyond life, of distortions which are yet verisimilar imitations, expressing a truth to reality and yet a higher truth also, controlled by the practical purpose, the mo[u]lding power, and, in almost every aspect, by the reason and morality of the poet.[39] □

This kind of concept is expressed in extended form in Sir Philip Sidney's *Apology for Poetry* (1595; also published in the same year under the title *The Defence of Poetry*). Dent concludes that the *Dream*, 'in offering a defense for its own existence', 'simultaneously offers us Shakespeare's closest approximation to a "Defense of Dramatic Poetry" in general', 'although one that expresses its view by indirection and without the emphasis upon strictly moral edification one commonly finds in more formal defenses'.[40]

Dent's essay was an important development of *Dream* criticism within the established parameters of the time; but the book that would really shake up interpretations of the *Dream* – and of Shakespeare more generally – appeared in English translation in 1964: Jan Kott's *Shakespeare Our Contemporary*.

JAN KOTT

Jan Kott's *Shakespeare Our Contemporary* unforgettably draws attention to the dark sexual potentials of the *Dream*. Kott asserts that the play 'is the most erotic of Shakespeare's comedies' and that 'in no other tragedy or comedy of his, except *Troilus and Cressida*, is the eroticism expressed so brutally'.[41] For Kott, the lack of individual characterization in the four lovers means that the entire action of the midsummer night 'is based on complete exchangeability of love partners'. In Kott's perspective, this 'mechanical reversal of the objects of desire', the 'reduction of characters to love partners' is the 'most peculiar' – and perhaps 'most modern' – feature of 'this cruel dream'.[42]

Kott finds that the 'metaphors of love, eroticism, and sex undergo [...] some essential changes' in the *Dream*. At first, they are wholly conventional: 'sword and wound'; 'rose and rain' (1.1.129, 130); 'Cupid's bow and golden arrow' (1.1.169–70). In Helena's soliloquy, which Kott sees as a coda (the concluding passage of a piece, typically an addition to the basic structure) to Act 1, Scene 1, 'two kinds of imagery' clash. Kott suggests that Helena's soliloquy is 'above her intellectual capacities' and that for a time it 'singles her out from the action of the play'. For Kott, the soliloquy is 'really the author's monologue' which states 'the philosophical theme' of the *Dream*, which is the tension between Eros, the sexual drive, and Thanatos, the death drive.[43]

As the *Dream* proceeds, 'animal erotic symbolism' becomes increasingly obtrusive, almost obsessive. Kott finds this passage through 'animality' *is* 'the midsummer night's dream, or at least this aspect of the *Dream* is the most modern and revealing' and provides 'the main theme joining together all the three separate plots running parallel in the play'.[44] 'Titania and Bottom will pass through animal eroticism in a quite literal, even visual sense'.[45] But even the four lovers 'enter the dark sphere of animal love-making'.[46] For example, Helena says to Demetrius: 'I am your spaniel; and, Demetrius, / The more you beat me, I will fawn on you. / Use me but as your spaniel: spurn me, strike me' (2.1.203–5); or, a little later: 'What worser place can I beg in your love / [...] / Than to be used as you use your dog?' (2.1.208–10).

In the forest itself, the lullaby sung by Titania's fairies 'seems somewhat frightening'.[47] It mentions 'spotted snakes with double tongue', 'Thorny hedgehogs', 'Newts', 'blindworms', 'spiders', 'Beetles black', 'worm[s]' and 'snail[s]' (2.1.9,10, 11, 20, 22, 23). Kott links these kinds of creatures with the kind of remedies for impotence or gynaecological problems found in medieval and renaissance prescription books, and connects the aversions which such creatures can arouse with some of the sexual neuroses with which psychoanalysis is concerned. Kott also finds sexual connotations in the kind of mammal whom Oberon imagines that Titania, under the influence of the magic flower, will fall in love with: 'lion', 'bear', 'wolf', 'bull', 'monkey', 'ape' (2.1.180, 181). The connotations are even more evident when Oberon actually drops the juice on Titania's eyes and says that she will love what she next sees, 'Be it ounce, or cat, or bear / Pard, or boar with bristled hair' (2.2.36–7). 'All these animals', Kott contends, 'represent abundant sexual potency, and some of them play an important part in sexual demonology'.[48] What Titania does see when she awakes, of course, is Bottom with the head of an ass. But, according to Kott,

■ in this nightmarish summer night, the ass does not symbolize stupidity. Since antiquity and up to the Renaissance the ass was credited with the strongest sexual potency and among all the quadrupeds is supposed to have the longest and hardest phallus.[49] □

If there is any kind of humour in this scene, Kott sees it as the 'cruel and scatological' humour found in the work of the poet and satirist Jonathan Swift (1667–1745).[50]

■ The slender and lyrical Titania longs for animal love. Puck and Oberon call the transformed Bottom a monster [3.2.6; 3.2.378]. The frail and sweet Titania drags the monster to bed, almost by force. This is the lover she wanted and dreamed of [...]; only she never wanted to admit it, even to herself. Sleep frees her from inhibitions. The monstrous ass is being raped by the poetic Titania, while she keeps on chattering about flowers. [...] Of all the characters in the play Titania enters to the fullest extent the dark sphere of sex where there is no more beauty and ugliness; there is only infatuation and liberation.[51] □

This is Kott's most sensational claim, challenging a well-established critical, theatrical and popular tradition which sees the *Dream* as a sexually innocent play. With Kott, *Dream* criticism comes of age. He puts sexuality on its agenda in a way no critic had ever done before. His methods infringe academic conventions to some extent; but he enlivens and enriches the field of *Dream* criticism. That field would be further enriched by David P. Young's substantial and more scholarly book, which we shall discuss in the next subchapter.

DAVID P. YOUNG

David P. Young's *Something of Great Constancy: The Art of A Midsummer Night's Dream* is the first full-length book devoted to the *Dream*. As well as skilfully synthesizing much previous criticism and scholarship (though Kott is not mentioned), Young introduces a new idea: that what he calls 'picturization' and 'panoramas' are unifying features of the *Dream*. In discussing 'picturization', Young claims that the *Dream* repeatedly offers 'not merely the glimpse afforded by an image, but a fully drawn picture' which is often a 'sketch [...] of human activity'.[52] His examples are Egeus's account of Lysander wooing Hermia (1.1.26–38), Theseus's evocation of the life of a nun (1.1.70–3), Bottom's demonstration of a tyrant ranting (1.2.27–34), Puck's vignettes of a gossip drinking from a bowl and an aunt falling from a stool (2.1.47–50) and Titania's image of Oberon in Corin's shape piping to Phillida (2.1.66–8). Although the pictures 'slow down the action', they 'realize the play's basic theme in a new and significant dimension' in 'their evocation of the imagination, their illustration of its follies, triumphs, and possibilities'.[53]

For Young, however, the 'most effective and memorable pictures in the play are not the [...] glimpses of single figures and activities' but what he calls 'panoramas': 'the larger representations, full landscapes with a remarkable sense of spaciousness and distance'. Act 1 hints at these panoramas in Theseus's picture of his wedding festivities (1.1.12–13) and in the exchanges of Hermia and Lysander (1.1.128–78), but with the entry of the fairies in Act 2 they start 'to dominate the play' and 'appear in profusion'. In reply to Puck's question 'Whither wander you?' the Fairy gives a wide-ranging answer (2.1.1–15). Puck itemizes the sites of Titania and Oberon's quarrels: 'And now they never meet in grove, or green, / By fountain clear, or spangled starlight sheen, / But they do square, that all their elves for fear / Creep into acorn cups and hide them there' (1.2.28–31). In her exchange with Oberon, Titania invokes 'the farthest step of India' (1.2.69) and Oberon speaks of Titania leading Theseus 'through the glimmering night / From Perigouna whom he ravishèd' (1.2.77–8). Titania offers an extensive picture of the disorder her quarrel with Oberon has caused in the world of nature (2.1.82–114), providing a 'cross section of geography, weather, and natural life', and goes on to supply 'a seascape, with herself and her "votaress" in the foreground and the "embarked traders" on the flood in the distance'[54] (2.1.123–34). After Titania's exit, Oberon presents a panorama and a vantage point from which to survey it when he recalls sitting 'upon a promontory' and hearing (and presumably seeing) 'a mermaid, on a dolphin's back' (2.1.149–54). He then offers a more ample panorama in his description of Cupid's arrow missing the 'imperial vot'ress' and falling on 'a little Western flower' (2.1.155–68).

Panoramic intimations occur even in the woods at night. Oberon's evocation of the 'bank where the wild thyme blows' is a mini-panorama (2.1.249–56). Puck speaks of girdling the earth in forty minutes (2.1.175–6) and Oberon says that he and Titania can soon 'compass the globe' (4.1.96–7); Hermia, as if echoing these global glimpses, visualizes, as a vivid impossibility, that the 'whole [i.e. solid] earth may be bored, and that the moon / May through the centre creep, and so displease / Her brother's [i.e. the sun's] noontide with th'Antipodes [i.e. the dwellers on the other side of the earth]' (3.2.53–5). Puck provides a wider picture when he compares the mechanicals who fly at the sight of Bottom translated to an ass to 'wild geese' or 'russet-pated choughs [...] / Rising and cawing at the gun's report' that '[s]ever themselves and madly sweep the sky' (3.2.20–3). Even Demetrius can open a panorama of distant mountains when, under the influence of the love-juice and enraptured of Helena, he evokes 'That pure congealed white – high Taurus' snow, / Fanned with the eastern wind' (3.2.142–3).

As day dawns in the *Dream*, the panoramic views come into their own again. Puck describes the approach of morning and the retreat of ghosts (3.3.379–88). Oberon paints a resplendent picture of the sun rising over the sea (3.3.390–4). With daylight now in command, Theseus announces that he will, as Young puts it, 'arrange a panorama of sight and sound'[55] on the mountain top with the 'musical confusion / of hounds and echo in conjunction' (4.1.109–10). Hippolyta recalls the 'musical [...] discord' of hounds in a hunt in a Cretan wood (4.1.111–17). Looking back on the night, Demetrius opens another brief panorama of mountains, which then metamorphose into visually similar and still distant but softer substances: 'These things seem small and undistinguishable, / Like far-off mountains turnèd into clouds' (4.1.186–7). Near the end of the *Dream*, Puck offers the final panorama of the menaces of the night which ends in a protected, semi-sacred domestic space: 'this hallowed house' (5.2.1–18).

Young contends that these panoramas, in 'their richness and variety', 'become a kind of metaphor' for the whole play:[56]

■ [The *Dream*] is itself a panorama of smaller scenes and characters, a great landscape with cities, woods, fields, mountains, valleys, rivers, ocean, and a host of figures representative of society and the supernatural [...] the panoramas contribute significantly to the play's atmosphere of magic, spaciousness, and limitless possibility, all attributes of the power of imagination which it both derives from and celebrates.[57] □

Although Young's book is a sober scholarly study, it does offer an exuberant account of the expansive aspects of the *Dream* which acts as a corrective – or perhaps a complement – to Kott's darker view. Stephen Fender provides a further perspective on the play, in the second book devoted to the *Dream* to appear in the 1960s.

STEPHEN FENDER

In his incisive study of the *Dream*, Stephen Fender suggests that possibly the most important point about the play is that 'the ideas and forces which Shakespeare makes his characters (and even locales) represent are in every case morally ambivalent'. The 'powers which are personified in the figures of Theseus, Hippolyta, the lovers, the fairies, Athens, the wood, are presented as potentially both "good" and "evil"'. This ambivalence 'is the source of the rather unusual complexity of the play'.[58]

Fender recognizes that the lovers in the *Dream* are not strongly individualized, but detects a development in their language under the pressure of experience:

■ [T]he action in the wood consists of the characters gradually forgetting the civilities of Athens as they meet with new experiences [...] the change in the kind of language they speak both reflects and makes explicit the changes that take place in their awareness of what goes on around them [...] they enter the wood speaking in a highly organized, witty, complicated manner, and leave it speaking much more simply. □

In the early part of the play, while the lovers are still in Athens, the courtly style in the exchanges between Lysander and Hermia seems appropriate, though there are sometimes, especially with Hermia, signs of strain, of a pushing against its formal qualities. Once the four lovers are in the wood, however, the courtly style seems less suitable. As Fender puts it: '[w]e get the feeling that the more strictly the stereotypes of rhetoric and metaphor are observed in this new context, the less they actually communicate'.[59] In 3.2.123–339, where the mounting tensions among the quartet explode into verbal and near-physical violence, courtly language gives way to pithy abuse (for example, 'juggler', 'puppet', 'maypole', 'vixen', 'dwarf', 'minimus', 'bead', 'acorn' (3.2.283, 289, 297, 325, 329, 330, 331)). When Theseus finds the lovers the following morning and asks them how 'gentle concord' has come about (4.1.142), '[t]heir first words fall naturally into the framework of the balanced court rhetoric which they know Theseus expects, but very shortly the pattern is modified':[60] Fender identifies the 'new feature of their language' as 'a congruence of rhythm and meaning'. 'The lovers have discovered not only themselves and their rightful partners, but a new rhetoric in which manner and matter at last become fused'.[61]

This discovery is not the end of the *Dream*, however; Act 5 shows the limitations of the human characters 'in order to suggest the providential power of the supernatural'.[62] Fender points out how two observations from the first scene of the play echo and qualify two elements of Theseus's speech on imagination (5.1.2–22). His description of the 'poet's eye' glancing 'from heaven to earth, from earth to heaven' (5.1.12, 13) links with Lysander's image of love as lightning which 'unfolds both heaven and earth' (1.1.146), and his view that the lover, as 'frantic' as the 'lunatic', '[s]ees Helen's beauty in a brow of Egypt' (1.1.8, 10–11) exemplifies Helena's general statement that '[t]hings base and vile, holding no quantity / Love can transpose to form and dignity' (1.2.232–3). When all these remarks are brought into conjunction, they invite us 'to balance Theseus's dismissal of imagination as merely delusive against the opposite view of imagination as a vision of a better world'.[63]

The lovers themselves, despite their momentarily enhanced awareness when they first try to tell Theseus what has happened to them during the night, fall back into the relative unawareness which they demonstrate when they watch the craftsmen's play. Fender asks: 'Should not this violent drama of crossed lovers – however absurdly produced – stir in them some memories of their own complaints at being crossed and their own violence?' Fender also – and this is very unusual in *Dream* criticism so far – suggests that the lovers' ridicule of the craftsmen's performance is unfair and unduly influenced by Theseus's attitudes: focusing on their mockery of Starveling as the Moon, he observes that, while the craftsmen 'may do their best to destroy dramatic illusion', 'their audience should surely be expected to make the imaginative leap from Starveling's iconography to what it "presents"'.[64] The lovers might also be expected to recall how they themselves behaved under the moon.

In their rejection or forgetting of the lessons of the night, Theseus and the lovers compare unfavourably with Bottom in his speech at the end of Act 4. The weaver may be, as his surname suggests, 'the "bottom" of the hierarchy of which Theseus is the top' and confuses those categories which Theseus aims to keep distinct. In Athenian society he is an ass and becomes literally so in the wood. But he is 'the one character to be granted a vision of the Fairy Queen'[65] and his inability to speak adequately of it, his recognition of its inexpressibility, is perhaps the best response to that vision. His speech is both comic and serious and can make Theseus's remarks on the lovers' story and on imagination, and the mockery of the craftsmen's play by Demetrius and Lysander, seem glib and superficial by contrast.

But Fender does not conclude that Bottom has the last word. Rather, Bottom presents one of three possible responses to the events in the night-time wood. Theseus's dismissive scepticism offers another possible response, at the opposite pole to Bottom's inexpressible wonder. A third possible response, mediating between Bottom and Theseus, is supplied by Hippolyta when she speaks of the lovers' 'story of the night' growing 'to something of great constancy' (5.1.23–6). But Fender sees the *Dream* as fully endorsing none of these views. Each of the three 'has a certain validity and each cancels the other out, to an extent'.[66] 'The real meaning' of the *Dream* 'is that no one "meaning" can be extracted from the puzzles with which a fiction presents its audience'.[67]

The books of Fender and Young provide a fitting end to this chapter on *Dream* criticism in the 1960s. Both are valuable works in their own right but they are also significant in a broader critical history. Young's study is, in a sense, the apotheosis of a critical approach to the *Dream* which sought its unity or harmony. Fender, in his stress on ambivalence, anticipates the alternative interpretations of the *Dream* which would burgeon in the later twentieth century. But as the next chapter of this Guide will show, those interpretations would take a little time to emerge.

CHAPTER FIVE

The 1970s: Tongs and Bones

The 1970s was a decade of transition in Anglo-American literary criticism, including the criticism of Shakespeare and of the *Dream*. Older critical modes were still active and fruitful to some extent, while the new and revived ones which were to forge ahead in the 1980s had not yet emerged – but intimations of their rough music, the sound of the tongs and the bones (Bottom's favoured instruments (4.1.29)) was starting to be heard. In this chapter, we shall first of all discuss Alexander Leggatt's view of the *Dream* in his book *Shakespeare's Comedy of Love*. We then explore Marjorie B. Garber's focus, in 1974, on dream and metamorphosis in the play, discuss David Bevington's essay, which seeks to assimilate but also to correct Kott, and consider the Marxist reading of Elliot Krieger, which offers a perspective on the craftsmen which had hardly been raised before.

ALEXANDER LEGGATT

In his 'Preface' to *Shakespeare's Comedy of Love*, Alexander Leggatt questions the value of seeking 'the inner unity of a work of art', seeing the desire to find such unity as 'normal, understandable [and] reasonable' but contending that '"[u]nity" can be too narrowly defined' and that 'when everything is seen as contributing to a central idea, a single pattern of images, or a particular kind of story, then individual scenes or characters may be denied their full life'.[1] His discussion of the *Dream* starts by stressing the differences between the four different groups in the play, who he defines as 'the lovers, the clowns, the older Athenians and the fairies'. According to Leggatt, 'each group [is] preoccupied with its own limited problems, and largely unaware of the others. When they make contact' – most notably in the encounter of Titania and Bottom – 'it is usually to emphasize the difference between them'. He further contends that all the groups 'are to some degree innocent, though [...] the degree of innocence varies'. But these differences, for Leggatt, do not ultimately mean fragmentation or disharmony: 'the play weaves them all together'.[2]

In the previous chapter of this Guide, we saw that Stephen Fender found the courtly language in the *Dream* becoming inappropriate or breaking down as the action moves from Athens into the wood. Leggatt, in contrast, is concerned to stress the persistence of such language throughout the play and to emphasize that 'the range of expression achieved within this framework of artifice is remarkable'.[3] He suggests that such artificial language 'helps to cool the terror' experienced by Hermia on awakening from her dream (2.2.151–62) and has a similar effect in other potentially distressing scenes with the lovers.[4] In this way, it can be seen to contribute to the distanced perspective on the lovers which, according to Leggatt, the *Dream* establishes. The experience in the wood which is 'chaotic' for the lovers is 'neatly organized' – Leggatt compares it in this respect to a farce by the French playwright Georges Feydeau (1862–1921) – and gives the audience 'pleasure' where the lovers experience 'pain'.[5] Leggatt does not raise the issue of whether gaining 'pleasure' from 'pain', even the transient pain of imaginary characters, might be at least slightly sadistic and his approach more generally plays down the issue of sexuality in the play. In this respect, he seems to engage in a hidden polemic with Jan Kott, not mentioning Kott by name but focusing on that passage where, in Kott's view, the 'monstrous ass is being raped by the poetic Titania, while she still keeps on chattering about flowers'.[6] For Leggatt, Titania's chatter about flowers is a poetic sublimation of sexual desire:

■ [T]he suggestion of bestiality in Titania's affair with Bottom is kept under control by the cool, decorative poetry as she leads him off the stage. [...] They are going off to bed, but there is nothing torrid [full of intense emotions arising from sexual love] about it. The forest might have been a place of unbridled eroticism but it is not: Lysander and Hermia are very careful about their sleeping arrangements [2.2.45–70], and Demetrius warns Helena to keep away from him so as not to endanger her virginity [2.1.214–19]. Normally, couples going into the woods mean only one thing, but the lovers of this play are aware of the energies the forest might release, and determined to keep those energies under control. On the other hand, the ideal of chastity, in Theseus's reference to Diana's nunnery [1.1.69–78], and in Oberon's description of the imperial votaress who is immune to love [2.1.155–64], is set aside as something admirable but too high and remote for ordinary people. The play is aware of both extreme attitudes to sex, but steers a civilized middle course appropriate to comedy.[7] □

Leggatt does not deny the erotic potential in the situations of the play – after Kott, it had become difficult to do this – but he does contend that it is controlled, partly by language, partly by a 'civilized middle course' (as he sees it) in regard to sexuality and chastity, and partly by the nature of comedy as a genre, which is, Leggatt implies, hostile to extremes. Leggatt is fond of the adjective 'normal' and his attitude to sexuality – and chastity – in the *Dream* is a normative one which makes the assumption that both eroticism and chastity are abnormal – an assumption which could be questioned.

Just as he is aware of the potential of sexuality, however, so Leggatt is aware, on a wider scale, of a range of threats which are present in the *Dream* and which need to be kept at bay:

■ Throughout the play, we seem to be witnessing a constant process of exorcism, as forces which could threaten the safety of the comic world are called up, only to be driven away. The play stakes out a special area of security in a world full of hostile forces: just as the mortal world is very close to the fairy world, yet finally separate from it, so the comic world of the play is very close to a darker world of passion, terror and chaos, yet the border between them, though thin, is never broken.[8] □

Leggatt tilts close to Kott here in his acknowledgement of the proximity of 'the comic world' of the *Dream* to 'a darker world of passion, terror and chaos', but he still believes the border is intact.

For Leggatt, however, the world of the *Dream* is fragile for another reason: it is an illusion and its illusory nature is stressed in the play itself, by the references to acting and to shadows. The *Dream* 'moves us freely in and out of illusion, giving us a clear sense of both its fragility and its integrity'.[9] The play ultimately achieves a sense of harmony through its artistic vision, but this vision has its limits, which are those of art itself:

■ The understanding of art is necessarily limited; it cuts out a lot of reality in order to create an ordered work. [In the *Dream*,] Shakespeare deals with this charge by admitting it, by (paradoxically) suggesting within the play some of the things that have been left out, so that we see the process of selection at work. Art, like love, is a limited and special vision; but like love it has by its very limits a transforming power, creating a small area of order in the vast chaos of the world.[10] □

Leggatt's account tries to maintain a view of the *Dream* as a harmonious, de-eroticized work. In doing this, he concedes quite a lot to the opposition, acknowledging the erotic and dark aspects of the play – and perhaps thus implicitly admitting that those aspects are necessary to the play's energy – but arguing that they are finally but firmly kept at bay. Leggatt also introduces a new element into the discussion of the *Dream* – a sense that art, or at least that kind of art, highly valued in 1950s literary criticism, which creates an ordered unity, is limited by what it leaves out (even if this gives it 'a transforming power') and that the *Dream* draws attention to the limitation and fragility of this kind of art. Thus, although Leggatt preserves a pre-Kottian view of the *Dream*, he also suggests aspects of it which might, in other critical hands, undermine that view. His idea of art is a modest one, its transformative power limited largely to the creation of 'a small area of order'. A more ambitious view of the transformative power of art, closely linked to the transformative power of dream and metaphor, is advanced in Marjorie B. Garber's analysis of the *Dream* in her book *Dream in Shakespeare: From Metaphor to Metamorphosis*.

MARJORIE B. GARBER

In *Dream in Shakespeare*, Marjorie B. Garber explores the ways in which Shakespeare used and developed classical and medieval notions of dreams in his plays and relates these to Freudian theory. For Garber, in the chapter 'Spirits of Another Sort', the *Dream* is 'consciously concerned with dreaming'. The play 'reverses the categories of reality and illusion, sleeping and waking, art and nature, to touch upon [its] central theme' – the theme of 'the dream which is truer than reality'.[11] In the *Dream* the key term, occurring several times, is 'vision', which counters the dismissive use of the word 'dream' elsewhere in the text to indicate a transient and meaningless phenomenon – for example, when Lysander says that true love, besieged by war, death or sickness, is 'Swift as a shadow, short as any dream' (1.1.144). In the *Dream*, according to Garber, 'vision' is 'a code word for the dream understood, the dream correctly valued'.[12] The dream in this sense 'is truer than reality' because it has a transformative power. This transformative power 'is the special prerogative of the dream state and the center of interest of the whole' of the *Dream*.[13]

Garber values this transformative power, which is 'part of the fertile, unbounded world of the imagination', more highly than reason – and in this, she challenges the emphasis of those critics who acknowledge that Theseus's rationality is limited but still feel that reason ultimately and rightly prevails in the play. For Shakespeare, Garber suggests, 'reason is a limiting rather than a liberating force', especially in the *Dream*. In Act 1 Scene 1, Theseus tries 'to impose a "reasonable" solution upon the lovers without regard for passion or imagination'.[14] 'Reason has no place in the dream state, which possesses an innate logic of its own. [...] The instinct of the mind is to set boundaries, while the process of dream blurs and obliterates those boundaries'.[15]

A 'series of vital contrasts', in Garber's analysis, partly controls and orders the 'pattern' of the *Dream*: 'the opposition of the sleeping and waking states; the interchange of reality and illusion, reason and imagination'; and 'the disparate spheres of influence of Theseus and Oberon'.[16] All these spheres 'are structurally related to portrayal of the dream state; while the lovers sleep, the world of dream and illusion inhabited by the fairies dominates the stage':[17]

■ [T]he world over which Oberon presides, peopled by Puck and Titania, by Peaseblossom and Mustardseed, is itself a dramatic metaphor for the dream world of the subconscious and the irrational. 'Spirits' are moods and energies as well as sprites, and the fruitful ambiguity may stand as a sign of the multiplicity of the world they inhabit. [...] The simultaneity of dream world and spirit world is central to an understanding of the special magic of [the *Dream*].[18] □

The spirit world stands for the dream state which is characterized by its creative capacity for change, metamorphosis, transformation.

This dream state with its metamorphic capacity is 'structurally analogous' to metaphor. The *Dream* constantly directs attention to 'the act of metaphor-making, the visible exchange of literal for figurative and fictive'. This act moves towards the 'act of artistic creation, so clearly a conscious parallel to the subconscious activities of memory and imagination'. The *Dream* brings the 'act of artistic creation' before us 'in a series of fictional artefacts: a sampler [the piece of embroidery which Helena recalls making with Hermia (3.2.203–6)], a ballad [the ballad which Bottom says he will ask Peter Quince to write (4.1.111–14) but which, within the *Dream*, never gets written] and a play ['Pyramus and Thisbe']'. Thus the 'availability of art as an ultimate form of transformation, a palpable marriage of dream and reason, emerges as a logical extension of the recognized dream state'.[19] It is interesting to note that here Garber does allow a role for reason provided that it is wedded to dream and to imagination.

Garber also recognizes that the irrational may be dangerous. She sees this danger approached and discharged in the *Dream* by the play-within-a-play. 'Pyramus and Thisbe' is partly a 'failed' and 'out of control' transformation, but ultimately it provides 'a countermyth for the whole' of the *Dream*, a 'transformed vision of the events of the play' which 'absorbs and disarms the tragic alternative, the events which did not happen'.[20] The rupture of the dramatic illusion in which Bottom and his fellow-craftsmen engage is comic but also functional, producing a disengagement from passions which might otherwise seem painfully tragic:

■ The prologue [to 'Pyramus and Thisbe'] serves as a deliberate breaking of the frame, paralleled by illusion-shattering asides from Wall, Moon, and

Pyramus in the body of the play [-within-a-play]. In the analogy of dream, these are manifest content and latent thoughts at once, and their clear purpose is to warn against the dangers of the irrational: for the world of art, the lion in the fictional forest; for the subconscious imagination, the equally frightening serpent of Hermia's dream. □

[2.2.151–6][21]

But the irrational, despite its dangers, remains preferable, in the *Dream*, to Theseus's 'cool reason' (5.1.6). Garber challenges the widely held view that the play criticizes the unreasonableness of the lovers.

■ [The *Dream*] is throughout a *celebration* of the irrationality of love, not a criticism of the failure of reason. The indistinguishable Athenian lovers and their changeable passions are emblems, not of love's disorderliness, but of its creative power, more akin to the logic of dream than to that of waking reason. [Guide author's italics].[22] □

It is, however, an element of the *Dream*'s 'design that none of the Athenians, including even Theseus and Hippolyta, should fully comprehend the lessons of the dream state'. Their lack of comprehension is partly due to 'the preoccupation with reason and the rational which dominated the civilized world of Athens'.[23] The limits of this world are marked by their inclusion within a wider 'dramatic world where dreams are a reliable source of vision and heightened insight, consistently truer than the reality they seek to interpret and transform'.[24]

In analysing the *Dream* as a play which reverses categories, Garber herself reverses the critical categories which place reason above irrationality, dream and passion. Her positive account transforms those darker aspects of the play stressed by Jan Kott. But those aspects were still troubling critics, and David Bevington returned to them in 1975 in an essay which we discuss in the next subchapter.

DAVID BEVINGTON

In '"But We Are Spirits of Another Sort": The Dark Side of Love and Magic in *A Midsummer Night's Dream*', David Bevington acknowledges that the quote which forms the first part of the title of his essay is also used by Garber (without the 'But') for the title of her chapter on the *Dream* in the book we have just have been discussing; he asserts, however, an 'essential' difference between his and Garber's 'critical purposes'.[25] Bevington finds 'a fundamental tension in the play between comic reassurance and the suggestion of something dark and threatening'. He acknowledges that the forest 'is potentially a place of violent death

and rape' and, like Alexander Leggatt, recognizes that it offers oppor-
tunities for sexual licence. In contrast to Leggatt, however, who seems,
as we noted earlier in this chapter, to be engaged in a hidden polemic
with Jan Kott, Bevington enters openly into debate with Kott. While
he judges Kott's emphasis on these aspects of the play 'overstated', he
nonetheless maintains that Kott's 'insight has something to commend
it' and that the reactions against Kott have been 'sometimes over-
heated'. Bevington's own declared aim in this essay is 'to suggest that
in its proper context the dark side of love is seldom very far away in
this play'.[26]

Bevington contends that '[n]ight-time in the forest repeatedly
conveys the sense of estrangement and misunderstanding' which
afflicts the lovers and gives them 'a glimpse of their inner selves'
which often 'suggests much about human nature that is not merely
perverse and jealous, but libidinous'. While Kott provides 'helpful
insights' in this area, he has 'surely gone too far'. Bevington points
out that the lovers' night in the wood 'has been a continuous series
of proposed matings without any actual consummations'.[27] For example,
when Hermia and Lysander settle down to sleep in the forest, Lysander
eventually accedes to Hermia's request that he '[l]ie further off. In
human modesty. / Such separation as may well be said / Becomes a
virtuous bachelor and a maid' (2.2.41–70). Demetrius too, according
to Bevington, 'would never presume to take advantage of Helena's
unprotected condition, however much he may perceive an opportunity for rape' (2.1.214–19) (though in this case Bevington (like Helena
herself at 2.1.215) may attribute too much virtue to Demetrius: the
overwhelming point in this particular exchange is that Demetrius
does not fancy Helena and is trying desperately to get away from her).
Bevington also charges that

■ Kott seriously distorts the context of the love imagery in this play when
he discovers sodomistic [sic] overtones in Helena's likening herself to a
spaniel [2.1.203–10]; her meaning, as she clearly explains, is that she
is like a patient, fawning animal whose master responds to affection with
blows and neglect.[28] □

The term 'sodomistic' in the version printed in Richard Dutton's New
Casebook on *A Midsummer Night's Dream* may be a misprint for 'sado-
masochistic' or 'masochistic' – the last adjective would come closest to
Kott's observation that in these lines 'a girl calls herself a dog fawning
on her master. The metaphors are brutal, almost masochistic'.[29]

Kott's observation, however, perhaps conveys a more accurate
sense of the depth of Helena's subjection than Bevington does. The
paraphrase in the passage from Bevington, which we have just quoted,

diminishes the violence in Helena's lines. When Helena says 'I am your spaniel, and, Demetrius, / The more you beat me I will fawn on you. / Use me but as your spaniel: spurn me, strike me' (2.1.204–5), the verbs 'beat' and 'strike' help to drive home the elements of aggression and pain which Helena claims she is willing to endure in her relationship with Demetrius. Whether or not we infer that this prospect gives Helena some masochistic gratification, her words stress its brutal aspect. Bevington's paraphrase also changes Helena's initial metaphor into a simile and thus makes her readiness to identify herself as a spaniel in relation to Demetrius seem more distanced than her own words at first suggest: Helena does not start by saying 'I am *like* your spaniel' but 'I *am* your spaniel' (2.1.203; Guide author's italics), although in the next line but one she does modulate into a more distanced form of identification by using a simile, thus interposing a preposition ('as' or 'like') between the two terms of her comparison: 'use me *as* your spaniel' 2.1.205; Guide author's italics). Moreover Bevington, in contrast to Kott, does not pick up the element of self-degradation in Helena's canine imagery. Her capacity to explain herself clearly, which Bevington highlights, may stress rather than soften the degree of this self-degradation; her readiness to be treated as a dog can seem more degrading precisely *because* she is so lucid and articulate.

Nonetheless, Bevington's fundamental point – that sexual consummations between the lovers do not take place – still stands and is a useful corrective to those moments in Kott when he comes close to giving the contrary impression. In this respect, as Bevington suggests, the *Dream* offers a 'representation of desire almost but not quite satisfied' which is 'titillating' but 'looks forward as do the lovers themselves to legitimate consummation in marriage and procreation'. According to Bevington:

■ The conflict between sexual desire and rational restraint is, then, an essential tension throughout the play reflected in the images of dark and light. This same tension exists in the nature of the fairies and of the forest. The ideal course seems to be a middle one, between the sharp Athenian law on the one hand with its threat of death or perpetual chastity, and a licentiousness on the other hand that the forest (and man's inner self) proposes with alacrity, but from which the lovers are saved chiefly by the steadfastness of the women. They, after all, remain constant; it is the men who change under the influence of the love potion.[30] □

Bevington goes on to suggests that the 'tension between licentiousness and self-mastery is closely related also to the way in which the play itself constantly flirts with genuine disaster but controls that threat through comic reassurance'.[31]

Bevington then turns to the question of 'love and sex among the fairies'[32] and to two issues in particular: the nature of Oberon's desire for the changeling boy and the relationship between Titania and Bottom. Taking up what he sees as Kott's suggestion that Oberon's desire for the boy is sexual, Bevington admits the possibility but asserts that, as with many of Kott's claims, 'the boy's erotic status cannot be proved from a reading of the text'. But neither can it be wholly denied: '[t]his slender evidence seems deliberately ambiguous'. Bevington contends that '[a]ny attempts to depict Oberon as bisexual surely miss the point that the fairies' ideas concerning love [interestingly, Bevington omits 'sex' here, though he has earlier coupled it with 'love' in discussing the fairies] are ultimately unknowable and incomprehensible'.[33]

Despite this point about the ineffability of the fairies' ideas about love, Bevington seems pretty sure he knows what Titania's ideas on the subject are in relation to Bottom, and they do not include sex:

■ Her hours spent with Bottom are touchingly innocent and tender. Like the royal creature that she is, she forbids Bottom to leave her presence. Even if he is her slave, however, imprisoned in an animal form, she is no Circean enchantress teaching his enslavement to sensual appetite. Instead, her mission is to 'purge thy mortal grossness so / That thou shalt like an airy spirit go' [3.1.152–3]. Rather than descending into the realm of human passion and perversity, she has attempted to raise Bottom into her own.[34] □

For Bevington, Titania and the ass do not constitute, as they do for Kott, an image of grotesque, bestial sensuality, but of a reconciliation of 'the tensions in the play between the dark and the affirmative side of love'.[35]

There is a tension here between Bevington's claim that the fairies' ideas about love are unknowable and his seemingly assured knowledge that Titania's motives towards Bottom are 'innocent'. As we have seen in this Guide, it is not only Kott who thinks differently, but also Donald C. Miller, back in 1940, and Paul A. Olson in 1957, who claims that Titania's 'erotic games with Bottom and the changeling fit the symbolic frame which Shakespeare has placed about her, since she is princess of sensual passion'.[36] Bevington does not mention these earlier critics, and although he is prepared to make some concessions to Kott, he clearly stops short at doing so in regard to Titania and Bottom, weaving a sacred circle around them which admits no gross intrusions. Bevington valuably emphasizes the tender and innocent verbal and visual aspects of the Titania–Bottom scenes, which any fully adequate sexualized reading of them has to take into account; but he does not really address Kott's charge that these aspects are merely displacements of a coarser desire ('The monstrous ass is being raped by the poetic Titania, while she still keeps on chattering about flowers'[37]); moreover, he dismisses the idea that any element of undue coercion may be involved in Titania's refusal to allow Bottom to leave the wood, attributing it instead to her 'royal status' – although this could seem to reinforce the coercive element and would not necessarily preclude an element of sexual desire (if Oberon were substituted for Titania and were forbidding Hermia or Helena to leave, the charge of coercion might, certainly today, be more difficult to avoid). In affirming the innocence of the Titania–Bottom scenes, Bevington shifts from the position of even-handedness, adjudicating between Kott and his opponents, which he has adopted earlier in his essay and which he has also attributed to the *Dream* itself. Now he comes down emphatically on one side.

It is clear, both from Leggatt's indirect response to Kott, and Bevington's more overt challenge, that the issue of sexuality in the play, especially in the Titania–Bottom scenes, is a deeply contentious one which involves intense identifications on the part of critics. The responses of Leggatt and Bevington show once again how firmly Kott had put sex on the agenda of *Dream* criticism. But there was another aspect of the *Dream* that had not yet received sustained attention: its relation to class and social conflict: the aspect that might be of particular interest to Marxist criticism. It is to a notable example of such criticism, by Elliott Krieger, that we now turn.

ELLIOT KRIEGER

In *A Marxist Study of Shakespeare's Comedies*, Elliot Krieger takes up the idea that Shakespeare's comedies can be analysed in terms of a 'primary world' and a 'second world'. The 'primary world' is 'the location in which the action begins or from which the characters have departed'; the 'second world' is 'the location toward which the characters, hence the action, move'. These 'locations' become 'worlds' because 'in Shakespeare's comedies setting seems to have an active effect on the behaviour and attitudes of the characters'. The 'second world' 'seems to exemplify and contain holiday, freedom, and harmony with nature' and it is this 'second world itself, rather than what the characters do while there', which appears 'to resolve the conflicts that had been established in the primary world'.[38]

According to Krieger, other critics who have taken up the 'two worlds' idea – he instances Sherman Hawkins and Clifford Leech[39] – have seen those worlds as separate and distinguishable alternatives which audiences are invited to compare with each other and with a posited real world outside the play. Krieger propounds a different version of the 'relation between the primary and second world', in which the two worlds are not 'juxtaposed alternatives' but 'part of the same continuous representation of reality'. Drawing on Harry Berger Jr,[40] he suggests that the 'second world' is 'a strategy developed in response to the primary-world contents'; it is 'part of a process rather than [...] a polarity within a structure, an independent perspective, a separate reality'. The 'second world' may be a new (fictional) place but is, more significantly, 'the protagonists' new or transformed attitude towards their environment'.[41]

In the *Dream*, the primary and second worlds do have imaginary spatial locations: the primary world is Athens, the secondary world the wood; but in Krieger's view, the primary world carries through into the second world. We can highlight an example of this view by contrasting the way in which Krieger and David Bevington interpret Hermia's request to Lysander to '[l]ie further off' from her (2.2.50), when they settle down to sleep in the wood. Bevington sees Hermia's request as evidence of a restraint that springs from 'the person she is' and that furthers the end of 'legitimate consummation in marriage and procreation'.[42] Krieger, however, regards Hermia's request as a demonstration that she and Lysander 'have transported to the forest the system of Athenian moral conventions'.[43] Krieger also points out that lying apart almost ends their relationship because it leads to Puck's putting the love-juice on Lysander's eyes because Puck assumes that the distance between the lovers means that Lysander has spurned Hermia. Moreover:

■ The separation between the virtuous bachelor and the maid can be taken as a dramatic representation – an emblem – of the Athenian social code, which separates people from each other and from their senses and emotions. The separation correlates with the Athenian law and the father's will, both of which try to dictate and enforce the responses of others, to replace subjective perception with external and imposed authority. The lovers flee Athens so as to win autonomy, but their actions remain systematic and codified, based on received ideas rather than their own judgments, visions or senses.[44] □

This passage indicates the difference between Krieger's perspective and those of Alexander Leggatt and David Bevington; whereas Leggatt sees the lovers as 'aware of the energies the forest might release' but 'determined to keep them under control',[45] and Bevington regards the lovers as practising 'rational restraint'[46] that is in consonance with their personalities, Krieger sees them as acting on the basis of received ideas which replicate the authoritarian codes and laws of Athens. Their courtly language contributes to this: '[i]n a sense, language and literary references function so as to recreate, in the forest, the prohibitions expressed, at court, by the laws of Athens: language keeps the lovers apart'.[47]

Theseus himself uses language and literary convention to defuse the 'process of rebellion enacted by the lovers' and indeed employs these more widely as a means of social control: he 'translates the political process of rebellion against authority into an aesthetic act, a revel'. By doing this, he turns 'the potential divisions that threaten the civil peace of his society and the autonomy of his class' into 'an aspect of a larger harmony and consistency'. This process of incorporation also assimilates the craftsmen. In practising the skills by which they earn their living – carpenter, tailor, joiner, weaver, bellows-mender, tinker the craftsmen would work on nature and thus, 'in the Marxist sense, create nature by bringing it within the control of human society and commerce'. In the *Dream*, the craftsmen are removed from the contexts in which they could employ their various skills, partly because the play is set in a time of revelry, of holiday. Instead of working on nature, they, 'more than any of the other characters in the play, become and are treated as objects of nature: Puck refers to them, with a term unfortunately adopted by many critics, as "rude mechanicals" [3.2.9], an epithet that objectifies the men and abstracts human skill from their work'.[48] Bottom, in particular, is turned into an object, his body partly transmogrified for the role he is to play in reconciling those of elevated social (albeit supernatural) status: Oberon and Titania. According to Krieger, 'Bottom's transformation [...] serves no end for Bottom himself, even though he experiences it after the fact as a mystical vision'.[49] Krieger does not appear to think that Bottom gained any erotic satisfaction in his encounter with Titania.

Without any context within the *Dream* which would enable them to exercise their trade skills, the craftsmen function only as sources of entertainment for the aristocracy: 'the play furthers the aristocracy's fantasy of its absolute social predominance by replacing the craftsmen's physical control of nature in the performance of their work with their inept verbal control of nature in an aristocratic performance'.[50] The imagination of the aristocrat can transform the craftsmen's artistic ineptitude into a tribute to the aristocracy, as Theseus 'pick'd a welcome' from those 'great clerks' whose nervousness made them botch their speeches to him (5.1.93, 100).

Krieger concludes his discussion of the *Dream* with a challenge to those critics – such as Peter F. Fisher and G. K. Hunter, discussed respectively in Chapters 3 and 4 of this Guide – who claim that the play 'concludes with restored harmony, with concord achieved out of discord, with an emphasis on variety, balance, or reconciled contrasts'. For Krieger, these claims obscure 'the central social issue' in the *Dream*, 'the strategy through which the ruling class maintains its autonomy'.[51]

This strategy involves the use of the imagination to create an aristocratic fantasy of 'harmony within nature and separation from those who work with the materials of nature'. The discords of nature and of labour cannot be wholly banished and indeed resurface near the end of the play: Puck issues reminders of natural threats – 'the hungry lion', 'the wolf' – and of human effort – 'Whilst the heavy ploughman snores, / All with weary task fordone' (5.2.1, 2, 3–4); Oberon's blessing conjures up dangers – 'the blots of nature's hand' (5.2.39) – even in supposedly keeping them at bay. But nonetheless the *Dream* 'ends by incorporating nature, with its attendant sense of danger, within the Athenian society: the forces of nature certify and bless the aristocratic predominance and autonomy'.[52]

Like Kott, Krieger presents a key challenge to established ideas of the *Dream*, but of a different kind. Whereas Kott finds sexuality, sometimes of a sadistic or predatory kind, underlying the apparently innocent beauty of the play and reaching its apotheosis in the Titania–Bottom relationship, Krieger discovers continued sexual repression, potentially conflictual class relations and a nature that can be threatening. This view, like Kott's, can be seen as inappropriate to the delicacy of the *Dream*; but both views, in their different ways, could also be seen as laying bare what that delicacy could otherwise conceal. Krieger is playing the tongs and the bones, disrupting delicate harmonies, but his music has its own sophistication and power and it finds enough echoes in the *Dream* to create a certain concordance. Krieger's analysis is a notable example of how *Dream* criticism was changing in the 1970s; but it was mild compared to the challenges of the 1980s, which we explore in the next chapter.

CHAPTER SIX

The 1980s: Shattering the Dream

In the 1980s, provocative, stimulating, insightful and controversial readings of the *Dream* began to emerge and contributed to the great upheaval of Anglo-American literary studies, as post-structuralism, deconstruction, feminism, new historicism and revised forms of Marxism and psychoanalysis shattered – without wholly destroying – previously dominant modes of interpretation. It was not only a matter of an internal transformation of literary studies; social and political change also made an impact. The changes in attitudes to sexuality and gender which began in the 1960s and which, despite much opposition, have continued in some form ever since, meant that the idea that Shakespeare's comedies ultimately affirmed marriage began to be regarded in a more sceptical light. In academic literary criticism, the residues of the aspirations to radical or revolutionary political change which had emerged in the 1960s led to a more interrogatory attitude towards the view that Shakespeare's comedies reinforced social hierarchy – an attitude which intensified as hopes of political change in the contemporary world seemed increasingly blocked.

We have seen in this Guide how, in the 1950s, a consensus emerged that the *Dream* was an ultimately harmonious whole which worked through confusion and disorder to show the final triumph of order, social hierarchy and heterosexual and implicitly procreative marriage. In the 1960s, this consensus largely continued and was developed by an exploration of how the play provided an affirmation of the imagination, even of a visionary capacity. David P. Young's rich, erudite and urbanely argued book was the apotheosis of the view of the *Dream* as attaining ultimate harmony. But other views began to emerge. Most notably, Jan Kott's stress on the dark, bestial and sexual elements of the *Dream* aroused outrage among academic critics who tried either to ignore or marginalize it; but it influenced one of the most memorable productions of the *Dream*, by the director Peter Brook, and it had changed the configuration in which the *Dream* was read. Stephen Fender's perceptive and insightful book took issue more quietly, but often tellingly, with the critical consensus and stressed the ambivalence of the play, the impossibility of fixing on any one meaning. The 1970s saw a subtle but definite change in *Dream* criticism; critics such as Alexander Leggatt and David Bevington conceded the dark elements of the play which Kott (and, earlier, G. Wilson Knight) had highlighted but ultimately reaffirmed a slightly modified consensus view; Marjorie Garber, however, challenged the idea of the ultimate triumph of reason in the play, stressing dream as a source of insight, and Elliott Krieger saw the play as promulgating – while also revealing – an aristocratic fantasy which served to reaffirm ruling class values. But it was not until the 1980s that the challenge to the consensus view really gathered momentum and acquired a force that made it unignorable. The first example of such criticism in this chapter is the feminist analysis by Shirley Nelson Garner.

SHIRLEY NELSON GARNER

In *'A Midsummer Night's Dream*: "Jack Shall Have Jill; / Nought shall go Ill"', Shirley Nelson Garner makes an unequivocal break from previous interpretations which have endorsed the ending of the play. She highlights and accepts the idea that the *Dream* is like 'a fertility rite' which concludes with the restoration of the 'green world' and 'with high celebration, ritual blessing, and the promise of regeneration';[1] but rather than finding this conclusion benign, she regards it as complicit with patriarchy and the circumscription of female bonding and power, and as acknowledging that heterosexuality is fragile.

Garner suggests that the 'exclusion of men and suggestion of love between women' in the relationship between Titania and the Indian queen 'threatens patriarchal and heterosexual values'. Like Donald C. Miller back in 1940, she affirms that 'Titania's attachment to the boy is clearly erotic', pointing out, like Paul A. Olson in 1957, the similarity between her bedecking of the boy and the bedecking of Bottom; but she maintains that Titania is attracted to the boy 'not only as boy and child, but also as his mother's son'. Moreover, in contrast to Miller and Olson, Garner contends that Oberon is also 'attracted to the child'.[2] Challenging the view that Oberon wants to free the boy from undue feminine influence so that he will grow up to be properly masculine, Garner points out that Oberon does not seem to want to return the boy to his father 'with whom he, as a human child, might be most properly reared'. Oberon's conquest of the boy is 'the centre of the play, for his victory is the price of amity between [Titania and himself], which in turn restores the green world'.[3] It is also a way in which Oberon secures 'the exclusive love of a woman' and the satisfaction of his 'homoerotic desires'.[4]

Theseus does the same when he marries Hippolyta. As Oberon points out, Theseus is notorious as a serial sexual predator, unable to commit himself to enduring relationships with women (1.2.77–80). But Hippolyta, an Amazon and huntress, is androgynous, mixing masculine and feminine traits: she is thus an all-in-one figure who gratifies Theseus's desire for the exclusive love of one woman and his homoerotic inclinations. Egeus also tries, though unsuccessfully, to gratify his desire for the exclusive love of one woman and his homoerotic inclinations by promoting Hermia's marriage to Demetrius. Hermia does not love Demetrius and Demetrius's previous behaviour with Helena (1.1.106–12) suggests that he may be an inconstant and unfaithful husband; thus Egeus may retain Hermia's love by confining her to a loveless marriage. Moreover, there are hints that Egeus especially likes Demetrius; Lysander's quip is particularly significant here: 'You have her father's love, Demetrius; / Let me have Hermia's: do you marry him' (1.1.93–4). In the last act, Egeus is thus doubly defeated: deprived of Hermia and Demetrius, he leaves the scene for good (in the Quarto version); his embittered presence would impair the festive celebration.

Hermia escapes patriarchal authority as administered by her father only to succumb to it again by marrying Lysander. Crucial to this process is the breaking of her bonds with Helena. Male intervention also divides Titania and Hippolyta from other women – Titania from her fidelity to her votaress, Hippolyta from her fellow-Amazons – but these divisions are less central to the plot than the sundering of Helena and Hermia. They are drawn into 'a demeaning quarrel' and come closer to physical combat than any other female character in Shakespeare's plays.[5] When they awake with their supposedly rightful male partners, there is no explicit reconciliation between them, and they say nothing in Act 5, suggesting that they are now obedient and properly silent wives.

Thus the 'harmony' at the end of the *Dream* comes at a price:

■ The cost of this harmony [...] is the restoration of patriarchal hierarchy, so threatened at the beginning of the play. This return to the old order depends on the breaking of women's bonds with each other and the submission of women, which the play relentlessly exacts.[6] □

The heterosexual bonding achieved at the end of the *Dream* is tenuous, however:

■ In order to be secure, to enjoy, to love – to participate in the celebration that comedy invites – men need to maintain their ties with other men and to sever women's bonds with each other. The implication is that men fear that if women join with each other, they will not need men, will possibly exclude them or prefer the friendship and love of women. This is precisely the threat of the beautiful scene that Titania describes between herself and her votaress. [2.1.123–34][7] □

This threat, Garner suggests, may have some actual basis but is also partly due to a male assumption that women who bond together will exclude men as men who have bonded together traditionally exclude women.

Garner, then, poses key challenges to the *Dream*'s representations of gender and sexuality – and to those critics who have accepted such representations as the 'natural' order of things. The next critic we shall discuss, David Marshall, makes further challenges in this area, which he relates to issues of dramatic representation.

DAVID MARSHALL

In 'Exchanging Visions', David Marshall puts a series of questions which are central to the more radical interpretations of the *Dream* which emerged in the 1980s and which critics in previous decades had not asked so directly:

■ How are we to take Demetrius' recovery from the 'sickness' of abandoning Helena and loving Hermia since it is just as much the product of enchantment as Lysander's abandonment of Hermia and love for Helena? Are we to be pleased by the success of Helena's subjection of herself to Demetrius or Titania's sudden and manipulated surrender to Oberon? What about Hippolyta's marriage to the soldier who vanquished her?[8] □

Pursuing the last question, Marshall points to Hippolyta's comparative silence – 'she speaks only once in the first scene – and she doesn't speak again until the fourth act' (though it should be pointed out that the latter is also true of Theseus). Marshall can find no 'sign of either happiness or willingness in Hippolyta's response to Theseus' impatience' in the opening scene. She speaks 'with dignity, reason, and diplomacy – as is appropriate for a queenly prisoner-of-war – but her words are restrained and noncommittal'. Hippolyta's silence in this scene, Marshall suggests, 'is an important key to the conflicts' of the *Dream*;[9] she is 'tongue-tied, as if she were the serious reflection of Bottom at the moment when Titania comically ravishes him with the command of her fairies: "Tie up my lover's tongue, bring him silently"' (3.1.194).[10] Hermia, 'wanting her father's voice' (1.1.54), is similarly tongue-tied. Others dictate what Hermia and Hippolyta should feel 'while they are silent or silenced'.[11] In these silencings, the *Dream* 'presents a political question: whether these women will be authors of their own characters or representations upon which the voices of others will be dictated and imprinted'. In dramatizing this question, the play also offers an image of the 'conditions of theater', in which a representation is imposed upon an audience.[12]

The questions Marshall raises about the women in the *Dream* are linked with his challenge to the idea that the play is an affirmation of marriage – he specifically cites here Paul A. Olson's essay, which we discussed in Chapter 3 of this Guide. Marshall claims that the *Dream* 'swerves away from festive comedy as it radically places in question a social institution that embodies relations of power and stages conflicts of imagination, voice, and vision'. This is not to say that the play is against marriage but that it explores a range of meanings which marriage may have. One key way that it does this is 'by considering the conditions of being sundered and being joined'. At the start of the play, Demetrius is sundered from Helena and wants to be joined to Hermia, and Hermia and Lysander are sundered and want to be joined to each other; Titania is joined to the changeling boy and sundered from Oberon. As Marshall puts it: 'The situations which separate, divide, part, and mismatch these various pairs provide the comedy of errors of the middle acts'.[13] In Act 5 the play-within-a-play shows 'the comic and tragic sundering of Pyramus and Thisbe'.[14]

In Marshall's perspective, it cannot quite be said that the *Dream* ends with the rejoining of those who have been put asunder. Marshall sees Helena as a particular problem. First of all, she displays qualities which are less evident in the other women in the play: 'defiance, self-respect, independence, dignity'.[15] Furthermore, her speech about wanting to possess Hermia's qualities (1.1.183–9) and her rich evocation of their earlier closeness (3.2.199–215), suggests that she has been sundered from Hermia and being joined in marriage to Demetrius may not be an adequate compensation for this.

The theme of sundering and joining also relates to the mechanicals. Their crafts – weaver, carpenter, joiner, bellows mender, tinker, tailor – all involve joining or repairing. In becoming actors, however, they sunder themselves, becoming another, in their roles, but still remaining, in some sense, themselves – a division emphasized when, in their rehearsal, Bottom says 'tell them that I, Pyramus, am not Pyramus' (3.1.19) and when, in the play-within-a-play itself, Snout announces that 'I, one Snout by name, present a wall' (5.1.155) and Snug declares '[t]hen know that I as Snug the joiner am / A lion fell' (5.1.221–2). The wall in the play-within-a-play, dividing Pyramus and Thisbe 'but also providing a method of communication' between the lovers and 'binding them in a union in partition', literalizes one of the *Dream*'s key images, providing a 'translation of a metaphor in a literal sense', as

Schlegel said of the ass's head placed on Bottom (see Chapter 1 of this Guide). As a literalized image of sundering and joining, the wall is also an image of the relationship, in any theatrical production, between audience and performance. It is not only the actors, but also the audience members, who are sundered from themselves in watching a production; but the audience is also, finally, sundered from the play, unable to merge with a representation.

Marshall's discussion of the significance of the wall leads him to pose further questions:

■ These reflections should lead us to wonder about what we are laughing at when we find the mechanicals ridiculous. (This is where the play might be laughing at us.) What, after all, is more ridiculous: to personate the wall that stands between us, thereby insisting that we see it, or to act as if the wall is not there? We are told that the mistake of the mechanicals is to leave nothing to the spectators' imaginations, but can we be trusted to see the invisible walls that confront us? Are we so much more observant than the spectators to the play within a play? □

[Marshall's italics][16]

The audience may not see its own sundering and doubleness but these are inherent in the experience of theatre. In this context, Puck's offer to 'mend' in his Epilogue (line 8) takes on the meaning of joining that which has been sundered. But can theatre, which makes us see with another's eyes, really do this? As Marshall puts it: 'The marriage of true minds that is the dream of theater presents the double prospect that it might mar us as it mends, steal as its restores'. 'What do we exchange for [the] visions' that theatre gives?[17]

Marshall links the idea that theatre 'steals' from its audience with a range of references to theft and possession in the course of the *Dream*. 'Hermia, Lysander, Helena, Demetrius, Egeus, Oberon, and Titania each "steal" or are stolen from or are stolen in the course of the play' and the changeling boy 'comes to represent all of the characters' in the *Dream* 'who are traded or fought over as property'. The other characters are also 'changelings', 'in the sense that the play's plot revolves around their exchanges: their substitutions and their interchangeability'. Furthermore, the actors who perform the play are in a sense changelings – exchanging their identity for another's – and the language of the play is full of changelings in the form of its figures of speech which partly change one phenomenon into another. The audience members are changelings too, partially exchanging their own identities for identification with the changelings who act on the stage, and, by the end of the play, those audience members may have been changed. Returning to the question of what we, as audience members or readers, exchange for our visions, Marshall suggests that 'we both give up visions in this exchange *and* get visions in return'.[18] This sort of 'exchange of visions' could be 'an alternative to the theft of visions in the play'. It would be a way of learning 'how you look': 'what you look like and how you see'. 'To learn this exchange of visions', Marshall asserts, 'would be to release others from the roles we cast them in'.[19]

Marshall's analysis is subtle, intriguing and challenging. It could, however, be charged with taking its favoured metaphors of the 'changeling' and of 'sundering' too far, extending them to cover a range of phenomena which could be better described and more precisely distinguished in more straightforward terms; Marshall, it might be said, sometimes loses his sense of proportion in a way which risks producing an inadvertently comic effect on the reader. This tendency to the perhaps excessive pursuit of specific terms and metaphors becomes more widespread in the 1980s and subsequently – for example, the focus on 'misjoinings' in Patricia Parker's analysis of the *Dream*, which is discussed in the next chapter of this Guide. Marshall's analysis can also be found wanting in its relative lack of concern with the contemporary historical resonances of the *Dream*. In this he contrasts with the next critic we shall consider, Louis Adrian Montrose, who offers what has subsequently become a classic New Historicist account of the play.

LOUIS ADRIAN MONTROSE

Montrose offers an 'intertextual study' of the *Dream* and 'symbolic forms shaped by other Elizabethan lunatics, lovers and poets', which interprets the play 'as calling attention to itself, not only as an end but also as a source of cultural production'. The term which Montrose takes from Theseus's speech on imagination in the *Dream*, 'shaping fantasies' (5.1.5) is meant 'to suggest the dialectical character of cultural representations: the fantasies by which the text' of the *Dream* 'has been shaped are also those to which it gives shape'. Montrose explores this dialectic 'within a specifically Elizabethan context of cultural production: the interplay between representations of gender and power in a stratified society in which authority is everywhere invested in men [...] except at the top', where Queen Elizabeth, a woman, reigns.[20] He mentions the suggestion, made by Harold F. Brooks for example, that Queen Elizabeth may have been present at the first performance of the play;[21] he finds this 'wholly conjectural' but affirms that 'her pervasive *cultural presence* was a condition of the play's imaginative possibility'.[22]

In a way that is characteristic of New Historicist practice, Montrose steps aside from what more traditional criticism might have seen as the primary text to discuss other texts which are not regarded as source texts or secondary texts but as intertexts, texts which can be seen as interrelated with another text (say, a Shakespeare play) in terms of themes and/or language, without assuming that one text is superior to another or that one text influenced the 'author' of another. One of Montrose's intertexts is an account by the astrologer and physician Simon Forman (1552–1611) of a dream he had on 23 January 1597, in which he was with Queen Elizabeth, a 'little elderly woman in a coarse white petticoat' who at one point received the attentions of a distracted weaver who kissed her, before Forman took her away. Later in the dream, Forman records, the Queen became 'very familiar' with Forman himself and 'would have kissed [him]'.[23]

The other two texts are descriptions by André Hurault, Sieur de Maisse, the ambassador extraordinary of King Henri IV (1553–1610; King of France, 1589–1610), of two audiences with Queen Elizabeth I. In the first, '[s]he kept the front of her dress open, and one could see the whole of her bosom' and in the second 'she often opened [her] dress and one could see all her belly, and even to her navel'.[24] Montrose uses these three texts, two by the same person, to suggest that the idea of erotic intimacy with the woman who was both the Queen and the symbolic mother of her nation was a more general cultural fantasy. He latches on to the detail that the man who first kissed Elizabeth in Forman's dream was a weaver to make the link with Nick Bottom, the weaver in the *Dream*: 'Bottom's dream, like Forman's, is an experience of fleeting intimacy with a powerful female who is at once mother, lover, and queen'. But Titania's power is circumscribed because she is an unwitting player in Oberon's plot, and Oberon is 'the play's internal dramatist' and 'a "King of Shadows"' (3.1.145–6) – that is, a master of actors, to whose company, on an amateur basis, Bottom belongs.[25]

■ [In the *Dream*, a] fantasy of male dependency upon woman is expressed and contained within a fantasy of male control over woman; the social reality of the player's dependency upon a Queen is inscribed within the imaginative reality of the dramatist's control over a Queen.[26] □

Both Forman's dream and Shakespeare's *Dream* are, Montrose contends, 'characteristically *Elizabethan* cultural forms'.[27] They occur in a situation in which an otherwise patriarchal society is ruled by a woman.

Montrose then turns to the 'mixture of fascination and horror' with which the Amazons were viewed in Elizabethan culture, for example in the account in the *Palace of Pleasure* (1566–7) by the translator William Painter (?1540–94), in Spenser's *The Faerie Queene* and in sixteenth-century travel narratives:

■ Amazonian mythology seems symbolically to embody and to control a collective anxiety about the power of the female not only to dominate or reject the male but to create and destroy him. It is an ironic acknowledgement by an androcentric [male-centred] culture of the degree to which men are in fact dependent upon women: upon mothers and nurses, for their birth and nurture; upon mistresses and wives, for the validation of their manhood.[28] □

The *Dream*, Montrose suggests, is 'in a dialectic with this mythological formation'.[29] Theseus has defeated Hippolyta, the Amazon, and is about to make her his wife; two other unruly women – Hermia and Titania – are subdued in the course of the play and – a point also made by David Marshall – the sisterly bonds between Hermia and Helena are broken. The changeling boy passes into male control. The *Dream* thus confirms key patriarchal attitudes but it also, at moments, subverts them. Oberon and Titania are personified as natural forces and, in accordance with the order of things, the male subdues the female; but their very personification within a play indicates that they are constructs of culture, not nature, and raises the question of whether their quarrel is culturally rather than naturally determined, a product of patriarchal anxiety and fantasy rather than of a female wilfulness which goes against the natural grain. As Montrose puts it, the 'all-too-human struggle between the play's already married couple provides an ironic prognosis for the new marriages' at the end of the *Dream*. Doubts are also cast at the end on the happy ending. Immediately after the lovers go to bed, Puck evokes 'an uncomic world of labor, fear, pain and death' (5.1.357–76). Oberon's blessing, invoking the dangers it is meant to keep at bay, suggests how fragile the situation is. The *Dream* 'ends upon the threshold of another generational cycle' – Hermia and Lysander, Helena and Demetrius are likely to become mothers and fathers themselves – but this renewed cycle has the potential for 'a renewal of the strife with which the play began'.[30] Montrose also suggests that the happy ending of the *Dream* is 'contaminated by a kind of inter-textual irony' because the 'mythology of Theseus', as related by Plutarch, 'is filled with instances of terror, lust and jealousy' and Shakespeare's play also contains traces of Seneca's *Hippolitus* and *Medea*.[31] Seductive and destructive women, rape and marital breakdown, are crucial in the legends of Theseus and they still figure, at some level, in the *Dream*.

The uneasy reaffirmation of patriarchal order at the end of the *Dream*, the lingering sense of anxiety and of a disruptive potential attributed to women, can be linked with the anxiety and fantasy which surrounded the woman who ruled the land, Queen Elizabeth. The cult image of Elizabeth, Montrose suggests, had three combined components: the 'unattainable virgin' (like the 'fair vestal' Oberon describes); the intractable wife (Titania); and the dominating mother (Titania). Oberon 'uses one against the other in order to reassert male prerogatives'. In this way, 'the structure of Shakespeare's comedy symbolically neutralizes the forms of royal [and female] power to which it ostensibly pays homage'.[32]

The metadramatic aspect of the *Dream*, its inclusion of references to imaginative and dramatic production, is not an auto-referential meditation on art but a claim for the cultural power of theatre, for the dialectical relationship between drama and society. The *Dream* is 'a cultural production in which the processes of cultural production are themselves represented; it is a representation of fantasies about the shaping of the family, the polity, and the theatre'. And it has the power, within its imaginary world but extending beyond, to reshape those fantasies. Thus, '[t]o the extent that the cult of Elizabeth informs the play, it is itself transformed within the play'. In this reshaping and transformation, the play challenges the royal claim for 'cultural authorship and social authority'. The *Dream* is, 'in a double sense, a *creation* of Elizabethan culture' which 'creates the culture by which it is created'.[33]

The *Dream* emerges from Montrose's account as a play of power which engages with pervasive perturbations in the Elizabethan era; it becomes a much weightier drama than many earlier critics had thought, fraught with cultural and political anxieties, a poetic casebook of sociological neuroses and a major player in key discursive contests of the time. James H. Kavanagh also sees the *Dream* as a weighty play, but he locates the anxieties primarily in its craftsmen.

JAMES H. KAVANAGH

James H. Kavanagh's discussion of the *Dream* adopts a view of ideology which was influential in literary criticism in the 1980s and which derived from the French Marxist thinker Louis Althusser (1918–90). In an Althusserean perspective, ideology is not simply a set of ideas constituting 'false consciousness' but a system of lived notions and practices which provides an imaginary resolution of real economic, political and social contradictions and thus engineers consent to an inequitable political order. Literature, as constructed by conventional literary criticism, contributes to this ideological work of providing imaginary resolutions. Kavanagh discusses the *Dream* as an appropriate illustration of 'the textual and linguistic management of significant ideological contradictions in a work whose concerns seem politically innocent'.[34]

Kavanagh joins the increasing number of critics who stress the darker aspects of the *Dream*: he finds 'a profoundly threatening and threatened aspect' in a play which is 'formed around questions of desire and obedience, representation and class power' and 'haunted throughout by the threat of death'. Female rebellion, particularly as represented by Hermia, is treated with qualified sympathy but shown as ultimately, and necessarily, submitting to a male power which is prepared to make occasional concessions (when Theseus overrules Egeus and permits Hermia to marry Lysander) but which broadly reaffirms a patriarchal and hierarchical order which permeates the family, the state and the cosmos. But the *Dream* also features a clutch of people who are, as Kavanagh points out, 'from a social order rarely so active on the Shakespearean stage' – the craftsmen.[35]

The craftsmen have a problem which may, on some level, be the same as that of the other characters – to accommodate themselves to a hierarchical order – but it takes a different form in that it involves producing 'an *appropriate* – that is, class-appropriate and therefore politically acceptable – dramatic representation'.[36] In their discussion about the danger of the lion frightening the Duchess and the ladies, the craftsmen effectively address the problem of their subordinate position; to try to impose their version of reality on an aristocratic audience – to frighten it – would be a threatening assertion of their own power which might result in their execution. The craftsmen are clearly aware of this danger. Quince warns that frightening the Duchess and the ladies to an extent that would make them shriek 'were enough to hang us all'. Snug, Flute, Snout and Starveling agree in unison – 'That would hang us, every mother's son' – and Bottom confirms their risk assessment: 'I grant you, friends, if you should fright the ladies out of their wits, they would have no more discretion but to hang us' (1.1.72–6). The craftsmen therefore decide that they must undermine any attempt to produce a convincing dramatic illusion and, by means of this undermining, signal their deference to their aristocratic audience; they will show clearly that they will not try to scare them. Thus they decide that the actor playing the lion must clearly indicate that he is not a lion. As Kavanagh points out, this is 'an inversion' of the kind of 'alienation effect' promoted by the German Marxist playwright Berthold Brecht (1898–1956) in that it draws attention to art as an illusion 'not in order to enable a working-class audience intelligently to assert its political power, but to enable the workers' troupe to *escape* the political power of a ruling class'. This is an interesting interpretation of the craftsmen's approach which suggests that their disruption of the theatrical illusion is not so much a result of bungling ignorance as an intelligent survival strategy. Kavanagh is concerned to stress that the craftsmen in the *Dream* do not represent, as they might in literature and drama which emerged during and after the Industrial Revolution, a 'working class' which could seem a serious danger to an aristocracy: 'the image of artisanal workers comically undercuts any sense of real threat, precisely because they are so marginal and politically impotent within the dominant *ideology* (if increasingly strong within the changing *economy*)'.[37]

Thus the craftsmen's enactment of their deference to aristocratic sensibilities contributes to the *Dream*'s imaginary resolution of real contradictions. But for Kavanagh, it seems that this resolution is primarily effected, not by action or plot, but by the 'supple capacity' of Shakespeare's language 'to achieve such a reconciliation effect'. This makes Shakespeare's language 'the recognition pattern for what we call "literature"' – that is, Shakespeare's language becomes the supreme model for the ideological work which 'literature', as constructed at a later stage of society in which bourgeois rather than aristocratic hegemony must be maintained, should perform.[38]

Kavanagh's sense that the craftsmen's concerns about offending their audience and risking death are to be taken seriously is also crucial to Theodore B. Leinwand's analysis, but he relates it less to a general theory of the way in which Shakespeare's drama contributes to ideological reproduction and more to specific contemporary events which suggest that the threat represented by the mechanicals might have been more serious than Kavanagh seems to suppose.

THEODORE B. LEINWAND

In '"I Believe We Must Leave the Killing Out": Deference and Accommodation in *A Midsummer Night's Dream*', Theodore B. Leinwand, like Kavanagh, takes seriously the craftsmen's fears that frightening their aristocratic audience might be their death warrant. As well as their concern that a lion might frighten the ladies, Leinwand points to their worry that their drawn swords may cause alarm: Bottom says that 'Pyramus must draw a sword to kill himself, which the ladies cannot abide' and Starveling expresses his belief that they 'must leave the killing out', before Bottom devises his 'device to make all well' and asks Quince to write him a prologue which 'seem[s] to say that we will do no harm with our swords', (2.2.9–10, 13, 15, 16–18). According to Leinwand:

■ The relationship that the artisans think they have with their superiors and the attitude that they assume their superiors have toward them betray considerable anxiety. [...] Performance, especially strife- and sword-filled performance, is potentially life threatening' [in the *Dream*].[39] □

If this is the case for the artisans the *Dream* portrays, it is also true for 'the artisan-playwright',[40] William Shakespeare; like the craftsmen, he must accommodate his work to the aristocracy to whom his drama has brought him close.

Some historical evidence suggests that hanging, which might be the consequence of theft prompted by unemployment and financial hardship, was a real threat for craftsmen in the Elizabethan era. Leinwand carefully stresses that he is not suggesting that Shakespeare was especially aware of artisanal discontent in the Elizabethan era, that he had a particular attitude to it, or that he responded to such discontent in the *Dream* or in other plays. But the element of tension in the relationship between Bottom and Theseus cannot be discounted and it can be related to tensions in the real world of the time. Bottom is a weaver and Leinwand quotes an Elizabethan weaver saying 'We can get no work, nor have we any money; and if we should steal we should be hanged, and if we should ask no man would give us'.[41] Leinwand suggests that this weaver's fear was both understandable and inflated. Theft, including that of goods worth more than one shilling, could incur the death penalty; although from 1550 to 1800, roughly a quarter to a half of all those charged with felony were acquitted and half of those condemned to death were not actually executed. Nonetheless, hanging for theft remained a real risk. Moreover, there was an unusual increase in crime in the 1590s, possibly due to economic difficulties: military expenditure on conflicts with Spain, soaring prices and falling wages in the early to mid-1590s and bad harvests and food shortages from 1592 to 1599 (to which the meteorological and agricultural chaos that Titania evokes in the *Dream* may refer (2.1.88–114)). Some artisans plotted revenge and rebellion: for example, in the town of Sandwich in Kent, a weaver, Thomas Bird, allegedly declared that he and three or four other textile workers 'intended to hang up the rich farmers which had corn at their own doors'.[42] In Oxfordshire in 1596, a carpenter, Bartholomew Stere and a miller, Richard Bradshawe, were said to have conspired with others to 'cast down enclosures, seize goods and arms, and then cut off the enclosers' heads'.[43] Like the artisans in the *Dream*, they met outside the town, at Enslowe Hill in Oxfordshire; though they abandoned their plan when only ten men gathered, their plot was discovered and the only surviving verdicts shows that two of the men were hung, drawn and quartered.

It might be objected that this has little to do with the *Dream*: Shakespeare's craftsmen meet in a wood not to plot insurrection but to rehearse a play and they are careful – as we saw James H. Kavanagh argue in the previous subchapter – to try to ensure that they do not alarm their aristocratic audience and to build a proper expression of deference into their performance. But Leinwand cites Keith Wrightson's argument, in *English Society 1580–1680* (1982), that the Enslowe Hill Plot has an element of performance in common with the discussions of the *Dream*'s craftsmen. Moreover, Wrightson, according to Leinwand, sees this performance element as characteristic of confrontations between artisans and the authorities in the Elizabethan era. Even when the artisans preached insurrection they did not necessarily really want it – rather, it was a strategy to try to wrest certain concessions from the authorities (which could of course lethally backfire, as in the case of the Enslowe Hill plotters). As Leinwand puts it: 'Elizabethan riots were rather orderly affairs' and the desire to maintain order came from 'below, as well as from above'.[44] The authorities took a paternalistic approach and the craftsmen's response, beneath their sometimes heated rhetoric, was one of accommodation and deference. A similar process spreads through the *Dream*: the play 'offers accommodation and deference, but on its margins we note raised swords and threatening gallows'.[45]

Leinwand develops an analogy between Oberon's approach to environmental disorder and paternalistic 'Elizabethan social policy':[46]

■ Confronted like Oberon with bad harvests and want of cheer, the Crown and Parliament tried to counter disorder with the 1563 Statute of Artificers, the Poor Laws of 1598 and 1601, the Book of Orders, issued in 1587 and 1594, and the enclosure act of 1598. Such statutes were meant to 'take what they mistake' [5.1.90] – to construe economic and social harmony where many poor labourers knew only cruel subsistence and chronic unemployment.[47] □

Oberon does not have legislative instruments in the usual sense (though Puck might be a good metaphor for the Elizabethan secret service, not least in his capacity for getting the wrong man). But Oberon does have Bottom, whom he uses 'to counter the sort of disorder in nature that was threatening so many Elizabethan wage earners, who were worse off in the 1590s than they had been for a century'.[48] And the last act of the *Dream* brings Bottom and his companions into a harmonious situation:

■ The proximity of artisanate and nobility, the mutual celebration of aristocratic nuptials, and the expected pension for the performers make for a community of shared interests. Order is restored in Athens when all levels of society celebrate together.[49] □

Even so, Puck provides a reminder, near the end of the play, of the 'hungry lion' (5.2.1), the howling wolf and the worn-out ploughman (5.2.1–4).

Leinwand finally returns to Shakespeare as artisan-playwright in an era in which '[p]laywrights deferred and yet criticized, and both City and Court responded with tolerance at one moment, imprisonment at another'. In his drama, Leinwand suggests, 'Shakespeare criticizes the relations of power in his culture, but does so with remarkable sensitivity to the nuances of threat and accommodation which animate these relations'.[50] Such nuances in the relations between artisans and aristocrats in the *Dream* can be linked to those in the relations between the players who perform and the patrons who permit the *Dream*:

■ The company that performs 'Pyramus and Thisbe' reveals the company that performs *A Midsummer Night's Dream* perhaps more than the latter would care to admit. The desire to be made men but to receive a pension for life, to leave the killing out but to 'gleek [jest pointedly] upon occasion' [3.1.139] – these express the reasonable longing of artisans throughout the Elizabethan age.[51] □

A third perspective on the craftsmen of the *Dream* is provided by Annabel Patterson, who relates them to festive theory.

ANNABEL PATTERSON

In *Shakespeare and the Popular Voice* (1989), in a chapter called 'Bottom's Up: Festive Theory', Annabel Patterson cites Leinwand's discussion of the Enslowe Hill plot and declares that it is now an indelible part of our consciousness that Shakespeare wrote the *Dream* in a society suffering the effects of poor harvests, economic privation and incipient rebellions. He would not have needed to know about the Enslowe Hill plot, which occurred late in 1596, to be aware of discontent. Patterson cites Brian Manning's claim that 'at least thirteen disturbances' took place 'between 6 and 29 June 1595', in the Midsummer season. In 1595, 'Shakespeare would have seen the social and cultural signs of unusual, economic distress; and he might even have noticed how frequently weavers were featured in the more public and violent protests'.[52]

Patterson aims to link this awareness with festive theory. She identifies three strands of festive theory which have been applied to the *Dream*. One is the occasionalist thesis, which connects the festive aspect of the play with a marriage celebration for which it was supposedly first written; as the Introduction to this Guide observed, and as Patterson stresses, there is no evidence for this. Patterson also suggests that the occasionalist thesis elides the play's challenge to the attitudes of Theseus and to increasing courtly control of the popular elements of drama. The second branch of festive theory, especially associated with C. L. Barber, whom we discussed in Chapter 3 of this Guide, links the *Dream* not to courtly celebrations but to the kind of popular ritual practices studied by anthropologists. But Patterson feels that Barber's emphasis is finally on the way that both primitive rituals and their echoes in Elizabethan drama 'functioned to reaffirm, through reconciliatory symbolic action, the hierarchical structure of society'.[53] A third branch of festive theory, exemplified in Shakespearean criticism by Robert Weimann's *Shakespeare and the Popular Tradition in the Theatre* (1978; 1987) and, in a more general way, in *Rabelais and His World* (1965) by the Russian critic and theorist Mikhail Bakhtin (1895–1975), sees popular cultural forms as subversive to a qualified extent.

In her analysis of the *Dream*, Patterson creates what she calls 'a gargantuan mingle-mangle of the strongest and boldest suggestions that these different festive theories proffer, while pushing them beyond their own aesthetic or procedural inhibitions'[54] – an approach which, Patterson suggests, the *Dream* itself adopts. For example, Theseus's festive revels, elevated though they are in some respects, incorporate a bawdy element in the references to the wall in 'Pyramus and Thisbe'; 'hole', 'chink', 'cranny' and 'stones' (which could mean 'testicles) all have sexual connotations. (Patterson also points to Thomas Clayton's argument that neither the Quarto nor Folio texts of the *Dream* have the stage direction 'Wall holds up his fingers' and that Pyramus and Thisbe may have been intended to try to kiss between Snout's legs.[55]) The bawdy, bodily element disrupts the division 'between courtly and popular entertainment'.[56]

If Theseus's festive revels cannot be seen solely in terms of elevated civility, the lovers' plot cannot be regarded solely as an assimilated fertility ritual. To some extent, Patterson suggests, it could be better understood in the kind of terms proposed by the anthropologist Victor Turner (1920–83), who argues that festive actions involve an 'exchange between rules and energies' and should be seen in relation to social norms of respect and obedience. But Patterson feels that there 'is no exchange between rules and energies in this tale of adolescent silliness' and that it is Bottom who 'marks, as [the four lovers] are incapable of doing, the sociological seriousness that their own festive plot implied'.[57] There is thus a further interchange between the courtly and the popular, where Bottom draws out the social implications of the lovers' plot, though in a further inversion, he does so, not through a popular form of drama but through an attempt at high tragedy.

The third festive plot, Patterson claims, is even 'more transgressive' – Titania's quarrel with Oberon which is only resolved 'by the most extreme example of status inversion and misrule which Shakespeare's canon contains, the infatuation of the Queen of Fairies with a common artisan'. While feeling that Louis Adrian Montrose, in the essay discussed earlier in this chapter, 'is true to the *Dream*'s mixture of light and dark, and subtle in its handling of the Elizabethan semiotics of gender', she argues that, in his use of psychoanalysis, Montrose does not do justice to the 'conscious analytic project' in which Shakespeare was engaged in the *Dream* and also plays down 'the socioeconomic component' in the linking of a queen with an artisan.[58] Patterson contends that Bottom, as 'visual pun and emblem', 'stands at the fulcrum of Shakespeare's analysis of the festive impulse in human social structures' and asks whether 'his (im)proper name, in symbolic alliance with his ass's head, invoke[s] [...] an enquiry into the way the lower social orders, as well as [what Bakhtin calls] "the lower bodily stratum", function'. Pursuing this question, she considers Bottom's account of his dream and points out that the passage from I Corinthians 2:9, which Bottom scrambles, goes on, in 1 Corinthians 12:14–15, to develop the references to bodily parts and faculties into an image of the harmonious body which is also a metaphor of an ideal Christian community:

■ [T]he parts of the body which seem to be weaker are indispensable, and those parts of the body we invest with greater honour, and our unpresentable parts are treated with greater modesty, which our more presentable parts do not require. But God has so adjusted the body, giving the greater honour to the inferior part, that there may be no discord in the body, but that the members may have the same care for one another.[59] □

In Patterson's perspective, the *Dream* invests the 'unpresentable parts' of the social body – represented by Bottom – 'with greater honour by their momentary affinity with a utopian vision'. Bottom judges that he cannot articulate this vision but 'its inarticulate message remains: a revaluation of those "unpresentable" members of society, normally mocked as fools and burdened like asses, whose energies the social system relies on'.[60]

In representing and elevating the unrepresentable, Shakespeare extends the scope of festivity in this play:

■ The *Dream* imagines a festive spirit deeper and more generous than the courtly revels that seemed, in the 1590s, to be appropriating plays and actors; an idea of social play that could cross class boundaries without obscuring them, and by those crossings imagine the social body whole again; and a transgressive, carnival spirit daring enough to register social criticism, while holding off the [...] dramatic scene of violent social protest.[61] □

This might make the *Dream* seem wholly benign, but Patterson adds a reservation in regard to an aspect of the audience's possible reaction. She points out that the rebels in the 1549 Norfolk uprising led by Robert Kett (1492–1549) seem to have been especially aggrieved that their plight was the object of mockery, that, as an account in 1615 put it, 'their miserable condition, is *a laughing stocke to most proud and insolent men*' [Patterson's italics]. Patterson suggests this has relevance to the response of the two audiences – onstage and off – of 'Pyramus and Thisbe' in the *Dream*:[62]

■ When Bottom and his fellows are mocked by the aristocratic audience, the audience outside the *Dream* has the opportunity to consider whether or not to laugh themselves, which sort of festive spirit to select for their own enjoyment. If laughter is necessary to mediate social tensions, Shakespeare's festive theory seems to argue, then let it be a laughter as far as possible removed from the red-hot iron of social condescension.[63] □

Thus the *Dream* emerges in Patterson's reading as a key text not only of festive comedy but also of festive theory – and it leaves the audience with the responsibility of choosing which aspect of festive theory to adopt in their own responses.

By the end of the 1980s, the field of *Dream* criticism had been radically reconfigured. Questions had been asked about the play's representations of gender, of sexuality, of order, of ideology, of artisans. There had been a marked shift from a stress on love to a stress on politics. If Jan Kott had put sexuality on the agenda of *Dream* criticism in the 1960s, the critics we have looked at in this chapter, from Shirley Nelson Garner to Annabel Patterson, put politics on the agenda in the 1980s, and they did so in ways that made them more difficult to marginalize than Kott had been. As this chapter has shown, there was nothing homogeneous about the interpretative approaches or the politics of these critics: they might employ psychoanalysis, Marxism, feminism, discourse analysis, empirical history and festive theory; they might focus on top-down or bottom-up practices, attitudes and events, from the iconography of Queen Elizabeth I to the stirrings of popular revolt. But it was clear, as the decade drew to a close, that the broad critical consensus on the *Dream* that had emerged during the 1950s, survived the shock of Kott in the 1960s, and screened the sound of the tongs and bones in the 1970s, had been shattered. This upset some traditional critics and scholars but it was, for the most part, liberating – the smashing of an enchanted glass. It meant, however, that critics in the 1990s would have to sift through the fragments, assembling them in old and new patterns, adding fresh facets, and observing the reflections that formed in the critical hall of mirrors. We will consider the most striking reflections in the next chapter of this Guide.

CHAPTER SEVEN

The 1990s: Sifting the Fragments

In the early 1990s, *Dream* criticism was furthered by the appearance of two books by established critics which assembled and elaborated material they had published earlier – René Girard's *A Theater of Envy*, a study of Shakespeare which includes substantial discussions of the *Dream*, and James L. Calderwood's book devoted to the *Dream* in the Twayne's New Critical Introductions to Shakespeare series. We shall consider each of these in turn. We shall then discuss two interpretations, the first by Terence Hawkes and the second by Patricia Parker, which to some extent pursue and innovatively extend the critical probings of the 1980s, and move on to the analysis of Margo Hendricks, which takes up the hitherto hardly explored topic of the *Dream*'s relationship to race and empire. We shall follow this by exploring the renewed attention to the relationship between the *Dream* and Ovid in Jonathan Bate's *Shakespeare and Ovid* (1993) and we shall conclude the chapter by considering Helen Hackett's book on the *Dream*, published in the Writers and Their Work series.

RENÉ GIRARD

The key concept which René Girard brings to Shakespeare in *A Theater of Envy* is that of 'mimetic desire' – desire which is imitative of the desire of another and which directs itself towards the same object which that other desires (as Demetrius and Lysander, in the *Dream*, both, for a time, desire Hermia and then Helena). In Girard's view, 'the mimetic desire that governs human relations in Shakespeare is mastered for the first time [in the *Dream*] and dramatized as a global system, the source of all social integration as well as disintegration'.[1] In the play, the 'Shakespearean focus on mimetic desire broadens into a total anthropological vision', making it 'compulsory reading for all modern anthropologists'.[2]

Mimetic or imitative desire can, in the same process, unite and divide people – and literary characters: 'Individuals who desire the same thing are united by something so powerful that, as long as they can share whatever they desire, they remain the best of friends; as soon as they cannot, they become the worst of enemies'. There is thus 'a perfect continuity between concord and discord' (Girard is not specifically discussing the *Dream* at this point, but it is interesting that he uses two key terms which occur in the play – in Theseus's line 'How shall we find the concord of this discord?' (5.1.60)). Mimetic rivalry can generate social bonding but is also 'the fundamental source of human conflict'.[3]

If mimetic desire is unsuccessful, however, it can turn into desire for one's successful rival, for what Girard calls the 'mediator' between the desiring rival and the object of desire. In the first scene of the *Dream*, Helena's desire for Demetrius has already reached this stage; she wants to *be* Hermia and although this is presented as a means to satisfying her desire for Demetrius, it seems that her desire for Hermia's being is stronger. As Girard puts it, she 'wants every part of her body to match Hermia's corresponding part. She wants the whole body of Hermia'. Girard dismisses the idea that Helena's desire to be Hermia has 'unconscious' homosexual connotations and instead sees those connotations as 'deliberate', a dramatization of a key aspect of Shakespeare's representation of mimetic desire:[4]

■ Shakespeare portrays the tendency of unsuccessful desire to focus more and more on the cause of its failure and to turn the mediator into a second erotic object – *necessarily* homosexual, if the original desire is heterosexual; the erotic rival is an individual of the same sex as the subject.[5] □

Thus Helena's desire to be Hermia is not primarily the emergence of a repressed homosexual desire but the result of a thwarted desire which directs itself towards the successful rival for the object of desire.

Just as mimetic desire is active in the lovers' plot in the *Dream*, so it is active in the craftsmen's desire to play parts, especially in Bottom's desire to take all the available roles. The lovers' plot and the craftsmen's plot have much in common: both start with roles being distributed, each of which should be played by one person, but each of which becomes confused and doubled. Demetrius and Lysander both play the role of Hermia's lover and then of Helena's; Bottom wants to play all the roles and to be Pyramus while also declaring himself to be Bottom; the lion wants to announce that he is also Snug the Joiner. As Girard puts it: 'In both subplots the fantastic apparitions result from the telescoping and *dismembering* of normally differentiated creatures, followed by a disorderly *remembering* that contradicts the culturally ordained differentiation of everyday life'.[6]

Girard contends that in the craftsmen's plot, 'Shakespeare reinjects the ingredient that the aestheticians always leave out – competitive desire', while in the lovers' plot, 'he reinjects the ingredient that the students of desire never take into account – imitation'. The 'real message' of the *Dream* is that the 'love of mimesis that sustains the aesthetic enterprise is one and the same with mimetic desire'. In this, according to Girard, the *Dream* challenges a whole 'Western philosophical and scientific [and anthropological] tradition' which divides the mimetic and the erotic into two independent spheres. 'Shakespeare's spectacular marriage of mimesis and desire is the unity of the three subplots [aristocrats, lovers, fairies] and the unity' of the *Dream*.[7]

Girard's case is an intriguing but overstated one – as a thinker, he is fond of finding one principle which will serve as universally explanatory and of shaping his data to conform to that principle. He is also dismissive and inaccurate about previous criticism of the *Dream*, claiming, for example, that, in the debate between Theseus and Hippolyta at the start of Act 5, the 'academic establishment has remained fully committed to the creed of Theseus'[8] whereas, as we have seen in this Guide, several critics who might be seen as members of 'the [or 'an'] academic establishment' have suggested the inadequacy of Theseus's statement when judged in the total context of the play in which it occurs. Nonetheless, 'mimetic desire' does provide a fascinating and illuminating concept to apply to the *Dream*, though it hardly seems as all-encompassing as Girard suggests. Another illuminating concept which can be applied to the *Dream* – that of anamorphosis – can be found in the next critic we shall consider, James L. Calderwood.

JAMES L. CALDERWOOD

The most original and intriguing aspect of James L. Calderwood's richly packed book on *A Midsummer Night's Dream* is his use of the idea of 'anamorphosis' – the ancient Greek term for 'transformation'. This is a device used by Renaissance painters in which an image that seems unidentifiable when viewed from the front becomes recognizable when viewed from a particular angle or with an appropriate mirror or lens. As Calderwood points out, the most famous example of anamorphosis is in the large painting in London's National Gallery usually known as *The Ambassadors* (1533), a double portrait of Jean de Dinteville (1504–55) and Georges de Selves (1508–41) by Hans Holbein the Younger (1497/8–1543). The odd shape in the lower centre foreground between the two confident and worldly diplomats resolves itself into a skull when looked at from the right angle and distance. Applying the idea of anamorphosis to the *Dream*, Calderwood contends that

■ [i]n [the *Dream*] Shakespeare does something similar to Holbein by creating a linear version of anamorphosis, converting the painting into a play which the audience sees from three different perspectives. We do not have to change seats during a performance to find the proper anamorphic angle; Shakespeare does our moving for us by making the 'seen' – that is, the scene – change, in effect presenting us with a painting in three panels. First he gives us a straight-on look at Athens, then shifts our perspective by obliging us to consider the night in the forest, then brings Athens back into the third panel and says, 'Look again'. The anamorphic effect arises from the fact that fairyland, though not exactly a blurry skull at the base of Theseus' palace, is a kind of crazed mirror of the Athenian world.[9] □

This is an interesting suggestion, although it is not pursued with quite the conceptual precision or attention to textual detail that would make it really productive and plausible. It would be worth linking it up with David P. Young's ideas of 'picturization' and 'panorama' in the *Dream* which we considered in Chapter 4 of this Guide, but although Calderwood occasionally mentions Young, he does not discuss Young's proposals about the pictorial aspects of the play. Nonetheless, Calderwood's exploration of the events and images which figure in the 'crazed mirror' of the forest is especially interesting for his discussion of a question which had, since Jan Kott, proved particularly vexing for critics: whether Bottom and Titania have sex.

Calderwood asserts 'Most arguments for a sexual consummation rely less on the text [of the Dream] than on mythic or fictional parallels'[10] – for example, with Pasiphaë, the wife of Minos, King of Crete, who mated with a sacrificial bull and gave birth to the Minotaur, or with the erotic exploits in Apuleuis's *Golden Ass*. Calderwood points to two textual moments which could have sexual implications: Titania's instruction to her fairies to light tapers 'to have my love to bed and to arise (3.2.163), where 'arise' could allude to a male erection, and the images she uses later when embracing Bottom: 'the female ivy so / Enrings the barky fingers of the elm' (4.1.42–3), where both the image of the ring around the finger and of the ivy embracing the elm have coital connotations. But Calderwood nonetheless contends that 'Titania's sexually ambitious metaphors are evidence not of what she and Bottom did or are doing but of what at worst she think she would like them to be doing'.[11]

Calderwood suggests that Titania's desire for Bottom is an aspect of a more general desire to be mortal and human. According to Calderwood, other aspects of this desire are her love for Theseus, her wish to be the pregnant Indian queen and her stepmothering of the queen's child'. Thus, Calderwood suggests, 'In this light, her surrender of the changeling child marks her reconciliation not merely to Oberon and patriarchy but also to her immutable destiny as an immortal'.[12]

Calderwood also draws attention to a feature of the *Dream* which marks the scenes in the forest as well as in Athens. He calls this absence 'the mystery of the missing mothers': in the play, 'the mothers are either dead (the mother of Titania's Indian boy) or puzzlingly absent (especially the mothers of Lysander and Hermia)';[13] even Thisbe's mother, though Starveling is cast for the part (1.2.54–6), never appears in the play-within-a-play (though neither, it should be said, do Pyramus's father, for whom Snout is cast (1.2.58–9) – though it could be argued that his role as the wall 'that parted their fathers' (5.1.345–6) makes him a patriarchal surrogate – or Thisbe's father, for whom Peter Quince casts himself (1.2.59)). The commonsense response to the missing mothers would be to say there is no mystery – as Calderwood acknowledges, they, or other relatives, do not have to be there and mothers are hardly prominent in Shakespeare's other comedies. But for Calderwood the *Dream* is different, because 'in it such a ferocious stress falls on fathers and on patriarchal authority, and such curious mention is made of stepmothers, that the absence of proper mothers looms larger than in other plays'.[14] Calderwood uses a psychoanalytic perspective derived from the French writer Jacques Lacan (1901–81) to suggest that these absent mothers, dead or repressed, 'remain elusively alive in the imaginary, where they appear as a series of substitutive (m)others [Lysander's dowager aunt to whom he and Hermia originally intend to flee, Titania as stepmother of the Indian boy] issuing promises of fulfilment which they can only partially and passingly keep'.[15] The mystery of the missing mothers will also come under scrutiny in Terence Hawkes's essay 'Or', which we shall now consider.

TERENCE HAWKES

Like James L. Calderwood, Terence Hawkes in 'Or' draws attention to the absence of mothers in the *Dream*, but suggests that there might be one who has hitherto passed unnoticed. In the opening scene of the play, Lysander refers to Helena as 'Nedar's daughter' (1.1.107) and in the first scene of Act 4 Egeus calls her 'old Nedar's Helena' (1.1.129). Insofar as readers have thought about Nedar at all, they will, Hawkes suggests, probably have assumed it referred to Helena's father. Hawkes challenges this assumption, asserting that the nearest ancient Greek version of the name is female, 'Neda', the name of a river and a nymph linked with Zeus. So 'old Nedar' might be Helena's mother. ('Nedar' is also, Hawkes points out, an anagram of 'Arden', the maiden name of Shakespeare's mother.)

Whether Nedar is taken as Helena's mother or father, however, the character 'seems superfluous'. 'As a parent, Nedar appears merely repetitive of a principle fully and powerfully presented elsewhere, perhaps in Egeus'.[16] Hawkes goes on to suggest that 'a repetitive mode invests the whole' of the *Dream*, 'almost to an extent that seems to insist on repetition as one of its central concerns'.[17] The start of the play is marked by delays and disruptions (for example, the slow approach of Theseus and Hippolyta's 'nuptial hour' (1.1.1), Egeus's vexed intervention, the blocked relationships of Helena and Demetrius, Demetrius and Hermia, and Lysander and Hermia); these are multiplied and echoed in the wood; and the play seems to make several attempts at ending – the main plot is resolved at the end of Act 4, but a fifth act follows containing a play-within-a-play which has difficulty in coming to a conclusion and when it does it is followed by a Bergomask dance and by the entries of Puck and then Oberon and Titania, and Puck's epilogue.

This repetitive, stop-start element in the *Dream* is illustrated, Hawkes suggests, in the language of the play itself, for example in the last two lines of Theseus's 'lunatic, lover and poet' speech: 'Or, in the night, imagining some fear, / How easy is a bush supposed a bear!' (5.1.21–2). Critics and editors have not always liked these lines and have felt they were an interpolation. Hawkes cites, for example, R. G. White, quoted by John Dover Wilson in his 1924 edition of the *Dream*: 'Would Shakespeare, after thus reaching the climax of his thought, fall a-twaddling about bushes and bears?'[18] Hawkes contends that the lines could be seen to reinforce Theseus's meaning – that 'strong imagination' can give 'a local habitation and a name' (5.1.18, 17) to both joy and fear by conjuring up images which correspond to those emotions – and that the real trouble is a word 'whose implications take us to the centre' of the *Dream* – and give Hawkes the title of his essay: the word 'or'. According to Hawkes, 'or', as used in this passage, 'links two polarities whilst maintaining the difference between them'. In a play which seems, as Hawkes has already suggested, invested with repetition on the level of action and of language, scholars who dislike the last two lines of Theseus's speech want 'or' to be 'and'. But 'and', in Hawkes's perspective, 'indicates "the same"', while '"or" implies difference'.[19] The *Dream* may seem committed to 'and', to the idea of repetition, as the mortal couples settle down at the end to marriage and procreation: but it 'also covertly offers to engage with an opposite mode represented by the word "or"'.[20]

Hawkes further suggests that in the *Dream*, 'or' can spring from 'and':

■ [A]s the plot unfolds, change seems to spring from the very stratagems designed to maintain sameness, to the dismay of those caught up in the process. The very idea of filial generation [expressed by Theseus], for example, whereby a father 'imprints' a 'form in wax' [1.1.49], deals in an evident sense of repetition through the metaphor of 'reproduction', and its links with printing and reprinting. Yet, as Egeus discovers, the notion that parents can thus safely 'repeat' themselves in their children runs full tilt into its opposite when the children seek to undertake liaisons in the world beyond the family. In fact, a central paradox emerges whereby the process of filiation, committed to an 'imprinting' repetition of the same, inevitably leads on to a social process of affiliation through marriage in this case, which must, willy-nilly, be committed to difference.[21] □

Of course – though Hawkes does not quite make this point – this means that 'or' folds back into 'and'; the difference of marriage provides a repetition of the institution of marriage. 'Or' and 'and' become 'and/or'.

Hawkes uses his distinction between 'and' and 'or' to make a more general point about literary criticism which is relevant to the developments in *Dream* interpretation which we have been tracing in this Guide. 'All criticism', Hawkes contends, intentionally or not, makes 'a potential space for "or"'[22] – it cannot avoid changing its ostensible object in a way which opens the door of difference. He advocates a 'critical stance which self-consciously seeks to raise this process to the highest power':[23]

■ The method of such a commentary would, of necessity, be 'to refuse absolutely to encounter the text on its own terms, to refuse the text's own hierarchy of character and event, and to read and re-read it seeking out what is suppresses, marginalises and silences as part of its own project.[24] □

Much of the *Dream* criticism considered in the previous chapter of this Guide and in this chapter exhibits this approach, to a greater or lesser extent. A further notable example, from a book by Patricia Parker whose very title highlights the 'marginal' – *Shakespeare from the Margins* – is the subject of our next subchapter.

PATRICIA PARKER

In *Shakespeare from the Margins,* Patricia Parker draws a link between the various kinds of 'joinings' with which the craftsmen of the *Dream* are associated in their trades and the idea that the 'proper "iogning" [joining] of words' was 'in the period contemporary with Shakespeare's *Dream* the foundation of the construction of order both in grammar, rhetoric, and logic, and in the social and political hierarchy their ordering reflected'.[25] Throughout the *Dream,* however, the craftsmen are always misjoining words (and other things) and their performance of 'Pyramus and Thisbe' 'disjoins or dismantles [...] theatrical illusion'. Parker proposes that 'there is an intimate relation between their laying bare of the joints and seams of theatrical spectacle [...] and their repeated disfiguring or deforming of what Theseus, the play's representative ruler, calls the ordered 'chain' of discourse, an order explicitly linked with 'government' (5.1.124, 123).

The exchange about Quince's prologue which takes place between Hippolyta and Theseus runs as follows:

■ Hippolyta: Indeed, he [Quince] hath played on this prologue like a child on a recorder – a sound, but not in government'. / Theseus: His speech was like a tangled chain – nothing impaired, but all disordered'. □

(5.1.122–5)

Parker further suggests that there are 'links between [the] suspect joinery [of the craftsmen] and the ending of this marriage play, with its conventional joining in matrimony' that set right 'the unlawful joining and misjoinings of the play's disordered middle in the woods'.[26] It is also important to Parker's argument that all the craftsmen can be 'associated by their names and trades with erotic counterparts to joining and fitting'.[27]

This association enables Parker to effect a joining of the mechanicals' plot and the love plot. In the 'disordered middle' of the *Dream*, the love plot is characterized by misjoinings which are also inversions of accepted hierarchies. In examining these inversions, Parker focuses on Puck's adverb for the turns of events which he likes most – 'prepost[e]rously' ('And those things do best please me / That befall prepost'rously' (3.2.120–1)) – a term that is also of particular interest to Douglas Green, as we shall see in Chapter 8 of this Guide. 'Preposterous', Parker suggests, 'was the term [...] for all inversions understood in the period as unnatural' and these are exemplified in the wood near Athens: 'maids pursue men as if the story of Apollo and Daphne were reversed' (2.1.231), 'Bottom the artisan is consort to a queen',[28] and 'a rebellious Titania temporarily overrules her husband and lord'.[29] The play's 'disordered middle' also includes a reference to a further possible inversion, which elevates same-sex relationships over heterosexual ones. This occurs in Helena's eloquent recollection of the closeness which she and Hermia enjoyed as girls growing together like 'a double cherry' (3.2.210). Even in the wood, however, this relationship is placed in the past rather than the present, and this is also the case, implicitly, with the woman-to-woman relationships of the Amazonian society from which Hippolyta has come. But these past same-sex bondings, like the temporary inversions of gender and hierarchical relationships in the wood, are nevertheless, Parker asserts, 'examples of potential joinings divergent from (and sundered by) the orthodox joining sanctioned by this comedy's conventionally consummating end, with its apparent coupling only of that which can lawfully be joined'.[30]

It is the craftsmen and their misjoinings, verbal and theatrical, which play a crucial role in suggesting that the 'conventionally consummating end' of the *Dream* is not natural but constructed, a joining that is a fabrication which works to preserve patriarchal and hierarchical power. As Parker puts it,

■ the rude mechanicals of Shakespeare's play – by their constant disruption of proper joining and disposition and by their inverse association, as artisans, with the appropriated metaphors of rule – also provide a perspective within the play from which to view this closural disposition and its righting as a frame that is itself constructed rather than cosmic or natural, a shaping of figuring that claims the prerogative to amend, or correct, both errant females and the artisans' apparently innocently disfigured production. And their insistence on laying bare the mechanics of theatrical illusion (on exposing the means of its construction rather than producing the seamless or naturalized) calls attention both within and beyond the confines of the play to the production of other illusions and spectacles, including the theatrics of power itself.[31] □

Parker's account of the *Dream* thus gives 'these too frequently marginalized artisans a crucial role in the ironizing of the telos, end, or final point of the play itself'[32] – though as Parker suggests, making a point similar to that of the critic we discussed in the previous subchapter, Terence Hawkes, the 'final point' of the *Dream* is an insecure concept to apply to a text that seems to have difficulty in ending.

Like Annabel Patterson, Parker puts the craftsmen more firmly on the map of *Dream* criticism. For Parker, they are not bumpkins, buffoons or clowns but key figures in the play's challenge to its own dominant assumptions. Parker is able to link the craftsmen's plot to the love plot through the metaphor of 'joining' which was used in the Elizabethan era to signify correct and fitting linguistic, sexual and governmental connections – though she may sometimes seem to extend the metaphor too far, like David Marshall with his metaphors of 'sundering' and 'the changeling', discussed in the previous chapter of this Guide. Staying within Parker's terms for the moment, however, we could point to another aspect of joining – and potential misjoining – which was developing in the early modern period, however, and this was related to race and empire. Parker herself observes the general absence of these topics from *Dream* criticism but sees Margo Hendricks as a critic who has recently drawn them out. We shall next consider Hendricks's analysis of the play.

MARGO HENDRICKS

In opening up the issue of race and empire in her 1996 essay '"Obscured by dreams: Race, Empire, and Shakespeare's *A Midsummer Night's Dream*', Margo Hendricks focuses on a figure who is much more marginal than the craftsmen: the Indian boy. The boy neither speaks nor, according to the text of the play, appears on stage (though some stage productions and films may insert him). On one level, as Hendricks acknowledges, the Indian boy is 'simply a plot device: he figures as the origin of the conflict between Oberon and Titania'. But, Hendricks asks, 'why does he have to be Indian? Why not describe the boy as merely a changeling child?' Or, given that the fairy sections of the play draw so much on English folklore, 'why not identify the changeling as the English boy?' But Puck immediately identifies the boy as 'stol'n from an Indian king' (2.1.22) and soon afterwards Titania offers 'an elaborate narrative of the boy's maternal ethnic origins' (2.1.123–35). Hendricks is interested in the 'implications about race and early modern England's mercantilist and/or colonialist-imperialist ideology' which might emerge 'from Shakespeare's use of India'.[33]

In pursuing these implications, Hendricks contends that 'literally and figuratively' the text of the *Dream* 'denotes cultural and temporal spaces' which she calls 'borderlands' – 'spaces that are clearly marked for recognition' The most evident borderlands in the play are 'between humans and fairies, male and female, Athenian and Amazon' but they also occur 'on an ideological level in the concept of race' – a concept which 'is neither wholly the older (and more feudal) idea based on class and lineage nor wholly the more modern idea based only on physical appearance (i.e., skin colour, physiognomy)'. Instead, the notion of 'race' in the *Dream* is 'an uneasy mixture – the miscegenation [...] – of these two views'. Hendricks argues that 'the figurative evocation of India localizes Shakespeare's characterization of the fairies' in the *Dream* 'and marks the play's complicity in the racialist ideologies being created by early modern England's participation in imperialism'. These ideologies do not only feature in Shakespeare but are also 'endemic to most [contemporary] textual representations of India'.[34]

Hendricks examines a range of examples of such representations. There are three possible sources for Shakespeare's portrayal of Oberon: the thirteenth-century romance *The Boke of Huon of Bourdeaux* which, in the translation of John Bourchier, Baron Berners (?1469–1533), appeared in at least three editions in the sixteenth century; Spenser's *The Faerie Queene*; and the play *The Scottish Histories of James the Fourth* by Robert Greene (?1560–92). Hendricks links these with two travel narratives: the first is the translation from Latin into English of the 1503 account by Lewes Vertomannus (a Latinized version of the name of the Italian traveller Ludovico de Verthema or di Varthema (1470–1517)) which was included in *The History of Travayle in the West and East Indies, and other countreys lying eyther way, towards the fruitfull and ryche Moluccaes* (published posthumously, 1577) by the collector and translator of travel narratives Richard Eden (?1521–76). The second, more briefly discussed, is the English translation of the book by the Dutch traveller Jan Huyghen van Linschoten (1563–1611), *Iohn Hvighen van Linschoten, his Discours of Voyages into ye Easte & West Indies; Divided into Four Bookes* (1598).

Hendricks suggests that the three possible source texts of the *Dream* link Oberon with India. At the end of *Huon of Bordeaux*, Oberon hands over his fairy kingship to Huon in Momur, 'the far-reaching district that was known to mediaeval writers under the generic name of India'. In Book 2 of Spenser's *Faerie Queene*, Sir Guyon reads a genealogy of his own ancestry in which a line of 'puissant kings' descends from Elfin, described as 'him [who] all *India* obayd / And all that now *America* men call' (Book 2, Canto 10, stanza 72, line 5) to 'the mightie Oberon' (Book 2, Canto 10, stanza 75, line 8). In Greene's *The Scottish Historie of James the fourth, slaine at* Flodden, *Entermixed with a pleasant Comedie, presented by* Oboram *King of* Fayeries, Oboram/Oberon, at the end of the first act, offers a dumb show which is linked with an Asian locale, depicting the defeat of the ancient Assyrian queen Semiramis, the coronation and death of Cyrus and the murder of the 'potentate' Sefostris.

These texts establish the literary image of 'an Asiatic or "Indian" Oberon' which was in cultural circulation at the time of the *Dream*. But the image of India itself was starting to change with the expansion of commerce, which began to produce, for example in travel narratives such as those of Vertomannus, another image of India as a place to be analysed and classified, partly in ethnographic ways. This new image did not drive out the exotic, fabulous and magical elements which had characterized the earlier image of India but mixed with them. This mixture of the magical and mercantile is exemplified in the *Dream*:

> ■ Like Athens, India is an actual geographic place, and, like fairyland, it is still figured as a place of the imagination. This simultaneity permits the articulation of a racial fantasy in [the *Dream*] where Amazons and fairies signify an alien yet domestic paradox in an otherwise stable, homogeneous world.[35] □

This mixture of elements is evident in Titania's 'poignant (and poetic) vision of female and mercantile fecundity' in her evocation of her relationship with the Indian boy's mother, when the fairy queen and her votaress would laugh at the sails of the trading ships growing 'big-bellied with the wanton wind' (2.1.129) and the votaress would imitate the ships as she 'sail[ed] upon the land' to fetch Titania trifles and returned as 'from a voyage, rich with merchandise' (2.1.134).

In Hendricks's perspective, Oberon's desire to possess the boy is not 'paternal'[36] or pederastic. Rather, he wants the boy as a status symbol; in this he anticipates those eighteenth-century aristocrats who sported non-European boys, especially African ones, as servants. To achieve this end, Oberon wants to distract Titania's attention from the changeling boy. The distraction is accomplished by means of the love-juice and of Puck's partial transformation of Bottom into a monstrous changeling by fixing an 'ass's nole' on the weaver's head (3.2.17) so that he becomes part-animal, part-human. But the adult Bottom, in Titania's bower, 'becomes a substitute' not only for the Indian boy but also for Oberon. As Hendricks sums up the situation: 'Once central to Titania's erotic desires, Oberon finds himself displaced twice: first by a changeling and then, in Bottom, by a monstrous "changeling" to boot'.[37]

The two changelings, Bottom and the Indian boy, contribute to what Hendricks sees as 'the defining trope' of the *Dream*: change. Hendricks links this trope with the Spanish term which emerged as European imperialism began to construct categories which the old ways of classifying people, in terms of class or nationality, could not provide: this is the term '*mestizaje*, or mixedness'[38] – the *cruziamiento de razas* (crossbreeding of races) or *conjunto de mestizos* (group of mestizos).

■ Both Bottom and the changeling child exemplify this hybrid state: in Bottom we see the *cruziamiento* of two species – human and equine (literally, the *mulatto*) – and in the Indian boy the possibility of human and fairy mixedness (the *mestizo*).[39] □

Hendricks acknowledges the difficulty of applying to the *Dream* a 'racial lexicon' that the play itself does not use, but feels that it is justified 'given Shakespeare's own framing of fairyland as a borderland between India and Athens'.[40] The two expulsions of the end of the play – of Bottom from fairyland and the Indian boy from Titania's bower – restore class and gender hierarchies but also 'leave [...] behind a vision of a new racial landscape [...] where the image of humanity is not the European but a changeling'. More significantly, the two changelings in the *Dream*, Bottom and the Indian boy, 'are haunted by the ghostly presence of the historical condition of *mestizaje* which occasions both Shakespeare's dramatic representation of India and the modern Western notion of race'.[41]

Hendricks's analysis, focusing on the Indian boy and extending the intertexts of the *Dream* to incorporate those travel narratives which were part of the early modern discourses of emergent imperialism, showed how far criticism of the play had come from the 1950s when critics largely concurred with what they took to be the dominant ideology of the play and hardly mentioned issues of gender, class and race. Hendricks's emphasis on change as the 'defining trope' of the *Dream*,[42] however, does form part of a strand which runs through both 'radical' and 'traditional' readings of the play: a concern with metamorphoses. This concern links up, implicitly or explicitly, with the relationship between Shakespeare and Ovid, which Jonathan Bate explores in his 1993 book. It is his analysis of the *Dream* in that book which we shall now consider.

JONATHAN BATE

In *Shakespeare and Ovid*, Jonathan Bate affirms that the *Dream* 'may be described as a displaced dramatization of Ovid'. It is 'deeply but not directly Ovidian'.[43] Shakespeare could have presented 'Pyramus and Thisbe' seriously and in a sustained way but offers a parody instead. Bate suggests that the reason for this lies in the Renaissance ideas of *translatio* and *imitatio*. As Bate defines these, *translatio* is 'to bring across'; 'to make a text from an alien culture speak in the distinctive language of the translator's culture' and to have the licence to alter that text so that it conforms to contemporary concerns and ideas – as in the 1611 translation of Homer's *Iliad* by the poet and playwright George Chapman (c. 1560–1634) which aims to draw out the likeness between Achilles in the ancient epic and the Elizabethan courtier, soldier and executed rebel Robert Devereux, the second Earl of Essex (?1566–1601). *Imitatio*, according to Bate, 'goes even further than translation in reconstituting the source-text in contemporary terms'. Thus for Edmund Spenser in *The Shepheardes Calendar* (1579), the 'imitation' of the ancient Greek pastoral poet Theocritus (c. 300–c. 260 BC) and the ancient Roman pastoral and epic poet Virgil (70–19 BC) offered a way of commenting on sixteenth-century church affairs. In the Renaissance, classic texts are precisely those which have the potential to achieve contemporary currency through translation and imitation.

Bate argues that the craftsmen in the *Dream*, in their dramatic endeavours, fail to grasp the real meaning of translation and make themselves laughable through their 'obsessive literalism'. He contrasts this with the way in which Arthur Golding, in his translation of the 'Pyramus and Thisbe' story, moralizes and makes connections to Renaissance ethical precepts. Quince's version lacks these elements and thus does not achieve any metamorphosis. In Bate's view, Shakespeare's incorporation of this impoverished *imitatio* into the *Dream* highlights the richness of his own *imitatio* elsewhere in the play. It is worth stressing Bate's own subtle metamorphosis of an established critical stance here. By this stage in the critical history of the *Dream*, the idea that the play-within-a play functions to show Shakespeare's superiority is a familiar one, but the superiority is usually located on the dramatic level – the *Dream* is a better play than 'Pyramus and Thisbe', Shakespeare a better dramatist than Peter Quince. Bate would not of course deny this – he points out later in his analysis that 'the medium of metamorphosis in Ovid is myth; in Shakespeare it is drama'[44] – but, considering Shakespeare in relation to Ovid, he locates the superiority implied by the play-within-a-play in the *Dream* primarily in the area of *imitatio*:

■ It is elsewhere in the [*Dream*], not in 'Pyramus and Thisbe', that we find all the marks of true Ovidianism: a philosophy of love and of change, the operation of the gods, animal transformation, and symbolic vegetation. It is the translation of these elements out of the play-within [a-play] and into the play itself that transforms [the *Dream*] into Shakespeare's most luminous *imitatio* of Ovid.[45] □

In dispersing Ovid throughout the *Dream*, Shakespeare shows himself to be, in terms of a distinction expressed by the Italian poet Francesco Petrarch (1304–74), a 'true son' rather than a mere 'ape'. Where the 'ape' seeks to reproduce the source-text as literally as possible, the 'true son' produces a text linked to but different from its source-text, generates, in fact, a metamorphosis. Bate proposes that 'the motto for the relationship between the [*Dream*] as a whole and the *Metamorphoses* is Helena's reversal of a typical Ovidian sexual pursuit':[46] 'The story shall be changed: Apollo flies, and Daphne holds the chase' (2.1.230–1). The inversion of the Apollo and Daphne story is striking and, as we have seen, of considerable interest to those critics who have seen the play as challenging the hierarchy of gender it ostensibly endorses. Bate also identifies a subtle and significant inversion which is exemplified in two other lines of Helena's: 'Love looks not with the eyes, but with the mind. / And therefore is winged Cupid painted blind' (1.1.234–5). This inverts the traditional 'etiological framework', as Bate calls it – 'etiology' or 'aetiology' is, in medical terms, 'the cause or causes of a disease or condition' and, more generally, 'the investigation or attribution of a cause or reason'. Traditionally, the cause of a condition would be attributed to the gods: winged Cupid – the god of love – is blind and *therefore* love looks with the mind rather than the eyes. Helena inverts this: love looks with the mind rather than the eyes, and *therefore* winged Cupid is painted blind. This is one example of the way in which the *Dream* 'shift[s] the balance of power away from the gods', making the play 'more anthropocentric' – human-centred – than traditional myth. As Bate puts it (his italics): 'the mortals [in the *Dream*] are the playthings of the gods, *but only playfully so*'.[47]

Shakespeare's *imitatio* of Ovid in the *Dream* involves modernization as well as inversion. The classical gods are updated; for example, Oberon is sometimes Neptune, the god of the sea, translated to a woodland rather than marine setting, and sometimes Jove, the president of the Gods, with the changeling boy in the role of Ganymede, the Trojan prince who was carried off to become Jove's cup-bearer and perhaps his catamite. Cupid becomes Puck, and this is why, Bate ingeniously suggests, Puck was not able to witness, as Oberon could, how Cupid's arrow, missing its original target, created love-in-idleness ('That very time I saw, but thou couldst not' (2.1.155)). As Bate puts it: 'one could almost say [...] Puck could not see Cupid because he *was* Cupid'.[48]

In focusing on Oberon's speech about the origins of love-in-idleness, Bate observes how Oberon, in that speech, 'seems to stray from [Ovid's] *Metamorphoses* to modern [i.e. Elizabethan] high politics'.[49] He acknowledges that it is 'hard to resist' the identification of the 'imperial vot'ress' (2.1.163) whom Cupid's arrow missed, with Elizabeth I, the Virgin Queen. Oberon's speech, Bate proposes, provides an etiology for doting love – a story of its origins – in terms of 'the knock-on effect of [the Queen's] chastity': 'where Ovid found causes in gods and ancient stories, Shakespeare finds it in contemporary history'. This both updates Ovid and upgrades Queen Elizabeth I to a mythical level. It is an unusual politicization of Ovid and may have been intended, Bate suggests, as a pre-emptive strike against the possibility that Elizabeth might be identified with Titania, a *de facto* married woman who is dubiously possessive about a changeling boy and only relinquishes him when she falls for an ass. Any such identification would have made the Master of the Revels refuse the play a licence. 'By identifying the Queen with the imperial votaress, Shakespeare denies the transgressive identification of her with Titania'. In this respect, Bate takes issue with Louis Adrian Montrose who, as we discussed in Chapter 6 of this Guide, sees Elizabeth as pervading the *Dream*: he judges that Montrose's reading, while 'ingenious',[50] appears contrary to Shakespeare's cautious placement of the allusion to Elizabeth in the past rather than the present time of the play.

For Bate, the 'business of Bottom and the ass's head is not a subversive historical allusion' but 'the play's most remarkable "higher imitation" of Ovid'. It combines 'classical and native elements'. The classical references are not to 'Pyramus and Thisbe' but to the two stories of the Midas myth: in the first, King Midas is granted his wish that everything he touches should turn to gold, only to find out its disadvantages (for example, that he cannot eat); in the second, Midas is given ass's ears after he awards the prize to Pan rather than Apollo in an ancient song competition. The native reference, probably drawn from Reginald Scot's *Discoverie of Witchcraft*, is to 'the power of witchcraft to give a man an ass's head'. In Shakespeare's combination and refiguration of these elements, Bottom, 'the poor man with the ass's ears', gains the love of the fairy queen but, 'in his beautiful naivety, his folly which is true wisdom, he does not want it – he wants only his ass's means of subsistence'.[51]

The Bottom–Titania relationship also rewrites the Ovidian scenes in which Jupiter, in the shape of a bull, a swan, or a shower of gold, violates a mortal woman: it inverts the usual gender hierarchy by making the sexual predator a goddess rather than a god and the mortal 'a wise fool', and it thus (in Bate's view) turns the situation into a comic one. The comic note is further sustained by the play's indications that Bottom's metamorphosis is a theatrical illusion, a point emphasized by the occurrence of the change during the rehearsal of the play-within-a-play. But this theatrical illusion does involve a *real* kind of on-stage metamorphosis, a 'displacement of the illusion [...] whereby when the character becomes an actor, the actor becomes the character'.[52] We apprehend, not the actor playing Bottom, but Bottom playing an ass. Thus, in the *Dream*, the activity of metamorphosis moves from poetry to drama: 'Shakespeare's capacity to metamorphose Ovid into a different medium is what makes art *imitatio* of the highest form'.[53]

Bate demonstrates how an attention to the Ovidian elements of the *Dream* – not as relatively inert sources, but as transformations – can prove highly illuminating. He also shows how some of the newer readings of the play – for example, the analysis of Louis Adrian Montrose – can be queried subtly rather than stridently. In a sense, Bate anticipates the reconciliatory tone which Helen Hackett would adopt more extensively in her book on the *Dream*, to which we now turn.

HELEN HACKETT

Helen Hackett's lucid, informed and balanced book on *A Midsummer Night's Dream*, in the 'Writers and Their Work' series, aims 'to explore how we might think about [the *Dream*] now, in the wake of all the recent diverse and fertile developments in Shakespeare criticism'.[54] It draws on feminism, new historicism, genre-theory and psychoanalysis to suggest 'ways in which they open up interpretative possibilities which readers will wish to contest or pursue for themselves'.[55] Some of the book covers ground we have already explored in this Guide, but its discussion of the generic instability of the *Dream* is especially valuable and interesting and we will focus on it in this subchapter.

Hackett sees the *Dream* as one of Shakespeare's happy comedies, but part of its happiness can be attributed to its consonance, not with the natural order of things, but with 'the relatively new ideology that marriage should be predominantly based on love'[56] (p. 54). But the play does not ignore the tragic possibilities of this ideology when it comes into conflict with the older ideology represented by Hermia's father or when two lovers desire the same woman or man. The *Dream* indicates 'other possible love-outcomes', and, 'along with them, potential generic divisions away from comedy into tragedy'. The first scene vividly dramatizes the patriarchal barriers to free choice in love and highlights the lethal consequences which might ensue from pursuing a love-based rather than father-directed marriage. Between this ominous opening and the festive finale, the middle of the *Dream* 'oscillates between tragic and comic potentials, to both of which love is central'.[57] The play contains two main tragic potentials: 'the wrong choice of love partner' and 'choice of the wrong kind of love, including sex outside marriage, homoeroticism, and self-slaughter for love'.[58]

The possibility of making the wrong choice of love partner is evident in the misalignments of the four lovers and it is finally averted by Puck's third intervention with the love-juice which results in their proper pairing. The possibility of sex outside marriage, particularly of a pre-marital kind, is indicated by the May Day references, with their connotations of sexual licence, and by the physical proximity of the lovers in the unchaperoned space of the wood. But while Demetrius warns Helena she is risking her virginity in the wood, she is safe from him, and Hermia clearly tells Lysander, when they decide to sleep in the wood, to 'lie further off', a request which, after some demur, he obeys. Homoerotic potentials are evident in Helena's account of her close girlhood union with Hermia; in Titania's account of her relationship with the 'votaress of her order', the mother of the Indian boy; and, implicitly, in Hippolyta's bonds with her fellow Amazons. Hackett argues, however, the play presents these as relationships which are already in the past and should be outgrown. In the passage in which Helena reminds Hermia of their girlhood closeness, the phrase 'sisters' vows' (3.2.199) echoes Theseus's threat that, if Hermia refuses to marry Demetrius, she must die or 'live a barren sister all [her] life'. Theseus's conclusion – 'earthlier happier is the rose distilled' (1.1.76) – 'overshadows Helena's nostalgic plea for a regression to pre-adolescence'.[59] Similarly, Titania must 'be educated away from her loyalty to a female bond [to her dead votaress], whose time is over, to renewed loyalty to her marital bond'. Hippolyta likewise 'must be wooed away from another form of all-female community, the sisterhood of Amazonian gynocracy [rule by women] which has been defeated and dissolved by the masculine force of Theseus'. Hackett contends that 'same-sex love undermines the argument of comedy' and features in Shakespeare's plays 'only to be averted or superseded'.[60] Once males and females have been heterosexually bonded, same-sex friendships can be allowed, but the latter are only 'a secondary supportive substructure to the primary unity of marriage'.[61]

The potential of 'self-slaughter for love' is dramatized in 'Pyramus and Thisbe'. The play-within-a-play suggests the fatal consequences that may ensue when the course of true love fails to run smooth and indicates what might have happened to the Athenian lovers if they had been in a tragedy rather than a comedy. But because its style of performance provokes laughter, it becomes 'a tragic tale which has comic effect'. Its echoes of the difficulties of the Athenian lovers emphasize how both tragedy and comedy 'depend upon mistaken identity, mishap, mistiming and misInterpretation'.[62] The *Dream* 'actively explores the intersections of comedy and tragedy and the fluidity of generic boundaries'[63] and 'offers particularly vivid illustration of [the] impurity and interdependence of genres'.[64]

The closeness between comedy and potential tragedy in the *Dream* enhances its celebratory conclusion:

> ■ The symmetries and parallels among the couples give a sense that the right ending has been achieved, while the sense that the means to achieve it were a matter of mere luck, of comedy fortuitously snatched from the jaws of tragedy, creates an air of relief and cause for celebration.[65] □

Hackett thus produces a version of the *Dream* as a happy comedy not in spite, but because of, its darker potentials, which throw the festive ending into relief. Her book is an impressive sifting and reassembly of the fragments of *Dream* criticism into a new synthesis, enriched by insights of her own, especially into the generic instability of the play. In the 1980s, the older critical perspectives on the *Dream* had been shattered, often fruitfully; by the end of the 1990s, as Hackett's book demonstrates, a creative reconstruction was under way which recognized the power and relevance of those new perspectives which had emerged in the previous decade and earlier in the 1990s themselves, but which also sought to assimilate aspects of those older perspectives which had caught elements of the *Dream* – its festive ending, for example – that could not be wholly discounted without limiting one's apprehension – and comprehension – of the play. The *Dream* was again becoming, as it had been for its pre-twentieth-century critics, a labyrinth, a maze – but it was now a much more complex one as successive, often competing critical explorers had sought to map its intricate paths, escape its blind alleys, navigate its enchantments, confront its chimeras, track down its monsters, fathom its fairies, find the key to its strangely compelling festivities. The next chapter of this Guide explores how, in the early twenty-first century, critics set about refiguring the maze.

CHAPTER EIGHT

The 2000s: Refiguring the Maze

In the early twenty-first century, the field of *Dream* criticism – and of Shakespeare criticism more generally – was interestingly varied. The kinds of critical-scholarly approach which had developed in the 1950s and remained dominant through the 1960s still persisted in some form, but within a configuration which had been strongly reshaped by the challenges that had emerged in the later twentieth century and which this Guide has traced in relation to the *Dream*. Those challenges themselves, however, no longer seemed quite so innovative and radical; they had become well established, their original practitioners were growing older and were, for the most part, more institutionally and personally settled (where they had not retired or passed on); and students encountered ideas and approaches which had once seemed subversive as a corpus of concepts and procedures which they were required to assimilate rather than rebel against. If this meant that some of the impetus which had initially fuelled the critical movements of the 1980s had diminished, it did, in a sense, make it possible to engage with Shakespeare's texts in a way less inflected by polemical considerations. But of course polemic continued, if in a quieter vein, and the first essay we shall consider in this chapter is an example of quiet polemic combined with erudite interpretation, by the most subtle of those critics who had emerged as defenders of what might loosely be termed a 'traditional' approach to Shakespeare: A. D. Nuttall.

A. D. NUTTALL

In '*A Midsummer Night's Dream*: Comedy as *Apotrope* of Myth', Nuttall seeks an accommodation between the benign and malign views of the play, arguing that while the *Dream* is largely (say ninety per cent) benign, there is a malign element of about ten per cent which is provided by the allusions of the play to dark aspects of myth, particularly of the myth of Theseus. The *Dream* performs an *apotrope* – a turning-away – of these dark aspects.

Nuttall begins by contrasting the *Dream* with a play which was first performed just over eighty years later: the French neo-classical verse drama *Phèdre* (1677) by Jean Racine (1639–99), in which Phaedra, then the wife of Theseus, falls in love with her stepson, Hippolytus, who is the child of Theseus and Hippolyta (also known as Antiope). The 'English comedy' offers 'moonlight, fairies and happy love', the 'French tragedy' presents 'sexual horror'. This leads Nuttall to ask whether the Theseus of the *Dream* is 'in any sense' the same as the Thesée of *Phèdre*. He points to an initial indication of similarity: in the opening scene of Shakespeare's play, Theseus tells Hippolyta – and the audience – that he wooed her with his sword (1.1.16), alluding to the war between Greeks and Amazons and Theseus's subsequent marriage to Hippolyta described in North's translation of Plutarch. As Nuttall puts it: 'Far more lightly than Racine but nevertheless unmistakably Shakespeare is touching on this Greek story',[1] reminding us, if very quickly, of Theseus's violent past in 'a prominent, *mind-setting* speech' very near the start of the play (Nuttall's italics).[2] If Shakespeare wished to make Theseus a wholly benign bridegroom, why let him speak of his sword?

Closely scrutinizing the four lines which begin 'Hippolyta, I wooed thee with my sword' (1.1.16–19), Nuttall points out that he does not say 'I won you by violence but now I will seek to gain your trust by a loving devotion'. Instead he makes him say – as Nuttall paraphrases it – 'I won you with my sword, but now we will proceed in joyous triumph'. Thus a statement whose grammatical form might initially make it look like an antithesis turns out to be only partly antithetical: 'triumph' – which has, as one its meanings, 'the processional entry of a victorious general into ancient Rome' (*Concise Oxford Dictionary*) – 'remains, obstinately, an arrogant, masculine word' which 'carries the idea of military victory into the new world of marriage'.[3]

Thus the 'suppression of dark forces is incomplete' at the start of the *Dream* and, in a way, 'remains incomplete throughout' the play. A further reminder of Theseus's dubious past occurs in the quarrel between Oberon and Titania, when Oberon speaks of Titania's love for Theseus: 'Didst thou not lead him through the glimmering night / From Perigouna, whom he ravished, / And make him with fair Aegles break his faith, / With Ariadne and Antiopa?' (2.1.77–80). The verb 'ravishéd' suggests sexual violence and violation and 'Antiopa' is an echo of Hippolyta's more usual mythological name. Nuttall concedes that not everyone will pick up these mythological references but those who do so will see a slightly different, darker Theseus in Shakespeare's play.

This dark penumbra does not shadow Theseus alone. The fairies in the *Dream* are benign but they 'carry the burden of a dark history' in folklore in which they could be feared figures. Oberon's 'promise' near the end of the play that the children-to-be of the married couples will be spared birthmarks and facial deformities is 'urgently required' because of the continuing fear that fairies may inflict such blemishes.[4] When Titania and the ass-headed Bottom get together, it recalls, via Apuleius's *Golden Ass*, Pasiphaë, who contrives to have intercourse with a bull by placing herself in an appropriate position within a specially built wooden cow – in the *Golden Ass*, Lucius compares a lustful matron into whom he inserts his vast member to Pasiphaë. Nuttall does not claim that a similar thing happens with Bottom and Titania but that the disturbing possibility is there: 'Bottom is a happily averted Minotaur, or Bull, Titania Pasipha[ë]'.[5]

Thus Nuttall inclines to the view that the 'suppression of sexual violence' in the *Dream* is 'laced with a nervous, intermittent memory of the matter suppressed'.[6] The *Dream* 'presents not the accomplished fact of terror disarmed but a feat of disarming' and to grasp this achievement, 'we must be aware in some degree, if only for a moment, of the background terror'.[7] This is an *apotrope* – a turning away – of dark aspects of ancient myth and also of 'incipient tragedy'. 'While Shakespeare is carefully *not* writing *Phèdre* the mechanicals are carefully *not* performing *Romeo and Juliet*'. But, as Nuttall concludes, '*apotrope* [is] not abolition'.[8]

In a sense, then, Nuttall aims to preserve and strengthen the benign view of the *Dream* by acknowledging a malign aspect which is kept at a distance and which, in a way, enhances the benignity because it makes a suitably primed audience (those with some knowledge of relevant classical mythology) aware of what might have happened (this is similar to Helen Hackett's argument, which we considered in the previous chapter of this Guide, that the happy comedy of the *Dream* is amplified by its potentially tragic elements). It is a view which might not have emerged prior to the more radical readings which were inaugurated by Jan Kott, but it is otherwise reasonably continuous with the style and approach of the *Dream* criticism of the 1950s which we discussed in Chapter 3 of this Guide. A much more radical approach, informed by queer theory, is offered by the next critic we shall consider, Douglas E. Green.

DOUGLAS E. GREEN

In 'Preposterous Pleasures: Queer Theories and *A Midsummer Night's Dream*', Douglas E. Green aims to explore some of the 'homoerotic significations' of the *Dream*, 'moments of "queer" disruption and eruption'.[9] He suggests that Shakespeare, though not necessarily 'a sexual radical', 'may work with distinct force for gay men and lesbians, simply because he didn't think he had to sort out sexuality in modern terms'.[10]

Drawing on such books as Jonathan Goldberg's *Sodometries: Renaissance Texts, Modern Sexualities* (1992) and Alan Bray's *Homosexuality in Renaissance England* (2nd edn, 1982), Green suggests that, in the early modern period, 'sodomy is a category that expands to signify and contain almost every sort of disruption of natural, social, and political order'.[11] Sodomy in this sense (which need not involve any equivalent physical act) is figured in the blanknesses and sensory confusions which characterize Bottom's attempt to describe his dream (4.1.200–19). His association with Titania and his production of 'Pyramus and Thisbe', release 'something treasonous, or at least "transgressive"', which 'evokes the natural and social confusion associated with sodomy even as the text suppresses its recognition as such'.[12]

This is evident in the scene in which Oberon witnesses Bottom's association with Titania:

■ The full comic force of the scene derives precisely from the inexpressibility of the 'undoings' of the moment where what is inconceivable finds its representation in what is proscribed: thus the scene may constitute from Oberon's voyeuristic position a re-enactment of the unthinkable (lesbian) love of Titania for her votaress (mother of the disputed changeling boy), now displaced onto the manifest bestiality of Titania's embrace of an 'ass', whose name – Bottom – may well conjure the anatomical pun, which introduces the (other) sodomy that is never mentioned or recognized as such but implied in Oberon's obsession with the changeling boy.[13] □

Once Oberon has the 'changeling boy', he is ready to release Titania from her 'dotage'.

Oberon himself applies the love-juice and its antidote to Titania, but he delegates other tasks to Puck – and Puck, in Green's view, 'represents that slippage between power and its exercise that affords some space, however minimal, for interests, desires, pleasures, and practices other than those consonant with the dominant ideology'. He figures in fairyland the potential for disorder, for 'the un- or mis-recognized possibility of preposterous pleasures' – Green cites Puck's remark 'And those things do best please me, / That befall prepost'rously' (3.3.120–1). By bringing Titania and ass-headed Bottom together, Puck furthers his master's desire to avenge himself on Titania and win the changeling boy from her: but Oberon's 'voyeurism implicates him in the bestiality he witnesses' and he has avenged himself by forcing her to re-enact, in a displaced form, the transgressive relationship with her votaress; moreover, his acquisition of the changeling boy by means of redirecting Titania's erotic attention towards Bottom suggests that Oberon is, as Green puts it, 'getting the bottom he desires, the ass he wants'. In a traditional reading, Oberon's manipulation of Titania restores a rightful patriarchal order; Green suggests, however, that at the same time 'it confirms sodomy not only as the paradoxically perverse sign of pervasive disruption(s) in nature and thus society but also as an unrecognized constituent of natural and social order'.[14]

Green acknowledges that the same-sex relationships between women in the *Dream*, even when eloquently evoked as in Helena's 'double cherry' speech (3.2.192–219), are located in the past, as stages already outgrown (Helen Hackett, discussed in the previous chapter of this Guide, makes a similar point). Nonetheless, Green asserts, the play 'provides a catalog of ways in which [upper-class] women not only comply with but also resist the mandate to marry that is designed to control their productive, particularly procreative activities [...] and to secure through this control the disposition of property'. For example, Hermia's request to Lysander to '[l]ie further off' (2.2.50) when they settle down to sleep in the wood may be interpreted as indicating, not her virtue or her continued compliance with courtly constraints, but a lack of desire or, as Green puts it, 'a sexual disinclination to what we call the heterosexual imperative'.[15] Green acknowledges that the text of the *Dream* does not encourage these readings but suggests that it does leave 'gaps', for example in supplying the motivations of its characters, which can be filled in ways that oppose 'dominant [...] ideological expectations', producing '"queer" moments' by 'reading consciously and conscientiously against the grain of the text'.[16]

Reading the play-within-a-play in Act 5 against the grain produces, for Green, a sense of how 'Bottom's exuberant imagination takes center-stage' and cannot be wholly constrained by the aristocratic discourses which surround it. It functions both to affirm and challenge the triumphant conclusion of the *Dream*:

■ [The] reintroduction of tragedy and death into the final act of the play, however laughably executed, do ostensibly exorcise these elements from the play's happy marital resolution, but only at the cost of reminding us that the world is bigger than the play, that plays shape but a small part of experience through dramatic conventions of characters, and that comedy, like other genres, functions like a lens that sharpens the focus here on the social desirability of marriage and procreation by filtering out other plots and perspectives.[17] □

The challenge of Bottom and the play-within-a-play in Act 5 of the *Dream* is amplified by that of Puck, 'the very possibility of the perverse operating within yet against such constraints'. Puck may seem at this point in the play to contribute to its exclusion of possibilities other than those of heterosexual, procreative marriage, but his return at the end of the play, particularly as 'speaker of the epilogue', 'reinscribes the impossibility of such a program [of exclusion] by reminding us of the play's potential for theatrical as well as ideological failure'.[18]

As we shall see in the next subchapter, however, Alan Sinfield is less optimistic about the queer potential of the Dream, especially when it is compared with the play that Shakespeare co-authored with John Fletcher, *The Two Noble Kinsmen*.

ALAN SINFIELD

In 'Cultural Materialism and Intertextuality: The Limits of Queer Reading in *A Midsummer Night's Dream* and *The Two Noble Kinsmen*', Alan Sinfield is concerned to challenge what he sees as the undue indeterminacy promoted by deconstructive criticism and, as his title suggests, to mark the boundaries of queer reading. In this, he juxtaposes the *Dream* and *The Two Noble Kinsmen* which, as he points out, have three aspects in common: in both, the wedding celebrations of Theseus and Hippolyta are interrupted; both show the problems of young heterosexual lovers; and both include people of humble station setting out to entertain aristocrats (though Sinfield lacks space to discuss this third aspect). He focuses first on the interruption to the wedding festivities of Theseus and Hippolyta, where three black-clad queens stop the procession to say that Creon has forbade them to retrieve the bodies of their dead husbands which are rotting on the fields of Thebes. They want Theseus to take arms against Creon in order to reclaim the bodies so that they may burn their bones and urn their ashes. Sinfield highlights how the Second Queen's address to Hippolyta elevates the Amazon and stresses her near-defeat of Theseus: 'thy arm, as strong / As it is white, wast near to make the male / To thy sex captive' (1.1.79–80). She concludes by asking Hippolyta to kneel, though only briefly, to Theseus to beg his help, and Hippolyta replies that she 'had as lief trace this good action with you / As that whereto I am going, and never yet / Went I so willing way' (1.1.102–4) – in other words, Hippolyta says she would as willingly take arms herself against Creon as marry Theseus, although she has never been more willing to do anything than to marry Theseus. Emilia, Hippolyta's sister, identifies even more thoroughly with the supplicating queens. *The Two Noble Kinsmen* thus, in Sinfield's view, evokes 'the potential of women together' and 'female independence' more fully than the *Dream*, where Hippolyta is 'reduced' to 'muted and captious silence'.[19]

Sinfield also draws attention to the 'intimations of same-sex relationships' in *The Two Noble Kinsmen*. When Pirithous exits to join Theseus's forces, Emilia says: 'How his longing / Follows his friend!' (1.3.26–7). Hippolyta refers to the 'knot of love' between the two men (1.3.41), which, Sinfield suggests, 'sounds remarkably like wedlock'.[20] Emilia compares and contrasts the 'more maturely seasoned love' of the two men with her 'innocent' love for her 'playfellow' Flavina, now dead (1.3.56, 60, 50):

> ■ The flower that I would pluck
> And put between my breasts (then but beginning
> To swell about the blossom), oh, she would long
> Til she had such another, and commit it
> To the like innocent cradle, where phoenix-like
> They died in perfume. □   (1.3.66–71).[21]

Emilia affirms that her relationship with Flavina demonstrates '[t]hat the true love 'tween maid and maid may be / More than in sex dividual' (1.3.81–2) and she confirms Hippolyta's summary of what she has said – that she 'shall never, like the maid Flavina, / Love any that's called man' (1.3.84–5). Hippolyta acknowledges that 'If I were ripe for your persuasion, you / Have said enough to shake me from the arm / Of the all-noble Theseus' but she proclaims her 'great assurance / That we more than his Pirithous possess / The high throne in his heart'. Emilia responds: 'I am not / Against your faith, yet I continue mine' (1.3.92–4, 95–8). In contrast to the relative frankness of these references to female bonding in *The Two Noble Kinsmen*, those in the *Dream* – Sinfield instances Helena's evocation in the 'double cherry' speech of her bonding with Hermia (3.2.199–215) – are subordinate to heterosexual priorities: in the 'double cherry' speech, Helena invokes her past bonding with Hermia 'reproachfully, in the light of Hermia's disruption of Helena's current heterosexual ambitions'. The contrast between the young men in *The Two Noble Kinsmen* and Lysander and Demetrius in the *Dream* is even greater: in the former play, Arcite describes himself and Palamon, when they are imprisoned together, as 'one another's wife, ever begetting / New births of love' (2.2.80–1). When they see Emilia from their cell and both fall for her, this is not, according to Sinfield, 'a replacement of male bonding by heterosexual passion, but its continuation by other means'. In the *Dream*, by contrast, Demetrius and Lysander 'pay only occasional attention to each other'.[22]

From Sinfield's perspective, same-sex passion vibrates most strongly in the quarrel between Oberon and Titania, where Titania is driven by her bonding with the mother of the changeling boy, and Oberon by his desire for that boy, to throw the natural world into disorder. 'Only acute sexual infatuation', Sinfield asserts, 'may plausibly move these great fairies to jeopardize the entire creation'. Sinfield points to the exploitation by Titania and Oberon of the changeling boy, in the early modern context of 'a casual traffic in boys, who, because they are less significant [than women], are moved around the employment-patronage system more fluently than women'.[23] Drawing partly on Margo Hendricks's essay, which we discussed in the previous chapter of this Guide, Sinfield argues that the changeling boy 'is being traded between Titania and Oberon, neither of whom consults his preferences'.[24]

Finally, Sinfield challenges what he sees as the widespread critical assumption that, in these plays, 'it is good when people get into couples – lately even same-sex couples'.[25] There are hints in *The Two Noble Kinsmen* that a *ménage à trois*, a triangular relationship, might be a possible alternative; for example Emilia, trying to choose between Palamon or Arcite, adumbrates even as she deprecates this possibility when she says: 'What a mere child is Fancy, / That having two fair gauds of equal sweetness, / Cannot distinguish, but must cry for both!' (4.2.53–5). But choosing both is not feasible in the early modern period as 'it would complicate the transmission of property' – as well as ensuring the collapse of 'half the plots of Elizabethan and Jacobean theatre'. Sinfield plays entertainingly with the idea of threesomes or even foursomes as a solution to the problems of a range of other Shakespeare plays, but he acknowledges that this is 'far-fetched' and does not suggest any such solution for the problems of the *Dream*.[26] *The Two Noble Kinsmen* marks the ideological limits of the *Dream*; it is possible to read or stage the *Dream* '*against the grain*' (Sinfield's italics), but doing so involves making a distinction between 'what [one believes] the play to be about' (the grain) and 'how [one] would like it to be' (an against-the-grain interpretation).[27] In the end Sinfield reinstates a relatively traditional interpretation of the *Dream* but takes his distance from it; he avoids any claim that there are elements in the play itself which might distance it from its own dominant ideology. In the next essay we shall consider, Thomas R. Frosch also offers what might seem a relatively traditional reading of the *Dream* in psychoanalytic terms, but, in contrast to Sinfield, he does not feel a need to take his distance from such an interpretation.

THOMAS R. FROSCH

In 'The Missing Child in *A Midsummer Night's Dream*', Thomas R. Frosch aims to analyse 'a psychological development in the play from an idealized voyage back to childhood to a return to a reconstituted adulthood and then [...] to a new and different idealization of childhood'.[28] He draws at various stages of his argument on Sigmund Freud, 'the ego psychology of Heinz Hartmann [1894–1970], the object relations theory of D. W. Winnicott [1896–1971]' and the kind of myth criticism influenced by Carl Jung (1875–1961). The action of the *Dream* starts in the oppressive patriarchal world of Athens but moves to a forest which has several features associated with early childhood. In the forest the mother is dominant, in the shape of Titania (who turns Bottom into a kind of infant), and the fluidity of identity and language which prevails in the forest setting is characteristic of what Freud calls 'the primary process, the mode of thinking characteristic of early childhood'. The forest scenes also suggest the early state of 'polymorphous perversity, culminating with bestiality in the relationship of Titania and the transfigured Bottom'. Puck exhibits 'voyeurism and sadism'; Oberon 'sadism and masochism';[29] Helena 'masochism' (when she asks Demetrius to treat her as his spaniel), Bottom 'orality and autoeroticism' in the bower and Helena 'homoeroticism' in her 'double cherry' speech (3.2.204–15). The forest voyage thus 'exposes the roots of eros in infantile sexuality'.[30]

Frosch suggests that Titania's feelings towards Bottom are 'both maternal and libidinous' and that this 'mingling of genital and maternal impulses towards the son and [the] fantasy of possessing him for ever as child/lover' might be called 'the Titania complex'.[31] (Similarly, he suggests that Oberon's desire to possess the changeling boy represents a wish, which might be called 'an Oberon complex', that the son should focus solely on the father and function as his father's 'servant and second self'.[32]) From the child/Bottom's viewpoint, the Titania complex is constrictive as well as comfortable: Titania says to Bottom: 'Out of this wood do not desire to go. / Thou shalt remain here, whether thou wilt or no' (3.1.144–5). So Bottom must escape from this position but when he does so he undergoes a 'symbolic castration'[33] (when Puck, under Oberon's instruction, removes the ass's head) and experiences a sense of loss and disorientation. The play-within-a-play provides a kind of cure for this, by turning Bottom as Pyramus into a figure, not of tragedy, but of fun. We laugh not only at his loss of Thisbe but also at his loss of Titania, and this checks the regressive impulse – the desire to return to the state of improved infancy he experienced in the forest. The play-within-a-play also diminishes the force of references to maternal and female figures which might, in a more serious vein, stir the regressive impulse: the 'pap of Pyramus' (5.1.292), the lion's dam (5.1.222), the furies (5.1.279), the 'sisters three' (5.1.330) with their milk-pale hands and castrating shears, the moon. The comments by the aristocrats on the play-within-a-play also encourage this detachment from the regressive temptation of the forest, and these comments, and the discussion of the lovers' story by Theseus and Hippolyta at the start of Act 5, 'show the important ego function of reality testing, of distinguishing fantasy from objective reality'.[34]

But the *Dream* does not stop there: 'after the play within the play [*sic*], the spirit of the mother returns not only in the indirect form of the fairies, the creatures of the forest, but also in Puck's closing assertion of the transitional vision',[35] which, like the 'transitional stage' posited in D. W. Winnicott's model of infant development, offers a protected space in which to negotiate between dream and reality. The missing child of the play, symbolized above all by the Indian boy who never speaks or shows himself in the text, reappears in the form of the unborn child of each of the three couples when the fairies bless the bride-beds. At this point, 'marriage appears not only as the end of courtship and as a complex new relationship but also as the beginning of family life'. The unborn child is 'a symbol of what is to come in general', 'the next generation', and 'the future of the entire comic community', which Puck's epilogue invites the audience to join.[36]

Frosch acknowledges that, in the case of Theseus and Hippolyta, the child-to-come was Hippolytus, who would play a key role in the tragedy of *Phèdre* (as discussed by A. D. Nuttall earlier in this chapter). As Frosch points out, '[i]t would be hard to imagine a more nightmarish future for characters who are supposed to live happily ever after'.[37] But for Frosch, this does not subvert the comic vision at the end of the play. No such doom hangs over the two other married couples in the *Dream* and the fate of Hippolytus is a potent reminder of what we already know – that things can go terribly wrong with marriages and with children. In Frosch's view, this 'does not invalidate marriage or the having of children or the blessings we have for the unborn'.[38]

Moreover, Frosch points out that the Hippolytus myth does not quite end with the brutal death he suffers after Phaedra has falsely accused him of raping her; according to Ovid's *Metamorphoses* (Book 15, lines 534–46) and Virgil's *Aeneid* (Book 7, lines 761–82), Aesculapius restored him to life and Diana took him to a sacred grove where, according to J. G. Frazer in *The Golden Bough*, he became, under the name of Virbius, the first priest-king of the golden bough. Thus, in Frosch's perspective, Hippolytus becomes, in this part of the myth, the son-lover of Diana, effectively playing the same role as the Indian boy and Bottom temporarily played for Titania. If we see the prospective child of Theseus and Hippolyta, not only as the tragic figure with whom Phaedra becomes obsessed, but also as the man who is reanimated to become the priest of Diana, then Hippolytus could be held to represent, in Frosch's psychoanalytical perspective, 'the child within the adult';[39] that regressive desire to return to the mother which persists and which can be creatively integrated into adult life if it can be held in balance with a proper attention to objective reality. The end of the *Dream* offers an image of this reintegration.

After focusing on Hippolytus as an image of the child-to-be at this stage in his argument, Frosch returns to his central idea that the Indian boy is the dominant missing child in the *Dream*:

■ Shakespeare uses [the Indian boy] to create a symbolic presence, looming over the world of the play, of the child of the future, who is still unborn; the child of the past, who is no longer visible; and the child of the present, who, after infancy, is never so much our visible possession as we want it to be.[40] □

Frosch also addresses himself to the question of why the boy is Indian – the same question Margo Hendricks considered, as we saw in Chapter 7 of this Guide. Whereas Hendricks answered that question in terms of the Eastern associations of Oberon in *Huon of Bordeaux* and the emergent discourses of European travel and imperialism, Frosch focuses on classical myth and links the Indian boy with the figure of the god Bacchus. In Book 4 of Ovid's *Metamorphoses*, the worshippers of Bacchus call him the 'puer aeternus' (eternal boy) who is 'formosissimus alto / conspiceris caelo' ('most lovely in the lofty sky'); one of his alternative names is Nyseus, meaning 'of Nysa', a city in India, and he is worshipped in the East: 'Oriens tibi victus, adusque / decolor extremo qui tinguitur India Gange' (lines 20–1) ('the Orient acknowledges your victory, even to the bounds where remotest Ganges waters swarthy India'). His worshippers also call Bacchus 'ignigenamque satumque iterum solumque bimatrem' (line 12), ('son of the thunderbolt, twice born, son of two mothers'), alluding to the story that he is the son of Jove and Semele but that, after Semele was burnt to death when Jove appeared to her in his thunderous glory, he was taken, still in an embryonic state, from his dead mother and sewn into Jove's thigh until he came to term, and was then brought up by his aunt Ino and subsequently by the nymphs of Nysa (see *Metamorphoses*, Book 3, lines 253–315) . Frosch suggests that the Indian boy, like Bacchus, has two mothers – the votaress who died and Titania. Bacchus, Frosch suggests, is the '[g]od of regressive ecstacy and frenzy' and thus, in psychoanalytic terms, 'the god of the primary process and the oceanic feeling', 'a version of the mythic archetype of the divine child', like 'another child who never appears onstage' in the *Dream*, Cupid. In contrast to critics such as Frank Kermode or Jonathan Bate (see chapters 3 and 7 of this Guide), Frosch finds Puck 'childlike' but not mythic or divine, but he does offer, in his epilogue, the chance 'to be on peaceful and friendly terms with the childlike'. And his last line – 'And Robin shall restore amends' (Epilogue, line 16) – takes the *Dream* 'beyond amity to the simple, primal ethos of comedy, leaving us with a sense of not an ending but a beginning'. In the *Dream*, 'the world has a future [...] in which things can be better. If you didn't like this play, come to the next one'.[41]

Frosch thus offers, against much of the most powerful *Dream* criticism which had emerged since 1980, a reading of the play as a happy comedy. Moreover, he does so by using the kind of psychoanalytical perspectives that had been displaced, in recent literary criticism by the revisionist psychoanalysis of Jacques Lacan and by some feminist critiques. His interpretation is also notable for its eschewal of any more than a peripheral concern with Elizabethan or present-day politics or history: a developmental model drawn largely from pre-Lacanian and pre-feminist psychoanalysis is treated as it if were universally applicable. But his reading is one index of the variety of *Dream* criticism in the twenty-first century, and of what might be called the return of the benign view of the play (the return of the repressed, perhaps, in Freudian terms). It is also possible to see, in recent *Dream* criticism, the return of the aesthetic, as Hugh Grady shows in the final essay we shall consider in this chapter.

HUGH GRADY

In 'Shakespeare and Impure Aesthetics: The Case of *A Midsummer Night's Dream*', Hugh Grady is concerned, from a radical viewpoint, to rehabilitate the idea of the aesthetic. As he points out, the aesthetic has been highly suspect since the emergence of the iconoclastic literary criticism of the 1980s; it has tended to be dismissed as a mystifying ideology, though it survives at the edges of critical discourse. Against this marginalization, Grady advocates an 'impure aesthetics – aesthetics conceived of as creative of an imagined realm separate from empirical reality, but one that draws its materials from that reality'.[42] Drawing on the work of the German Marxist philosopher Ernst Bloch (1885–1977), Grady is especially interested in the 'utopian potential' of art, 'its ability to create visions of the nonexisting, to embody desire and not just received ideas'. The project of an 'impure aesthetics' will contribute to a fuller understanding of Shakespeare:

■ [A] reinvigoration of impure aesthetics is a step towards a new appreciation of the specifically aesthetic content of Shakespearean drama and a deeper understanding of the imbrication of Shakespearean aesthetics with the social, the political, and the historical, in its original context and our own.[43] □

Grady affirms that the *Dream* 'is one of Shakespeare's fullest explorations of aesthetic ideas', a 'meta-aesthetic drama'.[44] He acknowledges that the term 'aesthetic' was an invention of the German Enlightenment philosopher Alexander Baumgarten (1714–62) in his book *Aesthetica* (1750) and that it may seem an unwarranted application of the present to the past – a form of 'presentism' – to apply it to a Shakespeare play. But he contends that the *Dream* 'implies' the concept of the aesthetic and indeed that the play 'uses the motif of the dream as its surrogate for the unnamed concept of the aesthetic'.[45] He also points out that *Dream* criticism really took off with Romantic critics such as Schlegel who were influenced by the idea of the aesthetic. Grady acknowledges that this led to a critical emphasis on the *Dream*'s unity which suppressed elements perceived as potentially disorderly – especially female ones. This was evident in some of the 1950s interpretations which we have considered in this Guide, such as Paul A. Olson's. Since the start of the 1980s, as this Guide has shown, critics have been much more inclined to challenge 'the play's hierarchies of domination' and 'become overwhelmingly political and/or historicist'. Grady sees this challenge and highlighting of political subtexts as 'essential to impure aesthetics' and indeed as drawing attention to elements that are part of the work's aesthetics. 'Impure aesthetics' permits the joint and simultaneous practice of criticizing ideology and analysing art. In the *Dream*, it is possible to discern the operation of 'antagonistic discourses' – above all, in relation to Grady's essay, 'an antagonism between two different representations of nature and the relation of humanity to nature'.[46]

The world of Oberon and Titania and the fairies mirrors the human world in that desire disrupts both worlds and patriarchal ideology dominates in both. But the fairy world 'is also utopian and aesthetic', 'an "as-if" structure in which the human and the natural are permeable to each other – a harmony expressed allegorically by the humanized spirits themselves'.[47] In this respect, Grady compares the *Dream* with Ovid's *Metamorphoses*: in both texts, 'nature is populated by naturalized gods serving as intermediaries between natural objects and human society'. This kind of representation of the gods is, for Grady, 'the very essence of the play's aestheticizing strategy'. To rewrite gods as aesthetic and fictional figures in order to release the element of truth concealed in them is a characteristic approach in the 'dialectic of enlightenment' – Grady takes the term from two other German Marxist thinkers associated with Bloch, Theodor W. Adorno (1903–69) and Max Horkheimer (1895–1973).

In this perspective, Titania, represented in an allegorical way which pays homage to Spenser, emerges not merely as 'an object of displacement for anxieties aroused' by Queen Elizabeth I or 'a marker in a power struggle':

■ [Titania] is a personification of natural fertility and its associated properties of sexuality and maternity; she is a kind of fertility and love goddess, and these qualities constitute a profound, and not merely ideological, connection of humanity and the natural.[48] ☐

Grady acknowledges that the invocations of India in the *Dream* link with emergent early modern imperialism but contends that they are 'translated into the play's aesthetic space and made to serve atmospheric, erotic, and aesthetic functions, as well as ideological ones'.[49] Oberon is also allegorized, if to a lesser extent than Titania, as a force of nature and desire in the *Dream* and their eventual reconciliation becomes an allegory of 'the restoration of natural order to the seasons'. He acknowledges that this restoration has a patriarchal aspect which should be criticized but affirms the continued validity of its aesthetic, utopian intimation of ultimate harmony between nature and the human.

The *Dream*'s view of aesthetics retains a materialist dimension. Bottom serves as a reminder of materiality in his association with Titania; the play-within-a-play stresses the material basis of its presentation, in its emphasis on the actuality of the actors and props. This acts as a corrective to idealist aesthetics, and Theseus's rationalism, while limited, works in a similar way. Hippolyta's reply to Theseus, however, in defending the coherence and consistency of the lovers' dream, defends the value of the aesthetic. Insofar as the audience members or readers of the *Dream* have let themselves partake of the magic of the play, they 'have implicitly found a value in imagination, in an aesthetic experience'.[50] But while creating and vindicating such an experience, the *Dream* does not, in Grady's view, endorse an exaggerated Romantic or idealist view of the imagination.

■ [The *Dream*] is a play that presciently constructs a modern concept of the aesthetic and at the same time shows us the constructedness of this concept, its relation not only to imagination and the aesthetic past, but to desire and labor as well.[51] ☐

Grady concludes that the *Dream* is 'Shakespeare's paean to, and anatomy of, impure aesthetics'.[52]

The project of reopening the issue of the aesthetic within *Dream* criticism – and, by implication, more widely – is a significant one in the early twenty-first century. It is interesting to see that part of Grady's argument involves a return to the founding moment of explicit aesthetic theory in the mid-eighteenth century, which is almost the starting point of the criticism we have covered in this Guide. In the mid-twentieth century, however, the medium which perhaps posed questions of impure aesthetics on the widest scale was cinema: here was a cultural form with global reach which drew rapaciously on popular and elite modes in drama, fiction, dance and music but which could not be adequately understood in terms derived from any of them; a cultural form which was, to use Grady's terms, imbricated with the social, the political and the historical but which could not be reduced to a mere epiphenomenon of these. If the *Dream* is indeed, as Grady suggests, an anatomy of impure aesthetics, it should be revealing to consider, as we do in the next chapter, what happens when it meets the strange compound of cinema.

CHAPTER NINE

1935–99: *Dream* on Screen

There can be no easy correspondence between the criticism of the *Dream* we have examined in the previous chapters of this Guide and the criticism of *Dream* films. For much of the twentieth century most literary critics disdained film, while critics could only tackle the new medium at full stretch when they had broken free of assumptions derived from literary criticism (at least of the more traditional kinds). There has nonetheless been a steadily growing body of criticism and related secondary material to accompany the now quite considerable corpus of *Dream* films. Kenneth S. Rothwell's *Shakespeare on Screen* (1999) lists eleven cinema and TV adaptations of the *Dream* between 1909 and 1996,[1] and in the very year in which Rothwell's book was first published, a further, highly significant version appeared. This chapter focuses on the critical response to the five adaptations which are, in varying degrees, closest to the original text: the 1935 version directed by Max Reinhardt (1873–1943) and William Dieterle (1893–1972); the 1969 version directed by Sir Peter Hall (born 1930); the 1981 BBC TV version directed by Elijah Moshinsky (born 1946); the 1996 version directed by Adrian Noble (born 1950); and the 1999 version directed by Michael Hoffman (born 1957).

THE 1935 FILM

Writing in the *Yale Review* in December 1935, the American film and theatre critic Richard Watts Jr. (1898–1981), felt that Max Reinhardt's 1935 film of the *Dream* was marred by the inadequate 'voice or voice-training' of some of the cast. For instance, Anita Louise (1915–70) 'was as exquisite a Titania visually as a poet could sensibly conceive, yet when she started to recite her lines you were aware of an unhappy feeling of being let down'. Similarly, Mickey Rooney (born 1920) as Puck was, 'despite connotations of Tarzan, admirably conceived pictorially', but 'as soon as he opened his mouth and emitted those strange animal out-cries, you were aware that much was amiss with this poetic drama'.[2]

Watts also found the film (which runs for 132 minutes) 'far too long'.[3] A more positive account of Reinhardt's *Dream* was provided by the English literary scholar Allardyce Nicoll (1894–1976) in his book *Film and Theatre* (1936). Although he found the film 'unsatisfactory as a whole' and 'tentative in its approach' in many scenes, he felt it nonetheless 'demonstrated what may be done with imaginative forms on the screen', in two key respects: it showed 'the power of the cinema to draw us near to an action or to a speaker' so that 'we could at will watch a group of players from afar or approach to overhear the secrets of a soliloquy', and it proved 'the ease with which the cinema can present visual symbols to accompany language'.[4] As an example of the latter in the 1935 film, Nicoll cited 'Oberon's appearance behind dark bespangled gauze' which, 'although too much dealt on and emphasised', 'gave force to lines commonly read or heard uncomprehendingly' by twentieth-century readers or audiences; Puck calls Oberon 'king of shadows' (3.3.348) but, in Nicoll's view, 'the phrase means little or nothing to us unless our minds are given such a stimulus as [the film] provided'.[5]

Other scholars and critics with a literary background tended to be dismissive. For example, Thomas Marc Parrott in *Shakespearean Comedy* felt that the film diminished 'the plot of the four young lovers' on which the structure of the *Dream* depends:[6] he charged that Reinhardt 'overloaded it with unessential, though fascinating, details from fairyland, and cut down the story of the lovers to the dimensions of a squabble between undergraduates in a co-educational college'.[7] Harold F. Brooks, in his introduction to his 1979 Arden edition of the *Dream*, declared that the fairies of Shakespeare's play 'are not the wisps of gossamer who stream through Reinhardt's film version'.[8] But in his book *Shakespeare and the Film* (1979), Roger Manvell (1909–87), a pioneer of film studies, located 'the principal value of the film, as a film' in 'the choreography and special effects'. (The choreography was by Bronislava Nijinsky (1890–1972), the sister of the celebrated Russian ballet dancer Vaslav Nijinsky (1890–87), and Nina Theilade (born 1916), who played the First Fairy). Manvell saw the concept of Reinhardt's production as a 'nineteenth-century one' which arose from a score that used the famous music of Felix Mendelssohn (1809–47) arranged by Erich Wolfgang Korngold (1897–1957).[9] This music, in Korngold's arrangement, 'pervades the atmosphere' of the film. Manvell concedes the objections to 'the characterization, to the truncated lines, to the speaking or nonspeaking, of Shakespeare's verse' but still finds that 'much of the film is still strangely effective in its own particular right'.[10]

In his book *Shakespeare, Cinema and Society* (1989), John Collick stresses that the 1935 film of the *Dream* is 'not just a movie interpreting a stage production which is, in turn, interpreting a text'. It is, rather, 'a process of appropriation' which is 'more emphatic' because it is taking place 'in the context of an American stage and film industry that has a very rigidly coded perception of spectacle and a very efficient production process'.[11] But there was, Collick suggests, a great similarity between the 'structures and images' characteristically used in the films produced by Warner Bros., the Hollywood company which produced the 1935 *Dream*, and the Symbolist, Romantic and Expressionist elements of Reinhardt's stage productions of the *Dream* in Germany. Thus 'the two styles merged easily' into a film that was 'a celebration of corporate wealth'.[12]

Collick's analysis constructs the 1935 film as one which is not merely 'glib escapism'[13] but which cannot escape from the constraints of 'the ideological structure of advanced bourgeois capitalism'.[14] Kenneth Rothwell, in *A History of Shakespeare on Screen*, recognizes the film as 'Shakespeare filtered through the Hollywood studio system', but also sees it as 'the *Dream* reimagined after Gothic films' like the silent Expressionist movie *Nosferatu* by the German director F. W. Murnau (1888–1931), adapted from the novel *Dracula* (1897) by Bram Stoker (1847–1912). Rothwell judges the 1935 *Dream* to be 'the best [...] major Hollywood Shakespeare movie'. It incarnates the 'fantasy world of mirror and reverse-mirror effects' in the play itself 'into a swirling electronic Masque of Light and Dark on the theme of the search for certainty in uncertainty'.[15] The imagery of the *Dream* 'translates into a feast for the camera's eye', with 'its swirling non-linear patterns of movement'. Rothwell asserts that the 'movie turns most filmic in the orchestration of camera work, editing, and theme music for the dazzling ballet sequence' and finds the subsequent Triumph of the Night scene, which ends with Nini Theilade's white hands melting into the darkness, '[p]oignant in the way that it manifests [the *Dream*'s] precarious equilibrium teetering between the forces of light and dark'. The scene would, Rothwell suggests, 'qualify as another talisman of wonder' in the 'masques' at the court of James I (1566–1625; King of England and Ireland 1603–25) on which the playwright Ben Jonson (1572–1637) and the architect and designer Inigo Jones (1573–1652) collaborated.[16]

After the 1935 film, it would be almost thirty-five years before another film of the *Dream* appeared, and this time it would be in the rather different cultural context of the 1960s.

THE 1969 FILM

According to its director, Peter Hall, the 1969 film of the *Dream* was significantly influenced by a literary critic, although not by a specific critical analysis of the play. Roger Manvell's *Shakespeare and the Film* includes an interview with Hall, in which the director makes clear his rejection of the style of the 1935 film:

■ I've tried in the *Dream* to get away completely from the expected Shakespearean setting, which is essentially nineteenth-century and Pre-Raphaelite. The kind of approach associated with Mendelssohn's incidental music. That's how the *Dream* has always been presented, [Hall is speaking, of course, before Peter Brook's 1970 production] culminating in Reinhardt's stage productions, and his film of the 1930s. None of these people could have really looked at the text. Or if they did, they chose deliberately to disregard it.[17]   □

Hall's emphasis on close attention to the text of the *Dream* is what links his film of the play with the literary critic whom he calls, in the interview, the 'greatest influence on me, and my generation': F. R. Leavis (1895–1978).[18] He acknowledges that Jan Kott's 'understanding of the ambivalence of Shakespeare has been as useful to us as Leavis's insistence on scrutinising the text for its real meaning'. But he expresses reservations about Kott's inability to grasp Shakespeare's humour and his view of the plays as 'neurotic'.[19]

For Hall, the use of close-up in the film is a way of focusing attention on its language: 'I wanted it close shot because this seems to me the only way to scrutinize the marked ambiguity of the text' which the cinema 'can do [...] better than the theatre'.[20] But he was concerned that 'the faces [of the actors] did nothing excessive in expression during the close shots' so post-synchronization was used for the dialogue. Hall thought 'an open-air acoustic would be wrong for the *Dream*' because it was 'an artificial play, not a natural one requiring natural sound'.[21] But while Hall did not feel that the film needed natural sound, he did believe that it was important that the film should convey a sense of the natural world and that, in order to convey this, it should be shot in an outdoor English location:

■ The *Dream* is quite clearly a play about an English summer in which the seasons have gone wrong. It is winter where it should be summer; everywhere is wet and muddy. [...] This is why I shot much of the film in the rain, during a bad-weather period lasting about six weeks. Titania's speech explaining this [...] is the essence of the situation [2.1.81–117]. The King and Queen of the Fairies, embodying animal nature, are quarrelling, and their quarrels have upset the balance of nature. This is what the play is all about. It is not a pretty, balletic affair, but erotic, physical, down to earth. All this, but with great charm and humour as well.[22]   □

In *Studying Shakespeare on Film* (2007), Maurice Hindle finds Hall's film so successful that it provides 'an object lesson in how [...] to use the whole text of a Shakespeare play in order to communicate the fullest range of meanings it suggests'.[23] The next adaptation of the *Dream* we shall consider also aimed for fidelity to the text, but this time on TV and within a major project of making television versions of all Shakespeare's plays.

THE 1981 TV FILM

The BBC TV *Dream* was part of a project, which ran from 1978 to 1985, to make television versions of thirty-seven Shakespeare plays (that is, all the plays in the 1623 Folio, and *Pericles*). Jonathan Miller (born 1934) was the producer of the series from 1980–2 and introduced a visual style which was marked by references to Renaissance painting, an approach shared by the director of the TV *Dream*, Elijah Moshinsky. The most notable reference in the *Dream* was to the work of the Dutch artist Rembrandt Harmensz. van Rijn (1606–69), particularly to *Danaë* (1636). Costume designer Amy Roberts (born 1949) is cited as mentioning another influence on the appearance of Titania in the TV version, *Danaë in the Pool*, which Roberts describes as 'that painting with a lady in her undershift';[24] this could refer to Rembrandt's *A Woman Bathing in a Stream* (1654) in London's National Gallery (which may be a picture of a subject from the Old Testament of the Bible (Bathsheba or Susanna), or the Diana of classical mythology). The designer, David Myerscough-Jones (born 1934) also points to the references to the Flemish painter and designer Sir Peter Paul Rubens (1577–1640) in the representation of the forest and of the hunting scene (4.1.102–37). There are also allusions to seventeenth-century Dutch genre paintings of tavern scenes and to the interiors of the Dutch artist Jan Vermeer (1632–75). This might seem to threaten to turn the film into a series of static tableaux, but Myerscough-Jones wanted a more mobile effect:

■ We wanted to get the feel of things rather than reproduce any particular painting. The overall conception, I suppose, was to try to take a painter's way of working – Rembrandt or Rubens or that school – but in a looser way. What we wanted was the triggering of the feeling of a canvas coming to life and you're not sure which.[25] □

In Susan Willis's view in her book on the BBC TV Shakespeare series, the film of the *Dream* moves between a stiffness and formality which is appropriate to the tensions of the court scenes and a 'more mobile' approach in the forest scenes, 'where every lover is part of the chase: moving, touching, kneeling, falling'.[26] Titania and the fairies move more slowly, as befits the stateliness of the Fairy Queen, but Puck is fast:

> ■ All Puck's motions are quick; he pops in and out of frame with sharp movements as if materializing instantaneously, and his curious, mischievous face, continually sniffing as he senses human presence, hovers in the midst of the lovers' confusions. [...] Puck's sprightliness in entering camera shots [...] establishes the suddenness, the unexpectedness of events in the wood on a midsummer's night. Moshinsky carries this device over to the lovers. [...] Puck's quick moves seem infectious.[27] □

The ending of the film is 'strangely sober' until the return of the '[i]rrepressible Puck' who sweeps the table for the fairies to 'swarm onto it' and deliver an 'unsentimental, almost businesslike blessing', and 'enjoys the incongruity of mastering the empty hall as he gives the epilogue. It has been their dream, not ours'. Willis locates 'the vigor and exuberance' of the film 'in the forest with the lyrical fairy queen, energetic Puck, and flower-crossed lovers, not with Bottom and the hempen homespuns – an uncommon balance of the play's possibilities'.[28] It is not wholly clear whether Willis approves of this balance, but Martin White, writing from a twenty-first-century perspective, is unequivocal; he claims that the film, like most of those in the BBC series, is 'a staid, safe and conventional work, torn between a desire to be theatrical or televisual, and producing neither exciting Shakespeare nor exciting television'.[29] But the film is arguably more interesting than this – even in the split between the theatrical or televisual (and the painterly), which is also, in part, a split between high and popular cultural forms (an issue which will arise in the critical discussion of Michael Hoffman's 1999 film). Moshinsky's version takes its place in the corpus of film and TV adaptations of the *Dream* which will be accessible to anyone in the twenty-first-century interested in the relationship between the text and its representations. It would not be until the 1990s that further film adaptations appeared and it is to the first of these, directed by Adrian Noble, which we turn next.

THE 1996 FILM

Adrian Noble's 1996 film of the *Dream* is notable for its introduction of a new, non-speaking character, the Boy – played by Osheen Jones – who is supposed to be dreaming the events of the play. Kenneth Rothwell follows many of the film's original reviewers in largely dismissing it as an 'ambitious film' which 'makes all the right gestures but never quite comes up with a protocol believable enough to attract the widespread audience generated by competing productions'[30] – for example, *William Shakespeare's Romeo + Juliet* (1996), directed by Baz Luhrmann (born 1962). Mark Thornton Burnett, however, offers a sustained defence of the 1996 film in 'Impressions of Fantasy: Adrian Noble's *A Midsummer Night's Dream*' (2000). He contends that Noble's production 'reinvents Shakespeare for the millennium, both recalling high Victorian decadence and looking ahead to the dawning' of the twenty-first century. It takes 'the various "impressions" or "forms" made by "fantasy" or the imagination' and presents them as 'a postmodern mixture of childhood reminiscences, self-conscious literary allusions, sexual awakenings and reminders of a turn-of-the-century environment'. The film 'rewrite[s] the play's imaginative topos [theme, territory]' mainly 'through the interpolated character of the Boy'.[31]

Burnett identifies a range of references in the film to children's literature which feature at key moments and reinforce the Boy's role. On his bed is a copy of the 1908 edition of the *Dream* illustrated by Arthur Rackham (1867–1939). He falls through the night sky and a chimney pot like Alice down the rabbit hole in Lewis Carroll's *Alice's Adventures in Wonderland* (it is interesting to relate this to Julia Wedgwood's observation, discussed in Chapter 1 of this Guide, that the Indian boy is the origin of a line of children's literature which leads to *Alice in Wonderland*, especially as the Boy in Noble's film at one point sees himself as the Indian boy). The Boy's night-time fall in Noble's film also recalls the tornado in *The Wonderful Wizard of Oz* (1900) by L. Frank Baum (1856–1919). The fairies employ flying umbrellas which allude to *Mary Poppins* (1934) by P. L. Travers (1899–1996) while the image of Bottom flying across the moon on his motorbike-with-sidecar evokes the escape of the title character in the film *E. T.: The Extra-Terrestrial* (1982). These allusions may seem to have little to do with Shakespeare, and Burnett concedes that in these respects the film offers 'less an experience of Shakespeare' and more 'an intertextual rehearsal of familiar children's stories, past and present'. But this rehearsal 'pushes back the perimeters of what constitutes "Shakespeare", combining elements from "high" and "low" cultural traditions and mixing "old" and "new" representational materials'.[32]

Burnett points to three aspects of the film's concern with childhood. Firstly, the echoes of children's literature and film indicate the wide range of forms which the imaginative impulse has taken over time. Secondly, those literary and cinematic echoes help the Boy to equip himself for adulthood, providing models of how to deal with life. Thirdly, the film dramatizes the Boy's negotiations with sexuality: by 'amalgamating a Shakespearean art form with the stuff of childhood "fantasies"', it 'reactivates the sexual dimensions that underlie all mythic archetypes'. The Boy encounters quasi-parental sexuality in a kind of primal scene (the witnessing of the parents' lovemaking by the child) when he first sees Theseus and Hippolyta approaching their 'nuptial hour' (1.1.1.); watching the craftsmen's rehearsals in a setting which alludes, as Noble acknowledged, to the TV comedy series about the British Home Guard in World War II, *Dad's Army* (1968–77), he encounters anxieties about masculinity in Flute and Bottom, both young enough for, but implicitly disqualified from, active service; he is associated with phallic imagery, for example the 'elongated handle of the sumptuous red parasol in which Titania drapes herself';[33] and he witnesses what the film suggests are homoerotic moments, for example when Demetrius and Lysander exit 'cheek by jowl' (3.2.338) or when Puck climbs on to Bottom's back just before turning him into an ass.

The elements that Burnett has identified in this film – its 'shifting sexual perspectives', 'ironic rewritings, invocations of modes of artistic production, confounding of the states of "fantastic" and "real", conjurations of competing marks and signifiers, and manipulations of forms and history' – indicate that it is 'a peculiarly postmodern phenomenon'.[34] 'Taking off from the 1590s', when the play was first written, 'the film addresses the 1990s via a detour of the 1890s, borrowing from a spectrum of fantastic "impressions" to reflect upon the future "forms" that the "Shakespearean" imagination will surely adopt or may never assume'.[35]

The second *Dream* film of the 1990s also 'addresses the 1990s' – and the early twenty-first century – by means of a detour, this time through the cusp of the nineteenth and twentieth centuries, the year 1900 – and it is, once again, a mixture of 'high' and 'low' cultural forms as well as being, in a sense, *about* the mixture of 'high' and 'low' cultural forms at a particular historical moment and through a specific new technology.

THE 1999 FILM

Michael Hoffman's *Dream* is the second Hollywood adaptation of the play after the 1935 film. As Judith Buchanan remarks in *Shakespeare on Film* (2005), it was, in some respects, the 'late-in-the-day response' of its production company, Fox Searchlight (a division of the studio which, from 1934 to 1985, was called Twentieth Century-Fox), to 'the film that its older competitor studio', Warner Bros., 'had produced sixty-four years earlier'.[36] The Hollywood of the 1990s is, however, rather different from that of the 1930s, even more profit-driven, and (partly because of the pressure to maximize profits) inhabiting a cultural space in which crossovers between high and popular cultural forms are more frequent than in the earlier decade. In Hoffman's film, there are two main areas of crossover: between film and Shakespeare, and between film and opera; or, more precisely, opera as mediated through sound recording. In 'Bottom and the Gramophone: Media, Class and Comedy in Michael Hoffman's *A Midsummer Night's Dream*', Peter Donaldson highlights how the 1999 film of the *Dream* 'combines Shakespeare adaptation with media story'. But though set in a period contemporaneous with the birth of film, and of filmed Shakespeare, its 'media story' focuses on the gramophone rather than on cinema, and especially 'on the gramophone as a medium for recorded opera'.

This concern with opera may seem to suggest that Hoffman's is an elitist film, insofar as opera requires specialized cultural knowledge for its appreciation and a fairly high disposable income to buy good seats in an opera house. But even before the advent of the gramophone certain operatic songs could escape from this high-cultural enclosure into a more popular zone, for example through street or music-hall performance; and the development of sound recording technology from the gramophone to today's iPod has greatly increased the dissemination of such songs (witness the huge sales in recent years of recordings of opera songs by celebrity opera singers). Recorded opera is represented in Hoffman's *Dream* by songs whose tunes, if not titles, are likely to be familiar to many people beyond the restricted circle of opera enthusiasts. These include 'Libiamo ne' lieti calici' ('Let's drink, let's drink from this merry chalice') from *La traviata* (*The Woman Who Strayed*) (1853) by Guiseppe Verdi (1813–1901); 'Una furtive lagrima' ('A furtive tear') from *L'elisir d'amore* (*The Elixir of Love*) (1832) by Gaetano Donizetti (1797–1848) and 'Casta diva' ('O pure goddess') from *Norma* (1831) by Vincenzo Bellini (1801–35). According to Donaldson:

■ The use of recorded opera [...] structures key moments of cross-class and fairy/human community in the film, and opens a cultural space in which (among other effects) the artistic (as well as romantic/erotic) aspirations of Bottom and the mechanicals can be treated more sympathetically than they commonly are in productions of the play.[37] □

The film alternates operatic and other music (for example, Mendelssohn's *Dream* overture) on the soundtrack with key moments in which a gramophone is actually shown playing recorded music. Near the start of the film, during the wedding preparations at Theseus's palace, two dwarfs steal cutlery, crockery and the bell of a gramophone; the dwarfs 'seem benign media pirates, "textual poachers", abetting the circulation of culture from the palace to the world outside'.[38] A little later, we see Hippolyta listening to a gramophone record, although we do not know what music she is hearing – Mendelssohn is on the soundtrack but barely audible at the point at which the gramophone appears on screen.

Theseus interrupts her to present her with a rose and her response suggests she is not wholly happy at this invasion of a private auditory experience. As Donaldson puts it: 'Hippolyta's ambivalence and emotional reserve are conveyed in terms of the protocols of the distinctively modern experience of listening to records'.[39] The craftsmen's rehearsal takes place in the square of the town of Monte Athena rather than the wood of Shakespeare's play and this locates them in a wider world and a social context: the soundtrack here plays 'Libiamo ne'lieti calici', a drinking song and duet that in *La traviata* itself crosses class lines – it is a toast and lovesong by Alfredo, an aristocratic dinner guest, to his host, the courtesan Violetta, who responds by affirming 'Godiam, fugace e rapido / e'il gaudio dell'amore' ('Let's enjoy ourselves, for the delight of love is fleeting and quick'). It became popular outside the opera house as a song or tune performed by street entertainers and then grew more widely available as a gramophone record. Applied to the craftsmen's rehearsal in the town square, 'Libiamo', Donaldson suggests, 'helps to redefine Shakespeare's artisans as participants in a rich and in some measure democratic culture'.[40]

After the rehearsal, during which Bottom is humiliated when boys tip wine over his white suit, he walks home with 'Una furtive lagrima', sung by Roberto Alagna (born 1963), on the soundtrack. Like 'Libiamo', this lends Bottom and his fellow craftsmen dignity by linking them with Romantic opera and it also suggests an association between the opera from which the song comes – *The Elixir of Love* – and the *Dream*: in both, an elixir of love is central to the plot. Donaldson draws further links between the performance of 'Una furtive lagrima' by Enrico Caruso (1873–1921) in the role of Nemorino, which made Caruso famous in stage opera and on records. Donaldson summarizes his argument in this way:

■ The character of Nemorino, then, and Caruso in the role of Nemorino, overlaps with elements of Shakespeare's portrayal of Bottom the Weaver, a proletarian who is granted 'a most rare vision' [4.1.102]. Hoffman works at the intersection of these personae and these texts, and in doing so deepens the romantic aspects of Bottom's character, and moves him into a milieu in which his dreams are nearly within reach.[41] □

For Donaldson, the central moment in the 1999 *Dream* is when Bottom reveals the true function of the gramophone and records which the dwarfs have brought to the bower. He plays a record of 'Casta Diva' which is a revelation to Titania and it at this point that she says 'hail mortal' and her fairies echo the salutation (3.1.166–9), which is thus 'counterpoised with the Druid Priestess Norma's address to the Moon Goddess' in Bellini's opera.[42] The scene can function, Donaldson suggests, 'as a replay of the moments of wonder experienced by the first audiences for recorded classical music'.[43] In *Studying Shakespeare on Film*, Maurice Hindle also praises this moment:

> ■ If there is one scene embracing the best elements of [Hoffman's] film it would have to be the three-minute one between Bottom and Titania in her bower, culminating in the 'Casta Diva' song from *Norma*. Just as Pfeiffer's Titania is stunned into admiration and love of Bottom for his seemingly magical creation of divine-sounding music, so does Kline's Bottom become quickly bewitched by her beauty and the romantic embrace of the moment.[44] □

It is possible to appreciate this scene, and other scenes in Hoffman's *Dream* which use recorded opera, without knowing anything about opera and indeed without knowing the title, lyrics or composer of the song being played; but our enjoyment and understanding of it, and of the rest of the film, can be enhanced by following up the operatic references.

If Bottom has brought the magic of recorded opera to the fairy world, however, he must leave that world. As Donaldson points out, 'Casta diva' moves from its link with Bottom, 'the wonder of the forest and the sanctity of moon and plants' to mark the reunion of Titania and Oberon, and 'Libiamo' shifts from the public square to the grounds of Theseus's palace where it is played less exuberantly by a quartet. Recorded opera does not feature centrally in the play-within-a-play, but the moving performance of Flute as Thisbe contributes to what Donaldson calls 'the film's broader allegory of democratic participation in the sphere of art'[45] in that Flute succeeds by drawing on his own emotional resources, in a way that resembles the approach systematized by the Russian actor and theatre director Konstantin Stanislavski (1863–1938). Nonetheless Bottom himself is a melancholy figure at the end of the film, left with only a souvenir of the kind which a later twentieth-century tourist might buy in a gift shop – a tiny ring, a reduced version of the golden laurel crown he wore in Titania's bower.

Although the idea of greater democratic participation in high culture is represented in Hoffman's *Dream* by the gramophone rather than directly by the cinema itself, the issues in regard to such participation which the film raises, and which Donaldson brings out in a fascinating way, have many resonances for filming Shakespeare. An adaptation of the *Dream* made for commercial cinema or TV is, almost inevitably, trying to widen democratic participation in Shakespeare, to reach out to wider audiences and that attempt will necessarily involve a complex crossover process, a difficult but sometimes delightful negotiation between 'high' and 'popular' cultural codes (as when 'Casta diva' plays on a record in Titania's bower). Much of the criticism of the *Dream* since the 1980s which we have considered in this Guide has also, in various ways, had democratic or liberatory aims and has had to nego-tiate between those aims, the rich density of Shakespearean criticism and scholarship, and the often difficult language of literary and cultural theory. In *Dream* criticism, as in *Dream* cinema, the results have been remarkable: the conclusion to this Guide looks back at the journey we have taken and asks where we go from here.

Conclusion: Dream On

We have come a long way since Samuel Pepys's dismissal of the *Dream* in 1662 as 'insipid and ridiculous'. But Pepys was not completely immune to the play's charm: he concluded his diary comment on the production he had attended by remarking: 'I saw, I confess, some good dancing and some handsome women, which was all my pleasure'.[1] In these respects, he did respond to two aspects of the play which, as this Guide has shown, have concerned later critics: its terpsichorean (dance-like) qualities and its engagement with matters of gender and sexuality (the latter of considerable interest to Pepys, as his diaries demonstrate). On some level, the play had touched him.

It has continued to touch audiences and to generate critical response ever since. At this stage of the twenty-first century, there is a rich body of criticism and scholarship which those who want to understand the *Dream* can draw on. The critical perspectives which came to fruition in the 1950s, in which the play is seen as achieving artistic unity and harmony and as endorsing heterosexual and procreative marriage and hierarchical social order, are still available and, at their best, are articulated with erudition, insight and commitment, as this Guide has aimed to show. They are indispensable to any future critical considerations of the play.

The scope of *Dream* criticism has, however, been immensely enlarged and enriched by those later criticisms which have challenged the play's apparent endorsements and drawn attention to the ways in which it both presents and suppresses alternative attitudes to gender, sexuality, marriage and social hierarchy. Those alternative attitudes are not impositions by politically correct critics; there is warrant for them in a text which does imply, in its language, structure and intertextual fields of reference, questions about the marriages it arranges; which does lyrically evoke same-sex relationships if only to (try to) fix them firmly in the past; which does put on stage craftsmen who are not mere buffoons but social actors engaging, comically, painfully and earnestly with difficult aesthetic issues in a strongly stratified and potentially brutal society. The radical criticism which has developed since the start of the 1980s has made visible and audible elements of the *Dream* which were repressed less by its text than by some of its critics.

Since we have reached this state of enhanced critical awareness, what future directions might be suggested for *Dream* criticism? Hugh

Grady, in the essay we discussed in Chapter 8 of this Guide, hints at the possibility of a 'green criticism' of the play[2] and the project of greening the *Dream* certainly seems worth pursuing. Ecological criticism has tended initially to focus on Romantic nature writing; but Gabriel Egan, in *Green Shakespeare: From Ecopolitics to Ecocriticism* (2006) argues that the correspondences in Shakespeare's plays between humanity, nature and the cosmos, often dismissed by recent radical criticism as mystifying and reactionary, anticipate a modern, scientifically informed ecological awareness:

■ Although he would not, of course, have used these terms, Shakespeare's plays show an abiding interest in what we now identify as positive- and negative-feedback loops, cellular structures, the uses and abuses of analogies between natural and social order, and in the available models for community.[3] □

Egan's book offers no detailed analysis of the *Dream*, seeing it as an example of Shakespeare's 'obviously green-world plays'.[4] But an ecocritical interpretation of the *Dream* could point out that Titania's speech about the disorder in the elements offers a peculiarly vivid sense of the seasons going wrong and could relate this to the modes of possessiveness which the play dramatizes: Titania and Oberon both want to possess the Indian boy, Theseus wants to possess Hippolyta, Egeus and Demetrius want to possess Hermia, Helena wants to possess Demetrius, Titania wants to possess Bottom, Bottom and his fellow-craftsmen want to possess the cultural skills which will enable them to put on a play which will please the aristocracy. These possessive desires are not simply those of individuals, which might be curbed by personal moral restraint; they are codified and encouraged in historically specific legal, economic and political situations. An ecocritical reading of the *Dream* might make links between the desire to possess human and cultural forms of otherness which are so vividly rendered in the play and the desire to possess the otherness of nature which gains new force in the early modern period and has perhaps culminated in our current ecological fragility. It could also be fruitful to begin an analysis of early modern, evolutionary and ecological perspectives by comparing what are probably the two most famous natural banks in English writing: Oberon's 'bank where the wild thyme blows' and the 'entangled bank' which provides an image of the struggle for existence in chapter three of *The Origin of Species* (1859) by Charles Darwin (1809–82).[5]

In considering the *Dream* in relation to the early modern period, we might also consider the ways it anticipates our world. It is indeed striking how much fairyland in the play resembles the way we live now: it is a land of rapid communication and transport, multiple manipulations of desire, surrogate motherhood (the votaress bears a child for Titania), custody battles over children, marriages sustained on medication (the juice on Demetrius's eyes), spectacular makeovers (Helena becomes an object of desire for both Demetrius and Lysander, Bottom becomes an ass). To suggest this is not to endow the *Dream*, or Shakespeare, with a quasi-magical power of prophecy but to analyse how the play's attunement to its cultural moment enabled it to pick up intimations of what that cultural moment was to develop into. To carry weight, such an analysis would have to attend carefully both to the details of the *Dream*'s language and structure and to the broader cultural patterns with which it may have been linked.

A further approach which would combine attention to the details of the play with an attention to broader cultural patterns would be to see it as both an example and an anatomy of the 're-enchantment industry' which aims to restore the magical qualities supposedly ebbing from a secularizing, fragmenting world. Elizabethan England, it may be suggested, was peculiarly well suited to the early development of this industry. It was a country which had, in the reign of Henry VIII (1491–1547; King of England 1509–47), undergone a process of un-enchantment with the repression of Roman Catholicism and its ritual and imagery and with the growth of the kind of state bureaucracy which had been necessary to carry through the Dissolution of the Monasteries and to try to secure civil order and monarchical rule in a rapidly changing society. The iconography which grew up around Elizabeth I was the most dominant example of the re-enchantment industry in Shakespeare's England and the *Dream* can be seen as playing a double part in relation to re-enchantment, both showing how magical illusions can be produced but also undermining them.

Any further developments in *Dream* criticism, however, will finally depend for their effectiveness on close attention to the text(s), the language(s), of the play – to its energies and containments, its instabilities and precisions, its intertextual and intercultural resonances. Criticism of the *Dream* begins in, and returns to, the encounter with a language that is complex and crystal-clear, difficult and delightful, copious and concise, ornate and ordinary, far-flung and familiar, magical and mundane. It is in this encounter that the text lives, moves and has its being; it is hoped that the end of this Guide, like the end of the *Dream*, will send its readers, their critical faculties sharpened, back to the beginning of the play, to the forces that are released by that first word which brings us into a vibrant present: Now.

Notes

INTRODUCTION

1. Quoted in Harold F. Brooks (ed.), *A Midsummer Night's Dream*, Arden Shakespeare third series (London: Thomson Learning, 2001), p. xxxiv [34].
2. Stanley Wells and Gary Taylor (eds), *William Shakespeare, The Complete Works* (Oxford: Clarendon Press, 1988), p. 311.
3. John Dover Wilson and Sir Arthur Quiller-Couch (eds), *A Midsummer-Night's Dream* (Cambridge: Cambridge University Press, 1924), p. x [10].
4. Brooks (2001), p. lxxxix [89].
5. Stanley Wells (ed.), *A Midsummer Night's Dream*, Penguin Shakespeare series (Harmondsworth: Penguin, 1967), p. 14.
6. Stanley Wells (ed.), introduction by Helen Hackett, *A Midsummer Night's Dream*, Penguin Shakespeare series (London: Penguin, 2005), p. lxxxvi [86].
7. David Marshall, 'Exchanging Visions: Reading *A Midsummer Night's Dream*', *ELH*, 49:3 (Autumn 1982), p. 554.
8. For a summary of the evidence suggesting that 'foul papers' provided the copy for Q1, see Peter Holland (ed.), *A Midsummer Night's Dream*, The Oxford Shakespeare series (Oxford: Clarendon Press, 1994), pp. 113–14.
9. See Holland (1994), pp. 265–8; Barbara Hodgdon, 'Gaining a Father: The Role of Egeus in the Quarto and the Folio', *Review of English Studies*, 37 (1986), pp. 534–42, collected in Richard Dutton (ed.), *A Midsummer Night's Dream*, New Casebook series (Basingstoke and New York: Macmillan, 1996), pp. 161–71; Philip C. McGuire, 'Egeus and the Implications of Silence', in Marvin and Ruth Thompson (eds), *Shakespeare and the Sense of Performance* (Newark, DE: University of Delaware Press, 1989), pp. 103–15; McGuire, 'Intentions, Options, and Greatness: An Example from *A Midsummer Night's Dream*', in Sidney Homan (ed.), *Shakespeare and the Triple Play: From Study to Stage to Classroom* (Lewisburg: Bucknell University Press, 1988), pp. 177–86.
10. R. A. Foakes (ed.), *A Midsummer Night's Dream*, New Cambridge Shakespeare series (Cambridge: Cambridge University Press, 1984. Updated edn, 2003), p. 12.
11. Quoted Brooks (2001), p. 136.
12. Quoted Brooks (2001), p. 134.
13. Quoted Brooks (2001), p. 136.
14. Apuleius, *The Golden Ass*, trans. William Adlington (1566), revised S. Gaslee, Loeb Classical Library series (London: William Heinemann; New York: Macmillan, 1915), p. xiii [13].

CHAPTER ONE

1. Samuel Pepys, *The Diary of Samuel Pepys: A New and Complete Transcription: Volume 3: 1662*, Robert Latham and William Matthews (eds) (London: G. Bell and Sons, 1977), p. 208.
2. John Dryden, 'The Author's Apology for Heroique Poetry and Poetique Licence', *The Works of John Dryden*: Volume 12: *Plays: Amboyna; The State of Innocence; Aureng-Zebe*, Vinton A. Dearing (ed.), (Berkeley, Los Angeles, London: University of California Press, 1994), p. 95.

3. W. K. Wimsatt (ed.), *Samuel Johnson on Shakespeare* (London: MacGibbon and Kee, 1960), p. 74.

4. Wimsatt (1960), p. 73.

5. Wimsatt (1960), p. 74.

6. Mrs. [Elizabeth] Griffith, *The Morality of Shakespeare's Drama Illustrated* (London: Frank Cass, 1971), p. 16.

7. Edmond Malone, in Judith M. Kennedy and Richard F. Kennedy (eds), *A Midsummer Night's Dream*, Shakespeare: The Critical Tradition series (London and Brunswick, New Jersey: Athlone Press, 1999), p. 67.

8. Charles Taylor, in Kennedy and Kennedy (1999), p. 70.

9. Taylor, in Kennedy and Kennedy (1999), p. 71.

10. Taylor, in Kennedy and Kennedy (1999), p. 73.

11. Ludwig Tieck, in Jonathan Bate (ed.), *The Romantics on Shakespeare*, New Penguin Shakespeare Library series (London: Penguin, 1992), p. 63.

12. Tieck, in Bate (1992), pp. 63–4.

13. August von Schlegel, *A Course of Lectures on Dramatic Art and Literature*, trans. John Black, 2 vols, vol. 2 (London: Baldwin, Craddock and Joy; Edinburgh: William Blackwood; Dublin: John Cumming, 1815), p. 176.

14. Schlegel (1815), p. 177.

15. Schlegel (1815), p. 177.

16. Schlegel (1815), p. 177.

17. Schlegel (1815), pp. 177–8.

18. Schlegel (1815), p. 178.

19. Schlegel (1815), p. 178.

20. Schlegel (1815), pp. 180–1.

21. William Hazlitt, *Characters of Shakespeare's Plays*, World's Classics series (London: Oxford University Press, 1939), p. xxviii [28].

22. Hazlitt (1939), pp. xxviii–xxix [28–9].

23. Hazlitt (1939), p. 103.

24. Hazlitt (1939), p. 104.

25. Hazlitt (1939), p. 105.

26. Hazlitt (1939), p. 106.

27. Hazlitt (1939), p. 106.

28. Hazlitt (1939), p. 108.

29. Nathan Drake, *Shakspeare* [*sic*] *and His Times: Including the Biography of the Poet* (London: T. Cadell and W. Davies, 1817), p. 299.

30. Drake (1817), p. 299.

31. Drake (1817), p. 300.

32. Drake (1817), p. 338.

33. Samuel Taylor Coleridge, *Coleridge's Literary Criticism*, with an introduction by J. W. Mackail (London: Oxford University Press, 1908; reprinted 1938), p. 198.

34. [William Maginn], 'Shakespeare Papers – No. IV: *Midsummer Night's Dream*. Bottom, the Weaver', *Bentley's Miscellany*, 2 (July 1837), p. 376.

35. Maginn (1837), p. 375.

36. Maginn (1837), p. 378.

37. Maginn (1837), p. 379.

38. Charles Knight, in Kennedy and Kennedy (1999), p. 125.

39. Knight, in Kennedy and Kennedy (1999), p. 128.

40. Joseph Hunter, in Kennedy and Kennedy (1999), p. 148.

41. 'Hermann Ulrici, *Shakespeare's Dramatic Art and His Relation to Calderon and Goethe* (London: Chapman, 1846), p. 270.

42. Ulrici (1846), p. 275.

43. Ulrici (1846), p. 271.
44. Ulrici (1846), p. 271.
45. Henry Norman Hudson, in Kennedy and Kennedy (1999), pp. 168–9.
46. G. G. Gervinus, *Shakespeare Commentaries*, trans. under the author's superintendence by F. E. Bunnètt, new edn, revised (London: Smith, Elder, 1877), pp. 188, 189.
47. Gervinus (1877), pp. 195–6.
48. Gervinus (1877), p. 194.
49. Daniel Wilson, in Kennedy and Kennedy (1999), p. 238.
50. Wilson, in Kennedy and Kennedy (1999), p. 238.
51. Wilson, in Kennedy and Kennedy (1999), p. 238.
52. Wilson, in Kennedy and Kennedy (1999), p. 240.
53. Karl Elze, in Kennedy and Kennedy (1999), p. 241.
54. Elze, in Kennedy and Kennedy (1999), p. 242.
55. Elze, in Kennedy and Kennedy (1999), p. 242.
56. Elze, in Kennedy and Kennedy (1999), p. 242.
57. Denton Jacques Snider, in Kennedy and Kennedy (1999), p. 245.
58. Snider, in Kennedy and Kennedy (1999), p. 246.
59. Snider, in Kennedy and Kennedy (1999), p. 246.
60. John Weiss, in Kennedy and Kennedy (1999), p. 264.
61. Weiss, in Kennedy and Kennedy (1999), p. 265.
62. Edward Dowden, in Kennedy and Kennedy (1999), p. 256.
63. Charles Ebenezeer Moyse, in Kennedy and Kennedy (1999), p. 271.
64. Moyse, in Kennedy and Kennedy (1999), p. 273.
65. Julia Wedgwood, 'The Midsummer Night's Dream', *Contemporary Review*, 57 (April 1890), p. 581.
66. Wedgwood (1890), p. 581.
67. Wedgwood (1890), p. 500.
68. Edmund Kerchever Chambers, in Kennedy and Kennedy (1999), p. 336.
69. Chambers, in Kennedy and Kennedy (1999), p. 336.
70. Georg Brandes, *William Shakespeare* (London: William Heinemann, 1920), p. 67.
71. Brandes (1920), p. 71.

CHAPTER TWO

1. G. K. Chesterton, '*A Midsummer Night's Dream*', in *The Common Man* (London and New York: Sheed and Ward, 1950), p. 10.
2. Chesterton (1950), p. 12.
3. Chesterton (1950), p. 13.
4. Chesterton (1950), p. 14.
5. Chesterton (1950), p. 15.
6. Chesterton (1950), p. 15.
7. Chesterton (1950), p. 12.
8. Chesterton (1950), p. 15.
9. Chesterton (1950), p. 16.
10. Chesterton (1950), p. 17.
11. J. B. Priestley, *The English Comic Characters*, The Week-End Library series (London: John Lane, The Bodley Head, 1928), p. 2.
12. Priestley (1928), p. 5.
13. Priestley (1928), p. 7.
14. Priestley (1928), p. 6.
15. Priestley (1928), p. 8.

16. Priestley (1928), p. 9.
17. Priestley (1928), p. 10.
18. Priestley (1928), p. 17.
19. Enid Welsford, *The Court Masque: A Study in the Relationship between Poetry and the Revels* (Cambridge: Cambridge University Press, 1927), p. 324.
20. Welsford (1927), p. 326.
21. Welsford (1927), p. 327.
22. Welsford (1927), p. 329.
23. Welsford (1927), p. 330.
24. Welsford (1927), p. 330.
25. Welsford (1927), p. 331.
26. Welsford (1927), p. 331.
27. Welsford (1927), p. 332.
28. Welsford (1927), p. 332.
29. Welsford (1927), p. 333.
30. Welsford (1927), p. 334.
31. G. Wilson Knight, *The Shakespearean Tempest*, Oxford Bookshelf series (London: Oxford University Press, 1940), p. 1.
32. Knight (1940), p. 3.
33. Knight (1940), p. 4.
34. Knight (1940), p. 141.
35. Knight (1940), p. 142.
36. Knight (1940), p. 142.
37. Knight (1940), p. 142.
38. Knight (1940), p. 143.
39. Knight (1940), p. 167.
40. Knight (1940), p. 144.
41. Knight (1940), p. 142.
42. Knight (1940), p. 148.
43. Knight (1940), p. 151.
44. Knight (1940), p. 153.
45. Knight (1940), p. 151.
46. Knight (1940), p. 146.
47. Knight (1940), p. 168.
48. Caroline F. E. Spurgeon, *Shakespeare's Imagery and What It Tells Us* (Cambridge: Cambridge University Press, 1952), p. 213.
49. Spurgeon (1952), p. 216.
50. Spurgeon (1952), p. 259.
51. Spurgeon (1952), p. 259.
52. Spurgeon (1952), p. 68.
53. H. B. Charlton, *Shakespearean Comedy*, University Paperbacks series (Methuen: London, 1966), p. 102.
54. Charlton (1966), p. 103.
55. Charlton (1966), p. 103.
56. Charlton (1966), p. 103.
57. Charlton (1966), p. 108.
58. Charlton (1966), p. 115.
59. Charlton (1966), p. 116.
60. Charlton (1966), p. 116.
61. Charlton (1966), p. 117.
62. Dorothea Kehler, '*A Midsummer Night's Dream*: A Bibliographic Survey of the Criticism', in Dorothea Kehler (ed.), *A Midsummer Night's Dream*: *Critical Essays*, Shakespeare Criticism series (New York and London: Routledge, 2001), p. 26.

63.   Donald C. Miller, 'Titania and the Changeling', in G. Kirchner, L. Whitbread, Donald C. Miller, A. H. King, Eilert Ekwall, Z. S. Fink, 'Notes and News', *English Studies: A Journal of English Language and Literature*, 22.1 (1940), p. 66.

64.   Thomas Marc Parrott, *Shakespearean Comedy* (New York: Oxford University Press, 1949), p. 133.

CHAPTER THREE

1.   Paul N. Siegel, '*A Midsummer Night's Dream* and the Wedding Guests', *Shakespeare Quarterly*, 4:2 (April 1953), p. 139.

2.   Siegel (1953), p. 139.

3.   Siegel (1953), p. 140.

4.   Siegel (1953), p. 141.

5.   Siegel (1953), p. 142.

6.   Siegel (1953), p. 142.

7.   Siegel (1953), pp. 10, 11.

8.   Samuel Pepys, *The Diary of Samuel Pepys: A new and complete transcription: Volume 3: 1662*, Robert Latham and William Matthews (eds) (London: G. Bell and Sons, 1977), p. 208.

9.   Siegel (1953), p. 143.

10.   Peter F. Fisher, 'The Argument of *A Midsummer Night's Dream*', *Shakespeare Quarterly*, 8:3 (Summer 1957), p. 307.

11.   Fisher (1957), p. 308.

12.   Fisher (1957), p. 307.

13.   Fisher (1957), p. 308.

14.   Fisher (1957), p. 308.

15.   Fisher (1957), p. 309.

16.   Fisher (1957), p. 310.

17.   Fisher (1957), p. 310.

18.   Paul A. Olson, '*A Midsummer Night's Dream* and the Meaning of Court Marriage', *ELH*, 24:2 (June 1957), p. 95.

19.   Olson (1957), p. 96.

20.   Olson (1957), p. 97.

21.   Olson (1957), p. 98.

22.   Olson (1957), p. 99.

23.   Olson (1957), p. 101.

24.   Olson (1957), p. 101, note 22, refers the reader to Nevill Coghill, 'The Basis of Shakespearean Comedy', *Essays and Studies* (1950), pp. 12–13 and *passim*, pp. 1–28.

25.   Olson (1957), p. 101.

26.   Olson (1957), p. 111.

27.   Olson (1957), p. 115.

28.   John Russell Brown, *Shakespeare and his Comedies*, 2nd edn, with a new chapter on the last comedies (London: Methuen, 1962).

29.   Brown (1962), p. 24.

30.   Brown (1962), p. 24.

31.   Brown (1962), p. 25.

32.   Brown (1962), p. 87.

33.   Brown (1962), p. 90.

34.   Brown (1962), p. 90.

35.   Brown (1962), p. 91.

36.   C. L. Barber, *Shakespeare's Festive Comedy: A Study of Dramatic Form and its Relation to Social Custom* (Princeton, NJ: Princeton University Press, 1990), p. 3.

37. Barber (1990), p. 11.
38. Barber (1990), p. 124.
39. Barber (1990), p. 135.
40. Barber (1990), p. 133.
41. Barber (1990), p. 135.
42. Barber (1990), p. 141.
43. Barber (1990), p. 142.
44. Barber (1990), p. 151.
45. Barber (1990), p. 154.
46. Barber (1990), p. 161.
47. Barber (1990), p. 161.
48. Barber (1990), p. 162.

CHAPTER FOUR

1. Bertrand Evans, *Shakespeare's Comedies* (Oxford: Clarendon Press, 1960), p. viii.
2. Evans (1960), p. viii.
3. Evans (1960), p. 34.
4. Evans (1960), p. 34.
5. Evans (1960), p. 36.
6. Evans (1960), p. 38.
7. Evans (1960), p. 40.
8. Evans (1960), p. 42.
9. Evans (1960), p. 44.
10. Evans (1960), p. 45.
11. Evans (1960), p. 45.
12. Frank Kermode, 'The Mature Comedies', in John Russell Brown and Bernard Harris (eds), *Stratford-upon-Avon Studies 3: Early Shakespeare* (London: Edward Arnold, 1961), p. 218.
13. Quoted Kermode (1961), p. 218.
14. Quoted Kermode (1961), p. 219.
15. Kermode (1961), p. 219.
16. Kermode (1961), p. 219.
17. Kermode (1961), p. 220.
18. G. K. Hunter, *William Shakespeare: The Later Comedies*, Writers and Their Works series no. 143 (London: Longmans Green for the British Council and the National Book League, 1962; reprinted with additions to bibliography, 1964), p. 8.
19. Hunter (1964), p. 9.
20. Hunter (1964), p. 17.
21. Hunter (1964), p. 10.
22. Hunter (1964), p. 11.
23. Hunter (1964), p. 18.
24. Hunter (1964), p. 17.
25. Hunter (1964), p. 12.
26. Hunter (1964), p. 13.
27. Hunter (1964), p. 13.
28. Hunter (1964), p. 20.
29. Hunter (1964), p. 19.
30. R. W. Dent, 'Imagination in *A Midsummer Night's Dream*', *Shakespeare Quarterly*, 15:2 (Spring 1964), p. 115.
31. Dent (1964), p. 118.
32. Dent (1964), pp. 118–19.

33. Dent (1964), p. 124.
34. Dent (1964), p. 126.
35. Dent (1964), p. 126.
36. Quoted Dent (1964), p. 127.
37. Dent (1964), p. 127.
38. Quoted Dent (1964), p. 128.
39. Quoted Dent (1964), p. 128.
40. Dent (1964), p. 129.
41. Jan Kott, *Shakespeare Our Contemporary*, trans. Boleslaw Taborski, 2nd edn revised 1967, University Paperback Drama Book series (London: Methuen, 1967), p. 175.
42. Kott (1967), p. 176.
43. Kott (1967), p. 179.
44. Kott (1967), p. 180.
45. Kott (1967), pp. 180–1.
46. Kott (1967), p. 181.
47. Kott (1967), p. 181.
48. Kott (1967), p. 182.
49. Kott (1967), p. 183.
50. Kott (1967), p. 183.
51. Kott (1967), p. 183.
52. David P. Young, *Something of Great Constancy: The Art of A Midsummer Night's Dream*. New Haven and London: Yale University Press, 1966, p. 75.
53. Young (1966), pp. 75–6.
54. Young (1966), p. 77.
55. Young (1966), p. 79.
56. Young (1966), p. 80.
57. Young (1966), p. 83.
58. Stephen Fender, *Shakespeare: A Midsummer Night's Dream*, Studies in English Literature series, no. 35 (London: Edward Arnold, 1968), p. 20.
59. Fender (1968), p. 40.
60. Fender (1968), p. 46.
61. Fender (1968), p. 46.
62. Fender (1968), p. 49.
63. Fender (1968), p. 50.
64. Fender (1968), p. 54.
65. Fender (1968), p. 55.
66. Fender (1968), p. 59.
67. Fender (1968), p. 61.

CHAPTER FIVE

1. Alexander Leggatt, *Shakespeare's Comedy of Love* (London: Methuen, 1974; reprinted 1978), p. xi [11].
2. Leggatt (1978), p. 91.
3. Leggatt (1978), p. 95.
4. Leggatt (1978), p. 110.
5. Leggatt (1978), p. 96.
6. Jan Kott, *Shakespeare our Contemporary*, 2nd edn revised, trans. Boleslaw Taborski, University Paperback Drama Book series (London: Methuen, 1967), p. 183.
7. Leggatt (1978), p. 111.
8. Leggatt (1978), p. 111.
9. Leggatt (1978), p. 112.

10. Leggatt (1978), p. 115.

11. Marjorie B. Garber, *Dream in Shakespeare: From Metaphor to Metamorphosis* (New Haven and London: Yale University Press, 1974), p. 59.

12. Garber (1974), p. 60.

13. Garber (1974), p. 62.

14. Garber (1974), p. 62.

15. Garber (1974), p. 65.

16. Garber (1974), p. 63.

17. Garber (1974), pp. 63–4.

18. Garber (1974), p. 64.

19. Garber (1974), p. 77.

20. Garber (1974), p. 81.

21. Garber (1974), pp. 83–4.

22. Garber (1974), p. 84.

23. Garber (1974), p. 84.

24. Garber (1974), p. 87.

25. David Bevington, '"But We Are Spirits of Another Sort": The Dark Side of Love and Magic in *A Midsummer Night's Dream*', in Siegfrid Wenzel (ed.), *Medieval and Renaissance Studies: Proceedings of the Southeastern Institute of Medieval and Renaissance Studies Summer 1975* (Chapel Hill: University of North Carolina, 1978), pp. 80–92; reprinted in Richard Dutton (ed.), *A Midsummer Night's Dream*, New Casebook series (Basingstoke and New York: Palgrave Macmillan, 1996), p. 35, note 1.

26. Bevington, in Dutton (1996), p. 25.

27. Bevington, in Dutton (1996), p. 30.

28. Bevington, in Dutton (1996), p. 31.

29. Kott (1967), p. 181.

30. Bevington, in Dutton (1996), pp. 31–2.

31. Bevington, in Dutton (1996), p. 32.

32. Bevington, in Dutton (1996), p. 32.

33. Bevington, in Dutton (1996), p. 34.

34. Bevington, in Dutton (1996), p. 34.

35. Bevington, in Dutton (1996), p. 35.

36. Paul A. Olson, '*A Midsummer Night's Dream* and the Meaning of Court Marriage', *ELH*, 24:2 (June 1957), p. 95.

37. Kott (1967), p. 183.

38. Elliot Krieger, *A Marxist Study of Shakespeare's Comedies* (London and Basingstoke: Macmillan, 1979), p. 1.

39. Krieger (1979), p. 171, notes 1 and 2 for Chapter 1, directs us to Sherman Hawkins, 'The Two Worlds of Shakespearean Comedy' *Shakespeare Studies*, 3 (1967), pp. 62–80, and Clifford Leech, *Twelfth Night and Shakespearean Comedy* (Toronto: University of Toronto Press, 1965), p. 9.

40. Krieger (1979), p. 171, note 3 for Chapter 1, directs us to Harry Berger, Jr., 'The Renaissance Imagination: Second World and Green World', *Centennial Review*, 9 (1965), pp. 36–78.

41. Krieger (1979), p. 2.

42. Bevington, in Dutton (1996), p. 31.

43. Krieger (1979), pp. 40–1.

44. Krieger (1979), p. 41.

45. Leggatt (1974), p. 111.

46. Bevington, in Dutton (1996), p. 31.

47. Krieger (1979), p. 42.

48. Krieger (1979), p. 59.

49. Krieger (1979), p. 60.

50. Krieger (1979), p. 61.
51. Krieger (1979), p. 65.
52. Krieger (1979), p. 69.

CHAPTER SIX

1. Shirley Nelson Garner, '*A Midsummer Night's Dream*: "Jack shall have Jill; Nought shall go ill"' (1981), in Richard Dutton (ed.), *A Midsummer Night's Dream*, New Casebooks series (Basingstoke and New York: Palgrave Macmillan, 1996), p. 84.
2. Garner, in Dutton (1996), p. 86.
3. Garner, in Dutton (1996), p. 87.
4. Garner, in Dutton (1996), p. 88.
5. Garner, in Dutton (1996), p. 94.
6. Garner, in Dutton (1996), p. 94.
7. Garner, in Dutton (1996), p. 96.
8. David Marshall, 'Exchanging Visions: Reading *A Midsummer Night's Dream*', *ELH* 49:3 (Autumn 1982), p. 548.
9. Marshall (1982), p. 549.
10. Marshall (1982), p. 550.
11. Marshall (1982), p. 551.
12. Marshall (1982), p. 553.
13. Marshall (1982), p. 557.
14. Marshall (1982), pp. 557–8.
15. Marshall (1982), p. 558.
16. Marshall (1982), p. 565.
17. Marshall (1982), p. 568.
18. Marshall (1982), p. 570.
19. Marshall (1982), p. 571.
20. Louis Adrian Montrose, '"Shaping Fantasies": Figurations of Gender and Power in Elizabethan Culture', *Representations*, 2 (Spring 1983), p. 61.
21. Harold F. Brooks (ed.), *A Midsummer Night's Dream*, Arden Shakespeare second series (London: Thomson Learning, 2001), p. lv [55]. 'It seems likely that Queen Elizabeth was present when the *Dream* was first acted'.
22. Montrose (1983), p. 62.
23. Quoted in Montrose (1983), p. 63. Montrose (p. 87, note 5) gives the following source: A. L. Rowse, *The Case Books of Simon Forman* (London [:Pan, 1976]), p. 31.
24. Quoted in Montrose (1983), pp. 63, 64. Montrose (p. 88, note 9) gives the following source: André Hurault, Sieur de Maisse, *Journal* (1597), G. B. Harrison and R. A. Jones (ed. and trans.) (Bloomsbury [:Nonesuch Press], 1931), pp. 25–6, 36–7.
25. Montrose (1983), p. 65.
26. Montrose (1983), p. 66.
27. Montrose (1983), p. 65.
28. Montrose (1983), p. 66.
29. Montrose (1983), p. 66.
30. Montrose (1983), p. 74.
31. Montrose (1983), p. 74.
32. Montrose (1983), p. 85.
33. Montrose (1983), p. 86.
34. James H. Kavanagh, 'Shakespeare in Ideology', in John Drakakis (ed.), *Alternative Shakespeares*, 2nd edn, Methuen New Accents series (London and New York: Routledge, Taylor and Francis Group, 2002), p. 155.
35. Kavanagh (2002), p. 156.

36. Kavanagh (2002), p. 156.
37. Kavanagh (2002), p. 158.
38. Kavanagh (2002), p. 159.
39. Theodore B. Leinwand, '"I Believe We Must Leave the Killing Out": Deference and Accommodation in *A Midsummer Night's Dream*' (1986), in Dorothea Kehler (ed.), *A Midsummer Night's Dream: Critical Essays*, Shakespeare Criticism series (New York and London: Routledge, 2001), p. 147.
40. Leinwand, in Kehler (2001), p. 145.
41. Quoted Leinwand (1986), in Kehler (2001), p. 149. Leinwand (in Kehler (2001), p. 162, note 11) gives the following source: J. S. Cockburn, 'The Nature and Incidence of Crime in England 1559–1625: A Preliminary Survey' in Cockburn (ed.), *Crime in England 1550–1800*, p. 61.
42. Quoted in Leinwand, in Kehler (2001), p. 150. Leinwand (in Kehler (2001), p. 162, note 21) gives the following source: Peter Clark, 'Popular Protest and Disturbance in Kent, 1558–1640', *Economic History Review 29* (1976), p. 367.
43. Quoted in Leinwand, in Kehler (2001), p. 151. Leinwand (in Kehler (2001), p. 162, note 23) gives the following source: Buchanan Sharp, *In Contempt of All Authority: Rural Artisans and Riot in the West of England, 1586–1660* (Berkeley: University of California Press, 1980), p. 20.
44. Leinwand, in Kehler (2001), p. 152.
45. Leinwand, in Kehler (2001), p. 153.
46. Leinwand, in Kehler (2001), p. 153.
47. Leinwand, in Kehler (2001), p. 158.
48. Leinwand, in Kehler (2001), p. 159. Leinwand (in Kehler (2001), p. 164, note 46) gives the following source: L. A. Clarkson, *The Pre-Industrial Economy of England 1500–1750* (London: Batsford, 1971), p. 212. In the same note, however, Leinwand also asks the reader to 'compare' D. M. Palliser, *The Age of Elizabeth: England under the Late Tudors 1547–1603* (London: Longman, 1983), p. 159.
49. Leinwand, in Kehler (2001), pp. 158–9.
50. Leinwand, in Kehler (2001), p. 160.
51. Leinwand, in Kehler (2001), pp. 160–1.
52. Annabel Patterson, *Shakespeare and the Popular Voice* (Cambridge, MA and Oxford: Basil Blackwell, 1989), p. 56. Patterson (p. 171, note 12) gives the following source for the figures: Brian Manning, *Village Revolts: Social Protest and Popular Disturbances in England, 1509–1640* (Oxford: Oxford University Press, 1988), p. 208.
53. Patterson (1989), p. 60.
54. Patterson (1989), p. 63.
55. For an argument in favour of the view that 'Pyramus' and 'Thisbe' should try to kiss between Snout's legs, Patterson (pp. 172–3, note 28) cites Thomas Clayton, '"Fie What a Question's That If Thou Wert Near a Lewd Interpreter": The Wall Scene in *A Midsummer Night's Dream*', *Shakespeare Studies*, 7 (1974), pp. 101–23.
56. Patterson (1989), p. 64.
57. Patterson (1989), p. 64.
58. Patterson (1989), p. 65.
59. Quoted in Patterson (1989), p. 68.
60. Patterson (1989), p. 69.
61. Patterson (1989), p. 69.
62. Quoted in Patterson (1989), p. 69. Patterson (p. 173, note 39) gives the following source for the quotation: Alexander Neville, *Norfolkes Furies, or A View of Ketts Campe: Necessary for the Malecontents Of Our Time, for their instruction, or terror; and profitable for every good Subject*, trans. R[ichard] W[oods], (London 1615), B2r [Patterson's italics].
63. Patterson (1989), p. 70.

CHAPTER SEVEN

1.   René Girard, *A Theater of Envy* (New York, Oxford: Oxford University Press, 1991), p. 30.
2.   Girard (1991), p. 31.
3.   Girard (1991), p. 3.
4.   Girard (1991), p. 43.
5.   Girard (1991), p. 43.
6.   Girard (1991), p. 64.
7.   Girard (1991), p. 64.
8.   Girard (1991), p. 68.
9.   James L. Calderwood, *A Midsummer Night's Dream*, Twayne's New Critical Introductions to Shakespeare series, no. 14 (New York: Twayne, 1992), p. 50.
10. Calderwood (1992), pp. 61–2.
11. Calderwood (1992), p. 63.
12. Calderwood (1992), p. 64.
13. Calderwood (1992), p. 2.
14. Calderwood (1992), p. 3.
15. Calderwood (1992), p. 4.
16. Terence Hawkes, 'Or', in Hawkes, *Meaning by Shakespeare* (London: Routledge, 1992), pp. 15–16.
17. Hawkes (1992), p. 16.
18. John Dover Wilson and Sir Arthur Quiller-Couch (eds), *A Midsummer-Night's Dream* (Cambridge: Cambridge University Press, 1924), pp. 141–2.
19. Hawkes (1992), p. 18.
20. Hawkes (1992), p. 19.
21. Hawkes (1992), p. 23.
22. Hawkes (1992), p. 38.
23. Hawkes (1992), p. 39.
24. Hawkes (1992), p. 39.
25. Patricia Parker, *Shakespeare from the Margins* (Chicago and London: University of Chicago Press, 1996), p. 89.
26. Parker (1996), p. 94.
27. Parker (1996), p. 95.
28. Parker (1996), p. 100.
29. Parker (1996), p. 101.
30. Parker (1996), p. 103.
31. Parker (1996), p. 106.
32. Parker (1996), pp. 106–7.
33. Margo Hen1dricks, '"Obscured by dreams": Race, Empire, and Shakespeare's *A Midsummer Night's Dream*', *Shakespeare Quarterly*, 47:1 (Spring 1996), p. 41.
34. Hendricks (1996), p. 43.
35. Hendricks (1996), p. 52.
36. Hendricks (1996), p. 53.
37. Hendricks (1996), p. 55.
38. Hendricks (1996), p. 55.
39. Hendricks (1996), p. 56.
40. Hendricks (1996), p. 56.
41. Hendricks (1996), p. 59.
42. Hendricks (1996), p. 55.
43. Jonathan Bate, *Shakespeare and Ovid* (Oxford: Clarendon Press, 1993; reprinted 2001), p. 131.
44. Bate (2001), p. 144.

45. Bate (2001), p. 132.
46. Bate (2001), p. 133.
47. Bate (2001), p. 140.
48. Bate (2001), p. 136.
49. Bate (2001), p. 139.
50. Bate (2001), p. 143.
51. Bate (2001), p. 142.
52. Bate (2001), p. 144.
53. Bate (2001), p. 144.
54. Helen Hackett, *A Midsummer Night's Dream*, Writers and Their Work series (Plymouth, Devon: Northcote House in association with the British Council, 1997), p. 3.
55. Hackett (1997), p. 4.
56. Hackett (1997), p. 32.
57. Hackett (1997), p. 34.
58. Hackett (1997), p. 36.
59. Hackett (1997), p. 40.
60. Hackett (1997), p. 41.
61. Hackett (1997), p. 42.
62. Hackett (1997), p. 45.
63. Hackett (1997), p. 45.
64. Hackett (1997), p. 46.
65. Hackett (1997), p. 43.

CHAPTER EIGHT

1. A. D. Nuttall, '*A Midsummer Night's Dream*: Comedy as *Apotrope* of Myth', *Shakespeare Survey: An Annual Survey of Shakespeare Studies and Production; 53: Shakespeare and Narrative* (Cambridge: Cambridge University Press, 2000), p. 49.
2. Nuttall (2000), p. 51.
3. Nuttall (2000), p. 52.
4. Nuttall (2000), p. 54.
5. Nuttall (2000), p. 56.
6. Nuttall (2000), p. 52.
7. Nuttall (2000), p. 53.
8. Nuttall (2000), pp. 58, 59.
9. Douglas E. Green, 'Preposterous Pleasures: Queer Theories and *A Midsummer Night's Dream*', in Dorothea Kehler (ed.), *A Midsummer Night's Dream: Critical Essays*, Shakespeare Criticism series (New York and London: Routledge, 2001), p. 370.
10. Green, in Kehler (2001), p. 371.
11. Green, in Kehler (2001), p. 378.
12. Green, in Kehler (2001), p. 375.
13. Green, in Kehler (2001), p. 376.
14. Green, in Kehler (2001), p. 378.
15. Green, in Kehler (2001), p. 380.
16. Green, in Kehler (2001), p. 381.
17. Green, in Kehler (2001), p. 385.
18. Green, in Kehler (2001), p. 387.
19. Alan Sinfield, 'Cultural Materialism and Intertextuality: The Limits of Queer Reading in *A Midsummer Night's Dream* and *The Two Noble Kinsmen*', in Peter Holland (ed.), *Shakespeare Survey: An Annual Survey of Shakespeare Studies and Production: 56: Shakespeare and Comedy* (2003), pp. 68, 69, 70.
20. Sinfield (2003), p. 69.

21. Quoted Sinfield (2003), p. 70.
22. Sinfield (2003), p. 72.
23. Sinfield (2003), p. 74.
24. Sinfield (2003), p. 74.
25. Sinfield (2003), p. 77.
26. Sinfield (2003), p. 78.
27. Sinfield (2003), p. 77.
28. Thomas R. Frosch, 'The Missing Child in *A Midsummer Night's Dream*', *American Imago*, 64:4 (Winter, 2007), p. 486.
29. Frosch (2007), p. 488.
30. Frosch (2007), p. 489.
31. Frosch (2007), p. 489.
32. Frosch (2007), pp. 505, 506.
33. Frosch (2007), p. 489.
34. Frosch (2007), p. 496.
35. Frosch (2007), p. 500.
36. Frosch (2007), p. 502.
37. Frosch (2007), p. 503.
38. Frosch (2007), p. 504.
39. Frosch (2007), p. 507.
40. Frosch (2007), p. 506.
41. Frosch (2007), pp. 507–8.
42. Hugh Grady, 'Shakespeare and Impure Aesthetics: The Case of *A Midsummer Night's Dream*', *Shakespeare Quarterly*, 59:3 (Fall 2008), p. 275.
43. Grady (2008), p. 277.
44. Grady (2008), p. 278.
45. Grady (2008), p. 295.
46. Grady (2008), p. 281.
47. Grady (2008), p. 282.
48. Grady (2008), p. 287.
49. Grady (2008), p. 288.
50. Grady (2008), p. 300.
51. Grady (2008), p. 301.
52. Grady (2008), p. 302.

CHAPTER NINE

1.   Kenneth Rothwell, *A History of Shakespeare on Screen: A Century of Film and Television* (Cambridge: Cambridge University Press, 1999; paperback edn, 2001), no page number.
2.   Richard Watts, Jr., 'Films of a Moonstruck World', *Yale Review*, 25:2 (December 1935), pp. 311–20. This quotation from extract in Charles W. Eckert (ed.), *Focus on Shakespearean Films* (Englewood Cliffs, NJ: Prentice-Hall, 1972), p. 50.
3.   Watts, in Eckert (1972), p. 52.
4.   Allardyce Nicoll, *Film and Theatre* (New York: Thomas Y. Crowell, 1936). This quotation from extract in Eckert (1972), p. 45.
5.   Nicoll, in Eckert (1972), p. 52.
6. Thomas Marc Parrott, *Shakespearean Comedy* (New York: Oxford University Press, 1949), p. 127.
7.   Parrott (1949), p. 128.
8.   Harold F. Brooks (ed.), *A Midsummer Night's Dream*, The Arden Shakespeare, third series (London: Methuen, 1979; Thomson Learning, 2001), p. cvii [57].

9. Roger Manvell, *Shakespeare and the Film,* revised and updated edn. (South Brunswick and New York: A. S. Barnes, 1979), pp. 25–7 (on the 1935 *Dream*), 119–27 (on the 1969 *Dream*).

10. Manvell (1979), p. 27.

11. John Collick, *Shakespeare, Cinema and Society* (Manchester: Manchester University Press, 1989), extract in Robert Shaughnessy (ed.), *Shakespeare on Film*, New Casebooks series (Basingstoke and London: Macmillan, 1998), p. 91.

12. Collick, in Shaughnessy (1998), p. 96.

13. Collick, in Shaughnessy (1998), p. 93.

14. Collick, in Shaughnessy (1998), p. 91.

15. Rothwell (2001), p. 34.

16. Rothwell (2001), p. 37.

17. Manvell (1979), p. 123.

18. Manvell (1979), p. 121.

19. Manvell (1979), p. 124.

20. Manvell (1979), p. 121.

21. Manvell (1979), p. 123.

22. Manvell (1979), p. 123.

23. Maurice Hindle, *Studying Shakespeare on Film* (Basingstoke and New York: Palgrave Macmillan, 2007), p. 45.

24. Quoted in Henry Fenwick, 'The Production', in *The BBC TV Shakespeare: A Midsummer Night's Dream* (London: British Broadcasting Corporation, 1981), p. 22.

25. Quoted in Fenwick (1981), p. 19.

26. Susan Willis, *The BBC Shakespeare Plays: Making the Televised Canon* (Chapel Hill and London: University of North Carolina Press, 1999), p. 152.

27. Willis (1999), p. 153.

28. Willis (1999), p. 154.

29. Martin White, *A Midsummer Night's Dream*: Shakespeare Handbooks series (Basingstoke and New York: Palgrave Macmillan, 2009), p. 134.

30. Rothwell (2001), p. 244.

31. Mark Thornton Burnett, 'Impressions of Fantasy: Adrian Noble's *A Midsummer Night's Dream*', in Burnett and Ramona Wray (eds), *Shakespeare, Film Fin de Siècle* (Basingstoke and London: Macmillan; New York: St Martin's Press, 2000), p. 90.

32. Burnett (2000), p. 92.

33. Burnett (2000), p. 94.

34. Burnett (2000), p. 95.

35. Burnett (2000), p. 98.

36. Judith Butcher, *Shakespeare on Film*, Inside Film series (Harlow, Essex: Pearson Longman, 2005), pp. 138–9.

37. Peter Donaldson, 'Bottom and the Gramophone: Media, Class and Comedy in Michael Hoffman's *A Midsummer Night's Dream*', *Shakespeare Survey 61: Shakespeare, Sound and Screen* (2008), p. 23.

38. Donaldson (2008), p. 25.

39. Donaldson (2008), p. 24.

40. Donaldson (2008), p. 26.

41. Donaldson (2008), p. 30.

42. Donaldson (2008), p. 31.

43. Donaldson (2008), p. 30.

44. Hindle (2007), p. 135.

45. Donaldson (2008), p. 35.

CONCLUSION

1. Samuel Pepys, *The Diary of Samuel Pepys: A New and Complete Transcription: Volume 3: 1662*, Robert Latham and William Matthews (eds) (London: G. Bell and Sons, 1977), p. 208.

2. Hugh Grady, 'Shakespeare and Impure Aesthetics: The Case of *A Midsummer Night's Dream*', *Shakespeare Quarterly*, 59:3 (Fall 2008), p. 289.

3. Gabriel Egan, *Green Shakespeare: From Ecopolitics to Ecocriticism*, Accents on Shakespeare series (London and New York: Routledge, 2006), p. 50.

4. Egan (2006), p. 175.

5. Charles Darwin, *The Origin of Species*, Gillian Beer (ed.), Oxford World's Classics series (Oxford: Oxford University Press, 1996), p. 62.

Select Bibliography

Wilson, John Dover and Quiller-Couch, Sir Arthur (eds). *A Midsummer-Night's Dream*. Cambridge: Cambridge University Press, 1924.

Wells, Stanley (ed.) *A Midsummer Night's Dream*. Penguin Shakespeare series. Harmondsworth: Penguin, 1967. New edn, with introduction by Helen Hackett. London: Penguin, 2005.

Brooks, Harold F. (ed.). *A Midsummer Night's Dream*. Arden Shakespeare, third series. London: Methuen, 1979; Thomson Learning, 2001.

Foakes, R. A. (ed.). *A Midsummer Night's Dream*. New Cambridge Shakespeare series. Cambridge: Cambridge University Press, 1984. Updated edn, 2003.

Andrews, John F. (ed). *A Midsummer Night's Dream*. Everyman Shakespeare series. London: J. M. Dent, 1993.

Holland, Peter (ed.). *A Midsummer Night's Dream*. Oxford Shakespeare series. Oxford: Clarendon Press, 1994.

Bate, Jonathan and Rasmussen, Eric (eds) *A Midsummer Night's Dream*. RSC Shakespeare series. Basingstoke: Palgrave Macmillan, 2008.

ANTHOLOGIES OF CRITICISM
Anthologies of general Shakespeare criticism which include key material on *Dream*

Bate, Jonathan (ed.). *The Romantics on Shakespeare*. London: Penguin, 1992.

Smith, D. Nichol (ed.). *Shakespeare Criticism: A Selection: 1623–1840*. World's Classics series. London: Oxford University Press, 1958.

Vickers, Brian (ed.). *Shakespeare: The Critical Heritage*, vols. 1–6. London and Boston: Routledge and Kegan Paul, 1974–81.

Anthologies of criticism specifically devoted to *Dream*

Cookson, Linda and Loughrey, Bryan (eds). *Longman Critical Essays: A Midsummer Night's Dream*. Harlow: Longman, 1991.

Dutton, Richard (ed.). *A Midsummer Night's Dream*. New Casebooks series. Basingstoke and New York: Palgrave Macmillan, 1996.

Kehler, Dorothea (ed.). *A Midsummer Night's Dream: Critical Essays*, Shakespeare Criticism series. New York and London: Routledge, 2001.

Kennedy, Judith M. and Kennedy, Richard F. (eds). *A Midsummer Night's Dream*, Shakespeare: The Critical Tradition series. London and New Brunswick, NJ: The Athlone Press, 1999.

Price, Antony W. (ed.). *Shakespeare:* A Midsummer Night's Dream*: A Casebook*. Macmillan Casebook series. Basingstoke and London: Macmillan, 1983.

INTRODUCTION

McGuire, Philip C. 'Egeus and the Implications of Silence', in Marvin and Ruth Thompson (eds), *Shakespeare and the Sense of Performance*. Newark, DE: University of Delaware Press, 1989, pp. 103–15.

McGuire, Philip C. 'Intentions, Options, and Greatness: An Example from *A Midsummer Night's Dream*', in Sidney Homan (ed.), *Shakespeare and the Triple Play: From Study to Stage to Classroom*. Lewisburg: Bucknell University Press, 1988, pp. 177–86.

Wells, Stanley and Taylor, Gary (eds). *William Shakespeare, The Complete Works*. Oxford: Clarendon Press, 1988, p. 311.

CHAPTER ONE: 1662–1898

Coleridge, Samuel Taylor. *Coleridge's Literary Criticism*, with an introduction by J. W. Mackail. London: Oxford University Press, 1908; reprinted 1938, p. 198.

Brandes, Georg. *William Shakespeare*. London: William Heinemann, 1920.

Drake, Nathan. Shakspeare [*sic*] and His Times: Including The Biography of the Poet. London: T. Cadell and W. Davies, 1817.

Dryden, John. 'The Author's Apology for Heroique Poetry and Poetique Licence', in Vinton A. Dearing (ed.). *The Works of John Dryden*: Volume 12: *Plays: Amboyna; The State of Innocence; Aureng-Zebe*. Berkeley, Los Angeles, London: University of California Press, 1994.

Gervinus, G. G. *Shakespeare Commentaries*, trans. under the author's superintendence by F. E. Bunnett, new edn, revised. London: Smith, Elder, 1877.

Griffith, Mrs. [Elizabeth]. *The Morality of Shakespeare's Drama Illustrated*. London: Frank Cass, 1971.

Hazlitt, William, *Characters of Shakespeare's Plays*. World's Classics series. London: Oxford University Press, 1939.

[Maginn, William]. 'Shakespeare Papers – No. IV: *Midsummer Night's Dream*. Bottom, the Weaver'. *Bentley's Miscellany*, 2 (July 1837), pp. 370–80.

Pepys, Samuel. *The Diary of Samuel Pepys: A New and Complete Transcription: Volume 3: 1662*, Robert Latham and William Matthews (eds). London: G. Bell and Sons, 1977, p. 208.

Schlegel, August von. 'Lecture XII', *A Course of Lectures on Dramatic Art and Literature*, 2 vols, trans. John Black. London: Baldwin, Craddock and Joy; Edinburgh: William Blackwood; Dublin: John Cumming, 1815.

Ulrici, Hermann. *Shakespeare's Dramatic Art and His Relation to Calderon and Goethe*. London: Chapman, 1846.

Wedgwood, Julia. 'The Midsummer Night's Dream', *Contemporary Review*, 57 (April 1890), pp. 580–7.

Wimsatt, W. K., Jr. (ed.). *Samuel Johnson on Shakespeare*. London: MacGibbon & Kee, 1960.

CHAPTER TWO: 1900–49

Charlton, H. B. *Shakespearean Comedy*. University Paperbacks series. Methuen: London, 1966.

Chesterton, G. K. '*A Midsummer Night's Dream*', in *The Common Man*. London and New York: Sheed and Ward, 1950, p. 10.

Knight, G. Wilson. *The Shakespearean Tempest*. Oxford Bookshelf series. London: Oxford University Pres, 1940.

Miller, Donald C. 'Titania and the Changeling', in G. Kirchner, L. Whitbread, Donald C. Miller, A. H. King, Eilert Ekwall, Z. S. Fink, 'Notes and News'. *English Studies: A Journal of English Language and Literature*, 22.1 (1940), pp. 66–70.

Parrott, Thomas Marc. *Shakespearean Comedy*. New York: Oxford University Press, 1949.

Priestley, J. B. *The English Comic Characters*. The Week-End Library series. London: John Lane, the Bodley Head, 1928.

Spurgeon, Caroline F. E. *Shakespeare's Imagery and What It Tells Us*. Cambridge: Cambridge University Press, 1952.

Welsford, Enid. *The Court Masque: A Study in the Relationship between Poetry and the Revels*. Cambridge: Cambridge University Press, 1927.

CHAPTER THREE: THE 1950s

Barber, C. L. *Shakespeare's Festive Comedy: A Study of Dramatic Form and its Relation to Social Custom*. Princeton, NJ: Princeton University Press, 1990.

Brown, John Russell. *Shakespeare and his Comedies*. 2nd edn, with a new chapter on the last comedies. London: Methuen, 1962.

Fisher, Peter F. 'The Argument of *A Midsummer Night's Dream*. *Shakespeare Quarterly*, 8:3 (Summer 1957), pp. 307–10.

Olson, Paul A. '*A Midsummer Night's Dream* and the Meaning of Court Marriage', *ELH*, 24:2 (June 1957), pp. 95–119.

Siegel, Paul N. '*A Midsummer Night's Dream* and the Wedding Guests'. *Shakespeare Quarterly*, 4:2 (April 1953), pp. 139–44.

CHAPTER FOUR: THE 1960s

Dent, R. W. 'Imagination in *A Midsummer Night's Dream*'. *Shakespeare Quarterly*, 15:2 (Spring 1964), pp. 115–29.

Evans, Bertrand. *Shakespeare's Comedies*. Oxford: Clarendon Press, 1960.

Fender, Stephen. *Shakespeare: A Midsummer Night's Dream*. Studies in English Literature series, no. 35. London: Edward Arnold, 1968.

Hunter, G. K. *William Shakespeare: The Later Comedies*, Writers and Their Works series no, 143. London: Longmans Green for the British Council and the National Book League, 1962; reprinted with additions to bibliography, 1964.

Kermode, Frank. 'The Mature Comedies', in John Russell Brown and Bernard Harris (eds), *Stratford-upon-Avon Studies 3: Early Shakespeare*. London: Edward Arnold, 1961.

Kott, Jan. *Shakespeare Our Contemporary*, trans. Boleslaw Taborski, 2nd edn revised 1967, University Paperback Drama Book series. London: Methuen, 1967.

Young, David P. *Something of Great Constancy: The Art of A Midsummer Night's Dream*. New Haven and London: Yale University Press, 1966.

CHAPTER FIVE: THE 1970s

Bevington, David. '"But We Are Spirits of Another Sort": The Dark Side of Love and Magic in *A Midsummer Night's Dream*', in Wenzel, Siegfrid (ed.), *Medieval and Renaissance Studies: Proceedings of the Southeastern Institute of Medieval and Renaissance Studies Summer 1975*. Chapel Hill: University of North Carolina, 1978, pp. 80–92. Reprinted in Dutton (1996), pp. 24–37.

Garber, Marjorie B. *Dream in Shakespeare: From Metaphor to Metamorphosis*. New Haven and London: Yale University Press, 1974.

Krieger, Elliott. *A Marxist Study of Shakespeare's Comedies*. Basingstoke and London: Macmillan, 1979.

Leggatt, Alexander. *Shakespeare's Comedy of Love*. London: Methuen, 1974; reprinted 1978.

CHAPTER SIX: THE 1980s

Garner, Shirley Nelson. '*A Midsummer Night's Dream*: "Jack shall have Jill; Nought shall go ill"' (1981), in Richard Dutton (ed.) *A Midsummer Night's Dream*, New Casebooks series. Basingstoke and New York: Palgrave Macmillan, 1996, pp. 84–100.

Kavanagh, James H. 'Shakespeare in Ideology', in John Drakakis (ed.) *Alternative Shakespeares*, 2nd edn. Methuen New Accents series. London and New York: Routledge, Taylor and Francis Group, 2002, pp. 147–69.

Leinwand, Theodore B. '"I Believe We Must Leave the Killing Out": Deference and Accommodation in *A Midsummer Night's Dream*', in Dorothea Kehler (ed.) *A Midsummer Night's Dream: Critical Essays*, Shakespeare Criticism series. New York and London: Routledge, 2001, pp. 145–64.

Marshall, David. 'Exchanging Visions: Reading *A Midsummer Night's Dream*'. *ELH* 49:3 (Autumn 1982), pp. 543–75.

Montrose, Louis Adrian. '"Shaping Fantasies": Figurations of Gender and Power in Elizabethan Culture'. *Representations*, 2 (Spring 1983), pp. 61–94.

Patterson, Annabel. *Shakespeare and the Popular Voice*. Cambridge, MA and Oxford: Basil Blackwell, 1989.

CHAPTER SEVEN: THE 1990s

Bate, Jonathan. *Shakespeare and Ovid*. Oxford: Clarendon Press, 1993.

Calderwood, James L. *A Midsummer Night's Dream*, Twayne's New Critical Introductions to Shakespeare series, no. 14. New York: Twayne, 1992.

Girard, René. *A Theater of Envy*. New York, Oxford: Oxford University Press, 1991.

Hackett, Helen. *A Midsummer Night's Dream*. Writers and Their Work series. Plymouth, Devon: Northcote House in association with the British Council, 1997.

Hawkes, Terence. 'Or', in Hawkes, *Meaning by Shakespeare*. London: Routledge, 1992, pp. 11–41.

Hendricks, Margo. '"Obscured by dreams": Race, Empire, and Shakespeare's *A Midsummer Night's Dream*'. *Shakespeare Quarterly*, 47:1 (Spring 1996), pp. 37–60.

Parker, Patricia. *Shakespeare from the Margins*. Chicago and London: University of Chicago Press, 1996.

CHAPTER EIGHT: THE 2000s

Frosch, Thomas R. 'The Missing Child in *A Midsummer Night's Dream*'. *American Imago*, 64:4 (Winter, 2007), pp. 485–511.

Grady, Hugh. 'Shakespeare and Impure Aesthetics: The Case of *A Midsummer Night's Dream*' *Shakespeare Quarterly*, 59:3 (Fall 2008), pp. 274–302.

Green, Douglas E. 'Preposterous Pleasures: Queer Theories and *A Midsummer Night's Dream*', in Dorothea Kehler (ed.) *A Midsummer Night's Dream: Critical Essays*. Shakespeare Criticism series. New York and London: Routledge, 2001, pp. 369–97.

Nuttall, A. D., '*A Midsummer Night's Dream*: Comedy as *Apotrope* of Myth', *Shakespeare Survey: An Annual Survey of Shakespeare Studies and Production; 53: Shakespeare and Narrative*. Cambridge: Cambridge University Press, 2000.

Sinfield, Alan. 'Cultural Materialism and Intertextuality: The Limits of Queer Reading in *A Midsummer Night's Dream* and *The Two Noble Kinsmen*', in Peter Holland (ed.), *Shakespeare Survey: An Annual Survey of Shakespeare Studies and Production: 56: Shakespeare and Comedy* (2003), pp. 67–78.

CHAPTER NINE: 1935–99: *Dream* on Screen

The BBC TV Shakespeare: A Midsummer Night's Dream. London: British Broadcasting Corporation, 1981.

Buchanan, Judith. *Shakespeare on Film*. Inside Film series. Harlow, Essex: Pearson Longman, 2005, pp. 121–49.

Burnett, Mark Thornton. 'Impressions of Fantasy: Adrian Noble's *A Midsummer Night's Dream*', in Burnett and Ramona Wray (eds). *Shakespeare, Film Fin de Siècle*. Basingstoke and London: Macmillan; New York: St Martin's Press, 2000, pp. 89–101.

Collick, John. *Shakespeare, Cinema and Society*. Manchester: Manchester University Press, 1989. Extract in Robert Shaughnessy (ed.). *Shakespeare on Film*, New Casebooks series. Basingstoke and London: Macmillan, 1998, pp. 83–102.

Donaldson, Peter. 'Bottom and the Gramophone: Media, Class and Comedy in Michael Hoffman's *A Midsummer Night's Dream*'. *Shakespeare Survey 61: Shakespeare, Sound and Screen* (2008), pp. 23–35.

Hindle, Maurice. *Studying Shakespeare on Film*. Basingstoke and New York: Palgrave Macmillan, 2007.

Manvell, Roger. *Shakespeare and the Film*, revised and updated edn. South Brunswick and New York: A. S. Barnes, 1979.

Nicoll, Allardyce. *Film and Theatre*. New York: Thomas Y. Crowell, 1936, pp. 175-81. Extract in Charles W. Eckert (ed.). *Focus on Shakespearean Films*. Englewood Cliffs, New Jersey: Prentice-Hall, 1972, pp. 43–7.

Rothwell, Kenneth. *A History of Shakespeare on Screen: A Century of Film and Television*. Cambridge: Cambridge University Press, 1999.

Watts, Richard, Jr. 'Films of a Moonstruck World'. *Yale Review*, 25:2 (December 1935), pp. 311–20. Extract in Eckert (1972), pp. 47–52.

White, Martin. *A Midsummer Night's Dream*. Shakespeare Handbooks series. Basingstoke and New York: Palgrave Macmillan, 2009.

Willis, Susan. *The BBC Shakespeare Plays: Making the Televised Canon*. Chapel Hill and London: University of North Carolina Press, 1999.

Select Filmography

A Midsummer Night's Dream (1935). 133 minutes. Black and white. USA. Warner Bros.

Directors: Max Reinhardt, William Dieterle
Writers: William Shakespeare, Charles Kenyon, Mary McCall Jr.
Cast: Ian Hunter: Theseus
       Verree Teasdale: Hippolyta
       Victor Jory: Oberon
       Anita Louise: Titania
       Mickey Rooney: Puck
       Olivia de Havilland: Hermia
       Jean Muir: Helena
       Dick Powell: Lysander
       Ross Alexander: Demetrius
       James Cagney: Bottom
       Joe E. Brown: Flute

A Midsummer Night's Dream (1969). 124 minutes. Colour. UK. RSC Enterprises/Alan Clore. Black and white. USA. Warner Bros.

Director: Peter Hall
Writer: William Shakespeare
Cast: Derek Godfrey: Theseus
       Barbara Jefford: Hippolyta
       Ian Richardson: Oberon
       Judi Dench: Titania
       Ian Holm: Puck
       Helen Mirren: Hermia
       Diana Rigg: Helena
       David Warner: Lysander
       Michael Jayston: Demetrius
       Paul Rogers: Bottom
       John Normington: Flute

A Midsummer Night's Dream (1981). 120 minutes. Colour. UK. BBC Shakespeare Plays.

Director: Elijah Moshinsky
Writers: William Shakespeare, David Snodin

Cast: Nigel Davenport: Theseus
        Estelle Kohler: Hippolyta
        Peter McEnery: Oberon
        Helen Mirren: Titania
        Phil Daniels: Puck
        Pippa Guard: Hermia
        Cherith Miller: Helena
        Robert Lindsay: Lysander
        Nicky Henson: Demetrius
        Brian Glover: Bottom
        John Fowler: Flute

A Midsummer Night's Dream (1996). 103 minutes. Colour. UK. Channel Four Films.

Director: Adrian Noble
Writers: William Shakespeare, Adrian Noble
Cast: Alex Jennings: Theseus/Oberon
        Lindsay Duncan: Hippolyta/Titania
        Finbar Lynch: Puck/Philostrate
        Monica Dolan: Hermia
        Emily Raymond: Helena
        Daniel Evans: Lysander
        Kevin Doyle: Demetrius
        Desmond Barrit: Bottom
        Mark Letheren: Flute
        Osheen Jones: The Boy

William Shakespeare's A Midsummer Night's Dream (1999). 116 minutes. Colour. USA/Germany. TCF/Fox Searchlight/Regency Enterprises (producers Leslie Urdang, Michael Hoffman).

Director: Michael Hoffman
Writers: William Shakespeare, Michael Hoffman
Cast: David Strathairn: Theseus/Oberon
        Sophie Marceau: Hippolyta/Titania
        Rupert Everett: Oberon
        Michelle Pfeiffer: Titania
        Stanley Tucci: Puck
        Anna Friel: Hermia
        Calista Flockhart: Helena
        Dominic West: Lysander
        Christian Bale: Demetrius
        Kevin Kline: Bottom
        Sam Rockwell: Flute

INDEX